PEREGRINE BOOKS
Y 76
WATERLOO TO PETERLOO
R. J. WHITE

WATERLOO
TO PETERLOO

R. J. White

PENGUIN BOOKS

Penguin Books Ltd, Harmondsworth, Middlesex, England
Penguin Books Inc., 7110 Ambassador Road, Baltimore, Maryland 21207, U.S.A.
Penguin Books Australia Ltd, Ringwood, Victoria, Australia

—

First published by William Heinemann Ltd 1957
Published in Mercury Books 1963
Published in Peregrine Books 1968

—

—

Made and printed in Great Britain
by Hazell Watson & Viney Ltd
Aylesbury, Bucks
Set in Linotype Juliana

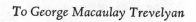

To George Macaulay Trevelyan

CONTENTS

PREFACE

THIS book was begun many years ago in an attempt to lay the ghost of a man called Jeremiah Brandreth. Brandreth, and two of his associates, suffered death by the rope and the axe for high treason on 7 November 1817. One of his associates, William Turner, cried out on the scaffold: 'This is all Oliver and the Government ....' Brandreth's last words were: 'God bless you all – and my Lord Castlereagh, too ...'

I lived for the first twenty-five years of my life in the Derby and Notts border-country where these things took place, and where their memory still lingered on among the grandchildren of the men who made 'The Pentrich Revolution'. It became a necessity of the imagination, almost an obligation of the heart, to attempt to rediscover and relive the thoughts and feelings of that vanished society, where a poor stocking-knitter could suffer the penalty generally reserved for traitors of noble birth, and where a broken-down master builder could figure as the villain in a drama which Shelley saw fit to raise to the level of a national calamity. Jeremiah Brandreth, Oliver the Spy, Shelley ... a Masque of Anarchy to challenge the mind and heart of a 'native'. And the challenge ended in a study of the whole troubled scene that occupied the four years between Waterloo and Peterloo. The Derbyshire Rising of 1817 remains the pivot of this book, but the subject ranges widely back and forth, before and after that event. Only so was it possible to understand it.

I have not attempted to write a history of Regency England. Nor is this book a study of parliamentary and party politics. Least of all is it concerned with the history of England in Europe at that time. It is a study in social transition, an essay in what may be called 'suspended revolution'. The materials on which it is based have all been used before, with the exception of certain local material employed for the writing of chapter 14. It makes but a small claim, therefore, to be a work of discovery. It may rather be described as a work of re-interpretation.

Chapter 1

WATERLOO

It was always Napoleon's object to fight a great
battle; my object, on the contrary, was to avoid to
fight a great battle.

WELLINGTON

1

THE battle of Waterloo was fought on 18 June 1815. On the fol-
lowing day, the Duke of Wellington composed his dispatch to Earl
Bathurst, His Majesty's Principal Secretary of State for the War
Department. It arrived in London late in the evening of 21 June,
and was printed in the *London Gazette* on the following morning.
So modestly was it worded, that the American Ambassador to the
Court of St James's went about for several days under the impres-
sion that the Allied armies had been defeated.

The great Duke was an Irishman, a good professional soldier, who
never fought a battle if he could avoid it, and detested the bloody
cost of heroism from the bottom of his heart. He preferred to leave
heroics to poets, politicians, women and Frenchmen. He had conquered Napoleon, but it was many years before his austere personality and tastes conquered his fellow-countrymen. His first victory,
on the home front, was at Haworth Parsonage, where the godlike
hero of the Brontë children's dream-world was to emerge in Mr
Rochester, the first strong man in English fiction. Nor was the
famous stiff-lipped, poker-faced manner ever to become the 'admired
characteristic' of Englishmen beyond the bounds of the small and
select governing class bequeathed to Victorian England by the public schools as they were remodelled by Dr Arnold. Certainly, in
Regency England, no one but John Quincy Adams was taken in by
the Waterloo dispatch. Its terse, matter-of-fact phrases were understood to be 'just the Duke's queer way'. Most Englishmen behaved
like the penurious painter, Benjamin Robert Haydon, who spent the
next three days reading it over and over until he had got it by heart.

Haydon, however, had heard the news from the lips of the

11

courier himself. Returning to his lodgings in Great Marlborough Street, a little before midnight on 21 June, he was crossing Portman Square when he heard someone running after him from the direction of Oxford Street. It was a fine night, with a high moon which did full justice to the neo-classic elegance of John Nash's London. All was quiet in the sleeping city, save for the subdued sounds of revelry that came from a house on the south side of the Square, where a rout was taking place. The courier ran straight up to Haydon and demanded to know which was the house of Lord Harrowby, the Lord President of the Council. 'For the Duke has beat Napoleon,' the man poured out, 'taking one hundred and fifty pieces of cannon, and is marching to Paris!' In his excitement, Haydon entirely forgot his whereabouts, and directed the courier to the same point in Portman Square that Lord Harrowby's house occupied in Grosvenor Square. Off ran the courier, straight up the steps and into the house where the rout was taking place. The violins stopped abruptly, cheering broke out, and Haydon went racing back to knock up his host of the evening in the Edgware Road and to shout, 'Huzza!' under the windows. 'How this victory pursues one's imagination!' he was reflecting, four days later. 'Great and glorious Wellington!' He prided himself on not having rubbed it in when talking to Leigh Hunt, who, as a Liberal, could not rejoice at a battle which seemed to spell the ruin of 'cosmopolite philosophy'. Hunt could only groan: 'Terrible battle, this, Haydon.' William Hazlitt, another Liberal, put on a crêpe band as a sign of mourning, and went about unwashed, unshaved, and in a state of intoxication for several weeks, because he chose to believe that Bonaparte had been the champion of liberty and enlightenment. *Chacun a son goût* .... Tory or Liberal, everyone agreed that the age that could produce such events was sublime. 'In this history of the world, never was there such a period as this of 1815', was Haydon's final verdict.

It was the age of the monstrous, the heroic, and the sublime. The ordinary civilian Englishman could still leave wars to be fought by the professional soldiers, together with what the Duke called 'the scum of the earth, enlisted for drink', while he sat at home and cheered, or groaned, at the distant thunder of the dynasts. The cult of sheer size, of the colossal, had been fostered

by the great Corsican himself – a little man who worshipped greatness in all things. The English had it, too. The colossal battles of
the Emperor, the huge symphonies of Beethoven, the enormous
monuments of the new Imperialism, these things were matched in
England by the vast canvases of Turner and Haydon, the endless
epics of Southey, the sublimities of the Minerva novels, the towering façades and arcades and pillars of John Nash, the cavernous
splendours of Carlton House, the voluminous cravats and quilted
waistcoats of the First Gentleman of Europe. This was no age of
the elegant miniature. The 'Big Bow-wow' of Sir Walter Scott
rather than the fine observation of Miss Austen reflected the taste
of the time.* The Duke himself thought it all rather vulgar. His
opinion of the Emperor was that he was 'no gentleman' † and he
found Nelson, at first acquaintance, insufferable.[1] He preferred
neatness, moderation, the elegant understatement. His men called
him (among other things) 'The Beau'. For so long as he played a
violin, he played Mozart. He was in a minority.

So the English gave themselves up to unashamed and exuberant
rejoicing. The coaches went dashing out of London, garlanded
with laurel and bay, to carry the wonderful tidings through
thronging crowds and beneath rocking steeples, to the four corners
of the King's dominions. For, after all, England had been at war for
twenty-two years, with scarcely an interval; and for more than
fifteen of them the shadow of Napoleon had rested upon the lives
of millions of men who had never seen the coasts of France and
who firmly believed that all Frenchmen had tails like monkeys.
Many could not remember a time when we were not at war with
the French. They had the memory of the amazing days of the nineties, when strange chattering prisoners crowded the quays at
Plymouth; when pedlars sold tiny guillotines carved out of mutton
bones by the captured 'Mounseers'; when parents had drawn down
the blinds and whispered : 'They have cut off the King of France's
head !' As Haydon observes : 'Boys were born, nursed and grew
up hating the name of Frenchmen .... We had thought of France
from youth as forbidden ground, as the abode of the enemies of our
country.' And now it was all over, and boatmen were taking the

* This contrast was instituted by Sir Walter himself.
† For such references see Notes pp. 205–14.

English citizenry to stare at the fallen Emperor on board the *Beller-ophon* in Plymouth harbour, and the tourists were discovering that the French 'absolutely had houses, churches, fields and children'.

The war had come home to most Englishmen in the form not of 'national service' but in the shape of high prices, still higher taxes, and plentiful employment. Few indeed, in proportion to the population, had seen any fighting, and fewer still had wished to see any. There was the occasional invasion scare, there were Gentlemen Volunteers, 'Bang-up Locals', Martello Towers, and a lively press-gang. No one, it has been justly observed, thought to inquire why Jane Austen's young gentlemen were not in uniform; and it might be added that still fewer of Jane Austen's young ladies inquired where their fathers' incomes came from. The English were a profoundly civilian race. Even at the height of the struggle, the English people resented the sight of regiments of horse and foot parading in England's green and pleasant land. It required all Pitt's tactical ingenuity to evade parliamentary opposition to the construction of barracks. The people were prepared to rejoice in the heroic or the sublime, but they still believed that wars should be fought at a suitable distance and by their salaried servants. They deeply distrusted soldiers in politics, and they were ready to snuff the threat of military rule in every tainted breeze from the continent of Europe.

The news of Waterloo itself was not the less joyfully received because it promised to put an end to the necessity of England's alliance with the despotic monarchies of eastern Europe which had made possible the overthrow of the upstart monarch of the west.* Since the death of Charles James Fox in 1806, avowed hostility to this alliance had, for the most part, given way to an attitude of grim and patient tolerance. Like a number of other unpleasant things, including the Income Tax and the postponement of much-needed domestic reforms, people had been prepared to submit to in a spirit of patriotic fortitude .... Now, by the summer of 1815, the despots had been fêted by the Prince Regent and his Ministers, politely cheered in the streets of London,†

* Distinguished from his enemies by Shelley as 'the only tyrant among them who was not a hypocrite'.

† See Mark Rutherford's novel, *The Revolution in Tanner's Lane* (1887).

awarded honorary degrees by the home of lost causes, and packed off home to their horrid haunts beyond the Elbe and the Danube. There was a widespread suspicion, however, that their English hosts had taken some highly un-English infection from their late allies, a suspicion which was not allayed by the retention of a large military establishment and the participation of Lord Castlereagh in a succession of European Congresses for the restoration of 'tranquillity' in the dominions of the lately restored sovereigns. The notion that Great Britain should have at once disbanded her armed forces and withdrawn from the councils of her late allies, after so many years of collaboration, was quickly shown to be an illusion, and the realization of that unpleasant fact was accompanied by dire prognostications for the future of English liberty.

2

Within little more than four years of the great and glorious victory of Waterloo, news reached London that a troop of the 15th Hussars, wearing their Waterloo medals, had massacred a peaceable assembly of unarmed men, women and children in St Peter's Fields, Manchester. A perfectly orderly rally of working-class people, assembled to hear Henry Hunt put the case for a reform of the House of Commons, had been brutally attacked by regular troops on the orders of the magistrates. On this occasion, no joyous courier ran through Portman Square in search of Lord Harrowby's house. The nation stood aghast. Then, in the fullness of time, a broken-down soldier, Arthur Thistlewood by name, girded himself and half a dozen followers in a stable-loft in Cato Street, off the Edgware Road, with swords, pistols and fire-bombs, with the intention of making their way into Lord Harrowby's house and there massacring the assembled Cabinet as they sat at dinner. 'High Treason was committed against the People of Manchester', Arthur Thistlewood declared. 'I resolved that the lives of the instigators of massacre should atone for the souls of murdered innocents.' However, Lord Harrowby was forewarned of Thistlewood's intentions. The arrangements for the dinner-party were allowed to go forward, but the members of the Cabinet were advised to dine elsewhere. The conspirators were rounded up or dispersed before they could

leave Cato Street, and shortly afterwards five of them were
executed for high treason.

'Peterloo', coming within five years of Waterloo, was the climax
of the prolonged post-war contest between governors and governed,
when it seemed to many that English politics were fast becoming
undistinguishable from the politics of continental countries, with
their tendency to oscillate perilously between reaction and revolution.* Shelley, awakened in distant Italy by the fratricidal
clamour of Peterloo, and viewing his country from the oblique
angle of the self-appointed exile, could see nothing but the grim
alternatives of despotism and revolution, alternatives which had
been sharpening year by year. 'The rich have become richer, and
the poor have become poorer; and the vessel of the state is driven
between the Scylla and Charybdis of anarchy and despotism.' Despotism had been 'notoriously gathering like an avalanche year by
year'.[2] And in the most ghastly of his poems, *The Masque of
Anarchy*, which was written in a paroxysm of anger upon hearing
of the Manchester massacre, he sent the 'despots' of Lord Liverpool's Administration riding down the road of historic memory in
a grisly Apocalypse which has obsessed the minds of their countrymen ever since at the mention of their names.

> I met Murder on the way –
> He had a mask like Castlereagh –
> Very smooth he looked, yet grim;
> Seven blood-hounds followed him. . . .
> He tossed them human hearts to chew
> Which from his wide cloak he drew.
>
> Next came Fraud, and he had on,
> Like Eldon, an ermined gown;
> His big tears, for he wept well,
> Turned to mill-stones as they fell. . . .

* On 16 February, Mrs Arbuthnot confided to her Journal some remarks
of the Duke of Wellington on returning from the funeral of King George
III. The Duke observed that, so great was the fear of assassination in France,
that the Government dared not indulge in funerals by torchlight, or even
permit nocturnal masquerades. On the following day, the Duke's words
were (as so often) proved prophetic by the arrival of the news of the assassination of the Duc de Berri. When, a week later, Mrs Arbuthnot recorded

And the little children, who
Round his feet played to and fro,
Thinking every tear a gem,
Had their brains knocked out by them.

Clothed with the Bible, as with light,
And the shadows of the night,
Like Sidmouth, next, Hypocrisy
On a crocodile rode by . . . .

The horrors of Shelley's doggerel almost match the ignorant injustice of his judgements.

There were others, better informed and less embittered by personal experience,* who nevertheless regarded Peterloo as the confirmation of those suspicions of a despotic, not to say a militarist, cast of mind which had characterized the Liverpool Administration from the beginning. The high European reputation of the Foreign Secretary, Lord Castlereagh; his diplomatically polite public references to the Tsar and his 'Holy Alliance' (which he described in private as 'a piece of sublime mysticism and nonsense'); his regular attendance at Congresses concerned with the suppression of liberal movements abroad: all these looked very dark indeed. 'Under our presiding influence', wrote the good Whig squire, Sir Robert Heron, in December 1815, 'the Monarchs are leagued against every exertion of popular energy.'[3] The *Black Dwarf*, most pertinacious of Radical newspapers, thundered week after week against 'Castlereagh and the Holy Leaguers'. His Lordship is regularly described as 'intriguing away his country's interests and bartering the prosperity of its inhabitants for blue ribands, stars, and personal advantages'. It was shameful that England, once the light of Europe, teaching nations how to live, 'had adopted the accursed principles of Legitimacy in her policy . . . .'[4] Among the horrid offspring of such treachery to the national traditions were to be accounted the employment of spies and informers, the employment of German mercenaries to flog English

the horrid news of the discovery of the Cato Street Plot, however, she appears to have indulged in no *arrières-pensées*. *Journals of Mrs Arbuthnot*, ed. Francis Bamford and the Duke of Wellington (1950), vol. I, p. 5.

* In 1817 Eldon had declared Shelley unfit to have the custody of his children by his first wife.

soldiers, and the refusal of the Government to intervene to save the life of Marshal Ney.

As for the Army, it seemed to be a settled policy with the Government not only to increase its size but to isolate it from the people. 'Our rulers are determined that we shall become a military nation', declared the *Black Dwarf*, in December 1817. The Militia, 'the army of citizens', had been allowed to decline while a standing army of processional soldiers had taken its place, 'presenting the prospect of a military government'. The old hatred of barracks, with which Pitt had had to contend during the war, was revived. 'The army and the people are therefore separated from each other altogether; and no intercourse must be allowed where it can be prevented lest the soldier should begin to remember that he is a man . . . .'[5] As early as 1810, Major Cartwright, a veteran of reform politics, had made an eloquent plea for the revival of the native militia, the 'Fyrd' of the liberty-loving Anglo-Saxons. 'Where are the armed householders?' he demanded. 'Without them, the nation must sink into a military despotism. Instead, we have 187 barracks and a standing army of which 60,000 are Germans, Sicilians, Portuguese, French and other foreigners.'[6]

As if to set at defiance these remonstrances, in 1818 the Duke himself was admitted to the Administration. Six months later came Peterloo. Hardly had the clamour of that tragic event died away, when the Government proposed still further to increase the size of the military establishment.

I am not apt to be alarmed [wrote Lord Brougham], but I confess these things do fill me with dismay. There is a character of violence and military vigour about them, quite foreign to the nature of Lord Liverpool. . . . I see Wellington distinctly in the measure, and I can hardly doubt that a design is formed of making the Government of this country less free – and permanently so.[7]

Brougham was a Whig, with Radical sympathies. But even that good Church-and-King man, Benjamin Robert Haydon, looking back on the Tory regime in 1830, was to give it as his opinion that 'the military vigour, the despotic feeling engendered by twenty-five years of furious war, rendered them unfit, perhaps, to guide the domestic policy of the country . . . .'

3

It has become the fashion to write history 'as it strikes a contemporary', or as a succession of 'past presents', and no doubt this
has supplied a salutary corrective to the operation of that rather
glib hindsight which afflicted the great Whig tradition of English
historical writing. Nevertheless, it remains the privilege and the
prerogative of the historian to set any given period of history
within a wider frame of reference than could possibly have been at
the disposal of contemporaries. Indeed, there is something to be
said even for hindsight, providing it is controlled by modesty and
discretion, and by a resolute resistance to the temptation of instituting historical parallels. On completing the second volume of his
great *History of the English People in the Nineteenth Century*,
Élie Halévy came to the conclusion that, so far from the spectacle
of the present (he wrote in 1923) having clouded his vision of the
past (he wrote of the period 1815–30), it had enabled him to see
the past more clearly as it really was.[8] In writing of the years
1815–19 in the year 1955, there is even more to be gained, in the
matter of historical understanding. Perhaps the isolationist mood
of the English people at that time is slightly more comprehensible
to an observer who has seen the English-speaking communities shy
away from European commitments not once, but twice, within
thirty years. Nor, perhaps, would the comparison of Lord Castlereagh's England with an Asiatic police-state, which was suggested
by Mr and Mrs Hammond in 1919,[9] be likely to suggest itself to
the historian of 1955. Indeed, Lord Castlereagh, and his fellow
monsters of *The Masque of Anarchy*, tend to take on the life-size
stature of country gentlemen and industrious clerks in an age
which has experienced Hitler, Mussolini, Stalin, and their legions.

A more legitimate extension of the frame of reference, however,
is essential to the understanding of these years of post-Waterloo
England. The key to the period is more likely to be discovered by
setting it against the past than by examining it in the light of the
future. For it is, more than most periods, one of rapid transition.
Its people and its problems, its tensions and its catastrophes, its
hopes and its fears, all are the phenomena of a society in the midst

of a process of precipitate change. A form of society which, with all its ways of living and thinking and feeling, had lasted for some fifteen hundred years, was precipitately giving way to another form which has now lasted for some one hundred and fifty. The precipitate nature of the change was largely fostered by the long war which ended in 1815. The war had at once hastened social change and postponed the attempt to solve the problems to which it gave rise. By focusing the energies of the nation upon a common cause, the war had served to supply the need for a centripetal force in a society which had become increasingly subject to the centrifugal forces of an industrial revolution. The war, wrote Coleridge in 1817, had 'brought about a national unanimity unexampled in our history since the reign of Elizabeth'.[10] A myriad discursive aims and interests had been temporarily harmonized in a common endeavour. The peasant could be dispossessed in the interests of economical farming; the artisan could be overworked and underpaid in the interests of large-scale production; machine-breaking could be identified with the sabotage of munitions; the tepid patriotism of the Whigs could be identified with defeatism, and the angry reformism of the Radicals could be identified with treason. Thus, with some hypocrisy, a good deal of selfishness, and still more 'double-thinking', the war had been won. Peace removed the danger, and the focus. The semblance of organic life was lost, and society reverted to a structure of classes, a multitude of individuals, an undisguised battlefield of governors and governed. 'The foundations of the State were loosened; there was no cohesion in the materials of which the State was built up.'[11]

Few people were at all aware of the true inward nature of what was happening. Only the poets seem to have been capable of sufficient detachment to discern how near to the surface of society were the forces of disruption: Coleridge looking down from Highgate Hill, Southey watching nervously from the Lake District, Shelley straining indignant ears and eyes at Geneva or Leghorn. A host of secondary Jeremiahs attributed the sad state of society to bad reading-habits, Sunday newspapers, the replacement of pantaloons by loose trousers, or even cheap champagnes.* The great mass of the people displayed no interest in the problem whatever. The

* See pp. 65–6.

England of the Regency was ebullient, self-confident, exuberant in
its self-belief. It delighted to talk of 'this enlightened age', and
never seriously doubted that all would work out for the best if
everyone minded his own business. The rich were ostentatious in
their riches; the middle classes grumbled at the high taxes, stormed
at the Chancellor of the Exchequer until he abolished the Income
Tax, and took blunderbusses to bed with them against the Luddites; the poor went through hell, and yet contrived to impress
foreigners as the proudest and jolliest poor in the world. The Home
Secretary smelled sedition and treason everywhere, and spent
sleepless nights over the bundles of papers which have loomed so
large in the minds of historians of this period ever since: those
long rows of files marked 'Disturbances' in the Public Record
Office, harbingers of the revolution which never came. The night
sky of the midlands and the north was red with the fires of iron
furnaces; the output of pig-iron had increased from 68,000 tons in
1788 to 300,000 tons in 1815. The stark bare lines of cotton factories were coming to dominate the skyline of Lancashire: there
were no steam-looms in Manchester until 1806, but by 1818 there
were two thousand of them. Men, women and children were congregating in mean streets around these rapidly-growing centres
of industry; Dale and Owen already employed 1,600 at the New
Lanark Mills, Strutt had nearly 1,500 at Belper and Millford, while
Horrocks were employing nearly 7,000 at Preston by 1816. There
was 'a wholesaleness, a monstrosity, about the great cotton mills
which marked them down for public notice'.[12]

Indeed, the inescapable and dominant feature of Regency England was it populousness. In the middle of the eighteenth century,
England had about seven million people. By 1815 she had about
thirteen million; and, of these, nearly a half were the more noticeable because they were concentrated in urban areas, while getting
on for a tenth of them lived in London itself. The dramatic thing
about all this was the speed with which population had increased
since the beginning of the new century, that is to say within the
very recent memory of the people of Regency England. In the last
fifty years of the eighteenth century, it is reckoned that some
three-quarters of a million people were added to the population
every ten years. After 1800, the addition amounted to about two

million every ten years. To talk of huge agglomerations of people in industrial towns would be foolish. But the little towns of the older England needed to grow very little in order to present urgent problems of administration for the primitive governmental machinery of the early nineteenth century. It is unlikely that a later generation will ever be able to recapture a sense of the bewilderment and dismay which settled upon the minds of Englishmen, a little more than a century ago, when they found themselves face to face with 'the new town', small as it may have been by any later standard of measurement. For 'the new town' really was new. Nothing like it had ever been seen in the history of western society. Perhaps Cobbett would have called London 'the Great Wen' at any time in its history; but it was a new thing to hear young men like Robert Southey describing a town as 'a fungoid excrescence from the body politic'. The governors of Regency England tried not to think about it at all.

Of course, they were compelled to think about it, from time to time. They were compelled to find out, for instance, what was happening among the hordes of people who now lived somewhere out of sight of squire and parson. That was one function of the spies who were employed so frequently in that unpoliced society. There had been a time, not very distant, when Sunday service at the parish church served as something in the nature of a 'call-over'. Now, not only were large numbers of people not going to church; there were not enough churches for them to go to. In 1818, Lord Liverpool devoted a good deal of his time to the passage of a Church Building Act, which provided a million pounds for the purpose of building new churches in London.

These new churches, designed as outposts in the battle against the advancing forces of Democracy and Dissent, frequently conformed to the classical taste of the age. The 'Waterloo churches', on the Lambeth side of the river, all had Greek porticoes. Elsewhere, the Gothic Revival was already putting up an ominous spire or two into the elegant Regency skyline. This was a pity, because the appropriate tone of the Regency was classical, as befittted England's first age of urban living since the departure of the Romans. Moreover, for the first time since the death of King Charles I, society was presided over by a Prince of informed taste and sincere concern for the visual arts. It is forgivable to laugh at the Brighton Pavilion: perhaps it was meant to be laughed at. But the new London, which the Prince Regent planned with John Nash, was a splendid birthday present for an urban society which had at last come of age.

The visual art of Regency London is the art of a public and populous society. These buildings were designed for large numbers of people, people who feel at home in the world, the world of man's own making. Here are no towering castles and cathedrals dominating a poor and thinly populated landscape, no remote and frozen faces peeping from niche and pedestal at a naughty world. These arcades and porticoes are spacious, but they do not dwarf humanity. They are an appropriate setting for a confident, populous, shameless multitude. Even the country house was a town house set down in the rural landscape. A college, a prison, a chapel, a cotton mill: each and every one of them was likely to conform to the stately classical model. Sometimes the note of confidence was strident and boastful. Sometimes it trumpeted the defiant tones of a cheerful cosmic impiety. And, of course, it could not last. The society which produced it had not solved, or even faced, the problems of social disintegration which threatened its destruction. A stone's throw to the east of Nash's Regent Street and the Prince Regent's Park, the dark courts and warrens of another London pullulated with the hidden life of another, and more awful, world, the world where Arthur Thistlewood and his outcasts brooded over the wrongs of the modern Babylon. Men were already using that ominous term. We even hear it in the mouth of Samuel Bamford, the weaver's boy from Lancashire, who saw it all and departed from 'the great Babylon, heartily tired of it', in the winter of 1816–17.[13] Even the splendid façades of the Regent's Park terraces were a flagrant and absurd sham, concealing 'rows and rows of identical houses, identical in their narrowness, their thin pretentiousness, their poverty of design'.[14] It was 'the Age of Stucco', and the stucco revealed its cracks even before it was dry. Soon, the Gothic was to return, with its sorrows and its sense of shame, and even the table-legs were to be concealed with chintz trousers in the great failure of nerve which is called 'Victorianism'. Waterloo ... Peterloo ... St Pancras Station ...

The men who presided over this scene of mingled squalor and bravura were not its children. Lord Liverpool assisted in, and approved of, the Prince Regent's plans. Indeed, it should be remembered that in this, the supposedly classic age of *laissez-faire*, 'the State was easily and by far the greatest initiator of building in London ... so great a proportion of public wealth can rarely have been spent on architecture in the capital in such a short time.'[15] The State paid for churches, the Law Courts, the Custom House, the Post Office, the Treasury's new home in Whitehall, and even for a royal palace and parks. 'The State' meant Lord Liverpool, Lord Castlereagh, Lord Sidmouth, Lord Eldon, and all the principal figures in *The Masque of Anarchy*. Yet these men were, one and all, children of the older world of the Manor House, the Parish Church beside the village green, the rural peace of the countryside. They could understand classical architecture, although they probably preferred Jacobean. They could understand the interests of a thriving business community, for they were one and all disciples of Mr Pitt and Adam Smith. They understood the wealth-producing possibilities of the new machines. 'Next to the spirit of her people,' Lord Liverpool declared, in a speech opposing Earl Stanhope's proposal to put a legislative limit to the employment of machinery, in 1820, 'England was indebted for her commercial power and greatness to her machinery.' A Watt, a Boulton, an Arkwright, his Lordship affirmed – these men were 'as useful to their country, in their generations, as any of the Legislators of old were in theirs'.* Yet, when they were faced with the social implications of these things, they reverted instinctively to the social attitudes and standards of their youth. It was very hard for them to change.

For they had won the war. They had, they claimed, made a wise and just settlement of the affairs of Europe. And now, deprived of the adventitious aid of a foreign war to focus the conflicting interests of society upon a common objective, they could do little more than bow their heads before the storm, strike blindly at hidden foes around them, and utter fervent but monotonous

* *Hansard Parliamentary Debates*, 1820, vol. I, 421. Stanhope's proposal was part of a wider Motion on means of providing employment for the poor.

appeals to Divine Providence and Adam Smith to see them through. More imaginative statesmen might have abdicated in face of such a maelstrom of centrifugal forces. They did not abdicate. They rode the whirlwind without pretence of controlling the storm. They continued to hold office for fifteen years with a good show of complacency, and they left office at the last with unshaken self-esteem.

To understand them, and the spirit in which they faced their task, it is necessary to turn to those imponderables which are ultimately more important in a nation's life than the price of bread and the policies of Cabinets. These imponderables change with time, no less certainly, and a great deal more subtly, than index figures or the fashion in hats. The imponderables of 1815 were different from those of 1750, or even of 1790. And the very last persons to respond to such changes are the men whom Burke and Wordsworth denominated 'routine statesmen', just as the first to respond are those who live closest to the primary sources of a nation's life. In Regency England, these last were the masters and men who lived their lives in mill and factory, farm and field, and in the free air which is inhabited by men of letters. The persons who retained longest the values of an earlier time were the men who lived their lives in office.

Persons who are nurtured in office [Burke once wrote] do admirably well as long as things go on in their accustomed order : but when the high roads are broken up and the waters are out, when a new and troubled scene is opened ... then it is that a greater knowledge of mankind and far more comprehension of things is requisite than ever office gave or than office ever can give.

No man ever came to the premiership with so long and varied an experience of parliamentary life and public office as Lord Liverpool.

It is necessary to turn now to the old England that was passing away, the world which bred the governors of Regency England, and whose values never ceased to dominate their attitude towards the new world that was coming into being. It is the world which William Cobbett, who shared so many of their prejudices, but who never shared their office, called the world of 'when-I-was-a-boy', or 'the Dark Ages'.

Chapter 2

OLD ENGLAND
SOCIAL LANDSCAPE

> If I have one wish more ardent than all others, it is
> this; that I, enjoying my garden and few fields, may
> see England as great in the world, and her industri-
> ous, laborious, kind and virtuous people as happy as
> they were when I was born ...
>
> WILLIAM COBBETT, 1763–1835

1

WILLIAM COBBETT was born in 1763, and in the course of
his long and stormy life he did more than any other single man to
create the myth of a 'Golden Age' which was destroyed by the
Industrial Revolution. No one any longer believes in either of these
terms, and yet there lingers a feeling that in some sense Cobbett
was right. It is easy enough to show where Cobbett was wrong.
He knew nothing about machinery. 'I never liked to see machines',
he tells us, 'lest I should be tempted to endeavour to understand
them.'[1] He knew scarcely more about the social effect of machine-
industry. Even when he visited Robert Owen's industrial community at New Lanark, where machine-industry was regulated by
a humane and enlightened industrial despot, he dismissed it as 'a
species of monkery'.[2] As for the celebrated 'Golden Age', which
machinery was supposed to have destroyed, it should be observed
that young Cobbett ran away from the drudgery of a ploughboy's
life at the earliest possible opportunity, in order to be a soldier, a
journalist, and finally a highly successful newspaper-proprietor,
and never went back to the land until he was in a position to buy
a house and some land in Hampshire. By that time he was a much-
travelled man of forty-three, and the nineteenth century was
already five years old. During the next thirty years, of which he
spent two in prison and two in the United States, he came to
know England better than most men have known it, although his

famous *Rural Rides* did not begin until 1821. In fact, the England that Cobbett knew best was England 'after the Deluge', if it is legitimate so to describe the onset of the machine age. When he looked back to the early years of the reign of George III, he instinctively removed from the landscape all those things which he most hated in the rural scene of the eighteen-twenties and thirties : commercially-minded landlords, nabobs, stock-jobbers, profiteers, fund-holders and Methodists. Likewise paupers, farm drudges and the overworked and underfed children of the cottage industries, which we know to have existed in large numbers in the older countryside, along with sturdy peasants and stout yeomen, all these simply vanished away.

Cobbett overstated his case, or rather he left out one side of the picture of Old England. He left out the rural slums, the wretchedness of the generations who toiled in the cottage industries, the town-bred landlords who had been buying up the land in every generation since the later Middle Ages. Where he was right – and this is truly remarkable in a man whom Coleridge likened to a political rhinoceros – was in his sense of the imponderables. 'With what serene conclusiveness,' Carlyle once exclaimed, 'a member of some Useful-Knowledge Society stops your mouth with a figure in arithmetic !'[3] It can be shown quite readily that Cobbett's healthy peasants never existed, that his stout yeomen rather flourished than declined between 1760 and 1830, and that the living conditions of both agricultural and industrial workers in terms of hours and wages were a good deal better when Cobbett died than they had been when he was born.[4] Yet the fact remains that the quality of living, in terms of the satisfaction of the whole nature of man, had steadily deteriorated, and that the old England of Cobbett's childhood had afforded the means to satisfy deeper and subtler needs of the human spirit than can well be reckoned by statistics. Cobbett knew this, perhaps more with his instincts than with his mind, and he said it in terms which are often confused by his tone of nostalgic and indignant lamentation.

For one thing, the old England was still a beautiful place. People did not yet need to go in search of the 'unspoilt'. The face of the land was still beautiful where men lived and worked, as one sees it in the exquisite backgrounds of Bewick's engravings of birds and beasts. Of course, there were black patches, as there had been for long enough, more especially where coal was mined. As early as 1798 we find Robert Southey, who lived at Bedminster, beside Bristol, giving thanks that 'the coal pits were in a different part of the parish, and the house ... at a sufficient distance from all annoyances'.[5] But the great treason to the spirit of man which was committed by nineteenth-century England was still to come. 'It was ugliness which really betrayed the spirit of man, in the nineteenth century,' D. H. Lawrence was to declare, when he, a miner's son, came to look back at the ruined midland countryside of his youth. 'The human soul needs actual beauty even more than bread.' It is almost as great a treason to suppose that the men and women who live and work in a ruined landscape are insensitive to their surroundings. Lawrence knew that the colliers of his generation 'had a peculiar sense of beauty'.[6] Southey knew, in his generation, and Cobbett knew, as Lord Macaulay did not know. Reviewing Southey's *Colloquies on the Progress and Prospects of Society*, in 1830, Macaulay regretted that it was

not from bills of mortality and statistical tables that Mr. Southey has learned his political creed. ... Mr. Southey has found out a way, he tells us, in which the effects of manufacturers and agriculture may be compared. And what is this way? To stand on a hill, to look at a cottage and a factory, and to see which is the prettier ...[7]

Cobbett himself is a faithful example of the natural good taste fostered by a society of the kind for which he spoke. It is to be seen not only in his direct, muscular and vivid prose, but in his scorn for the pretentious pseudo-Gothic style affected by city gentlemen who 'improved' old country-houses, and in his keen delight in every comely artifice of human labour and skill, from a fine field of wheat to a stage-coach. 'Next after a fox-hunt, the finest sight in England is a stage-coach just ready to start. A great sheep or cattle fair is a beautiful sight; but, in the stage-coach you see more of what man is capable of performing ...'[8]

Cobbett marvelled at the performance of the London–Exeter stage-coach, which kept up a steady eight miles an hour, 'and that, too, upon very hilly, and, at some seasons, very deep roads'. In 1804, it took forty-eight hours to travel from Lancashire to London, a distance of some two hundred miles. Roads were neglected, except where the turnpike trusts had made some pretence of putting them in order, and travel was no more speedy (and it was probably a good deal less comfortable) than it had been in the days of the Roman occupation. Few people travelled at all, except the well-to-do. When the artisan or the labourer had any cause to travel, he walked. A young weaver like Samuel Bamford thought nothing of walking from Lancashire to London and back, keeping up his twenty or thirty miles a day, begging milk and bread at farmhouse kitchens and sleeping in hayricks. The walking feats of the men of that age, undertaken in the course of ordinary business, read like athletic contests in the twentieth century.* And, after all, there was hardly ever any need to get anywhere urgently. Time seems to have been less important than it has ever been since. Uncle Cobley, Haydon tells us, came to Plymouth on a six weeks visit, 'got embedded in the family, stayed thirty years, and died'. No one thought it remarkable. The eminent musicologist, Dr Burney, returning to England on the Calais–Dover packet-boat, forgot to disembark and was carried back to France. No one thought this remarkable, at least in an eminent musicologist.

Living their lives in remote villages, forgotten hamlets, and sleepy country towns, the people of the old England lived at a tempo which matched the slow, grave beauty of the land. They could tell the time by the sun, moon and stars, and their calendar was regulated by the great Feast Days of the Christian religion and the principal events of the farming year, plough-time, lambing-time and harvest-home. News of the great world came to them slowly and by devious channels. Often it was a rumour in the mouth of a packman or a pedlar. Sometimes, in places where a highway ran along the valley or the spine of the hills, a stage-coach came lumbering along at infrequent intervals, and men in the distant fields would straighten their backs at the sound of the coachman's horn. Perhaps a newspaper would be dropped at the Hall, to find its way presently to the Rectory, and at last to the inn, where the schoolmaster would be in demand to read it to the company. The news was generally old news, because the coaches were

* Thomas Holcroft records that his father often walked sixty miles in a day as a matter of course. See Hazlitt's *Life of Holcroft* (1816; World's Classics edition, 1926), ch. 2.

slow-coaches, and there was an infinitude of time to chew it over at the inn, at the smithy, or at the cobbler's shop. And the little towns and villages, where most people lived, were full of 'meditative professions', occupations which afforded time for reflection while one was engaged upon the daily task. The bookseller in a country town, the village schoolmaster, the smith at his anvil, the cobbler at his last: these men had time, if not to stand and stare, at least to think while they worked. They needed no other music for that purpose other than the small sounds of their tools. What they thought matters little. The important thing about their lives is the fact that the old England gave them time to think at all.

Haydon's father, the bookseller, appears to have thought that public spirit was thoroughly compatible with fervent loyalty to established institutions in Church and State. He 'loved his Church and King', his son tells us, 'believed England to be the only great country in the world and swore that Napoleon won all his battles by bribery ....' The cobbler often reached different conclusions. With 'the solitary and meditative generation of cobblers', meditation seems often to have led to radicalism in politics and free-thinking in religion. Indeed, the village cobbler was often the village atheist. Nor were the shoemakers much better. Thomas Hardy, the father of the first working-class reform club, was a shoemaker. So was William Benbow, the fiery Lancashire advocate of the General Strike. There was a cobbler among the ten prisoners tried at York after Peterloo. Wherever the spirit of reform is stirring we are likely to find a cobbler. As for the schoolmaster, as like as not he was a kindly old vagrant, devoid of depressing considerations about the future of his pupils or the country in general, content to let his boys pick up the rudiments of learning in school-hours, and loving to drink his tea and smoke his pipe in the long summer afternoons. Such was Haydon's preceptor, the Rev. Dr Bidlake: 'a poetical, tea-drinking, organ-playing, cottage-sketching idler', who thought it more important to take his boys to see a fine sunset from Bickley Vale than to make them perfect in *propria quae maribus*. With the schoolmaster went the apothecary, for a man who could brew potions and prescribe herbs was regarded as in some sort a learned man in country places. Such a man was Bamford's friend, 'Doctor' Healey, a village character, barely able to write his own name, who supposed that he got into the surgical profession by deriving a taste for it from his father. Healey, examined by the Privy Council in 1817, earned that rare distinction of making Lords Castlereagh and Sidmouth laugh .... Finally, among the meditative trades, there were the blacksmiths. In that age of the horse, there were about twenty thousand village smiths. The forge, or its doorway, has provided a forum for the village politicians from time immemorial. Here they talked while the sparks flew upwards. There was time for it. The slow, measured tempo of that talk, and of the thought that went with it, and of all the mental processes of that vanished age, was the strangest, and not the least precious, thing that died with the coming of the machine.

Cobbett's wilful refusal to comprehend machinery represents old England's instinctive recognition of the enemy that was to ravage its beauty, shatter its peace, and substitute its own rhythm for the rhythm of nature. Similarly, his repudiation of 'formal schooling' for country boys was not ignorant rhetoric. He was saying, rather more boastfully, what his favourite *bête noire*, Adam Smith ('that old Scotch tax-gatherer'), had said in *The Wealth of Nations* ('I could make neither top nor tail of the thing') as long ago as 1776. 'In barbarous societies', where husbandry is still in that 'rude state ... which precedes the improvement of manufactures' (no wonder Cobbett hated the 'Old Feelosofer'), men are obliged to be inventive, resourceful, personally responsible for making choices at every hour of their daily lives, and thereby 'the mind is not suffered to fall into that drowsy stupidity, which, in a civilized society, seems to benumb the understanding of almost all the inferior ranks of people.'[9] Only at this stage, when work becomes routine labour, are schools necessary, as an antidote to the soporific effects of mechanical toil. Cobbett agreed. He was always ready to admit that 'schools are very proper things in many cases: in large cities and towns ....' True, the admission plainly carries with it an unspoken 'God-help-them'. The best way to be an educated man, Cobbett held, with all the solid wisdom of old England's experience behind him, was not through the formal instruction of a school, but through experience of 'the little labours and cares' of a craft or a trade from one's earliest years. 'Education means *rearing-up*, not teaching to read and write. He is a learned man,

31

who has great knowledge in his profession or calling; and not he who can read about the knowledge of others.'[10] That is to say, education is the by-product of a way of living. When a meddling woman said of one of his sons: 'Bless me, so tall, and not learned anything yet!' – Cobbett *père* replied: 'Oh yes, he has. He has learned to ride, and hunt, and shoot, and fish, and look after cattle and sheep, and to work in the garden, and to feed his dogs, and to go from village to village in the dark.'[11] He once went so far as to assert that 'the nature and qualities of all living things are known to country boys better than to philosophers.'[12] But then, Cobbett always minced the name of philosophers into 'feelosofers'.

The most destructive and the most resented oppression of the machine age, when it overtook the old England, was not 'the capitalist system', or any such abstraction. Capitalist control of the means of production was as old as the hills. Nor was it the onset of long hours and low wages. The country people who underwent the rigours of an industrial age were accustomed to long hours of back-breaking toil for a mere pittance. There were factories in old England, too: Lombe's huge silk mill, with its five storeys, its wondrous mechanism, and its large-scale employment of women and child labour, had been flourishing since 1719, and was in most respects the prototype of the Lancashire cotton mills of the following century. Nor, it might be added, were urban slums to prove very much more unhealthy than the rural slums of the 'domestic system'. The real tyranny was the substitution of the rhythm of the machine for the rhythm of nature in the daily lives of people.* It was hated because it was senseless in its monotony; because its final purposes were incomprehensible in human terms; and because it seemed to bear no evident relationship to the familiar tempo of living things. There was, of course, plenty of monotony about field-labour, and Francis Place has told us of the deadly monotony of the domestic industries which would fill the workman with a 'sickening aversion' for his work and drive him to seek solace in bouts of drunkenness. 'We are the most *lazy–diligent* nation in the world', wrote Defoe. 'There is nothing more frequent than for an Englishman to work till he has

* See the excellent discussion of this in J. L. and B. Hammond, *The Town Labourer* (1917), ch. 2.

got his pockets full of money, and then go and be idle or perhaps drunk till 'tis all gone ....' The point, here, however, is that
the Englishman *could* 'go idle', *could* get drunk, when the
monotony of toil became intolerable. It was this very possibility
of relief, this cherished tradition of irregularity, which made the
factory bell so hateful to the first generation of factory workers.*
It required many schools, and particularly Sunday schools, with
their lessoning in the industrial virtues of diligence, thrift, and
especially 'regularity', to turn the people of the fields and the cottages into the people of the factories and the back-streets.

2

The cherished 'irregularity' of old England, within the ancient and
familiar rhythms of nature, must appear to a later age – as at the
time it so often appeared to foreigners – 'a licensed anarchy', or a
particularly large edition of bedlam. Old England was famous for
individual eccentricity and a tendency to suicidal mania. Here
was one of the most prosperous communities in the world, and it
possessed neither a standing army nor a police force. It let people
commit crimes, and then proceeded to punish them severely. It
had no censorship of the press, and a savage law of libel. It locked
up William Combe in the King's Bench prison for most of his life
because he refused to pay what he chose to regard as an unjust
debt, and allowed him to run a highly successful legal business in
the City by virtue of 'the day-rule'. It provided no schools for its
people, and yet any odd fellow you met on the top of a stage-coach
might tell you the height of a church steeple by squinting at it
along the lines of his three-cornered hat. Its laws were an archaic
jumble, and its educational 'system' non-existent, and nobody
seemed to mind very much, except Jeremy Bentham, and he was the
greatest eccentric of them all. Indeed, the mesh of the huge net
which has come to be known as state regulation was so large that
there was ample opportunity for people to grow into very queer
fish indeed.

* This paragraph owes much to the excellent discussion of the old English
working-habits by Dorothy George in her *England in Transition* (1931;
reprinted with additions in Penguin Books, 1953). See especially ch. III.

At the time of the Battle of Waterloo, Élie Halévy observed, with all the incredulity of a Frenchman when faced with a disorderly society which nevertheless maintained itself with remarkable success,

the central government did nothing to secure the public safety, provided no schools, made no roads, gave no relief to the poor. With the solitary exception of the postal service, the State performed no function of immediate benefit to the tax-payer. In the eyes of the public the State appeared only as the power that enlisted men and levied taxes.[13]

This meant, as Halévy came to see, that England was 'in very truth the country of self-government, the country which in the deepest sense – the moral and religious sense – of the phrase "governs itself", instead of being governed by an external authority'.[14] It was, indeed, the very anarchy of English society which enabled the country to remain institutionally so stable. Edmund Burke, who lived at the heart of the old society, saw this when he said: 'Nations are not primarily ruled by laws .... The laws reach but a very little way.' Nations are ruled by the prudence and uprightness of ministers, by the easy and widespread observance of certain traditions of behaviour (both public and private), and by the conformity of the laws to the basic – and often unspoken – conventions of society. Indeed, in the old England, which so considerably perplexed the foreign observer, with its paradoxical combination of a superficial irregularity with a fundamental stability, it was the immense binding-force of social conventions which made formal laws both infrequent and unimportant.

These conventions were hierarchical. They took it for granted that society was a graded order of persons and classes. At the basis of this order was the ancient devotion to *lares et penates*, the cult of filial piety. Children at school wrote home to 'Honoured Parents'. Fathers were still Roman fathers. They beat their sons and spent their wives' portions for them by an unquestioned prerogative.* Among the well-to-do, marriage was still what it had always been, and what it still is in France, a matter of solemn and businesslike negotiations between the families of bride and bridegroom. When young Walter Scott decided, in the year 1797, to take 'the

* There was no Married Women's Property Act until 1882.

34

most important step which I can possibly take in life', he assured his parents that his judgement and his affections had been equally consulted. His own professional exertions, along with his prospective wife's private income, he told his father, 'will enable me to hold the rank in society which my family and situation entitle me to fill'.[15] And this, again, was one of the most important conventions of old England: the duty of maintaining oneself in one's proper station. Social climbers were plentiful, then as always, but the process remained intricate, and its exponents were suspect. It was thought to take three generations, at the very least, to make a gentleman. The accepted view of the social hierarchy remained very much that of the Book of Common Prayer. 'Enable me', prayed Patrick Fraser Tytler, the young Evangelical, in 1810, 'to discharge my duty amiably in that situation in life in which it has pleased God to place me.'[16] Robert Southey observes with satisfaction: 'I *am* in that state of life to which it has pleased God to call me, *for* which I am formed, *in* which I am contented.'[17]

When they write their autobiographies, these children of old England are always at great pains to make perfectly clear on which step of the social ladder they were born. Their pains are more than ordinary when they possess the least shadow of a claim to be known as 'gentlemen' – a description which seems to have had a clearer meaning at that time than it has ever had since. The safest passport to gentility, of course, was the possession of landed property, however small the amount. Scott tells us that his ancestors lived on their own landed property: therefore, 'I was a gentleman, and so welcome anywhere.'[18] Haydon observes: 'Both by my father's and mother's sides I am well descended and connected; the families always residing on their own landed property.'[19] George Borrow, who was at pains to point out that Walter Scott was the son of a pettifogging lawyer and the descendant of a long line of cattle-stealers, was nevertheless careful to put it on record that his own father 'sprang from a family of *gentilâtres*', who had a coat of arms and 'lived on their own property'.[20]

Once one departs from this indefeasible material qualification, however, the test of gentility becomes more complex, and it is possible to proceed only by a process of elimination. It is safe to say that the term 'gentleman' excluded all who made things with their own hands, with tools, or with machinery; all who sold things over a counter; all who owed services in return for wages – as distinct from a stipend or salary. It is apparent that it was a very wide term indeed. At the higher levels it included all those whose daughters were eligible to marry the younger sons of peers: clergymen, lawyers, officers of the army and navy, surgeons, university professors, knights of the shire, landed men above the rank of tenant farmer. There were marginal cases of some difficulty. The poor curate, for example: although William Jay, an Evangelical preacher, tells us, 'In the established Church let a clergyman's appearance and poverty be what it may, he is always treated as a gentleman, and is entitled by right of his sacred office to be admitted, and is received, into the best company upon a footing of equality.'[21] When we remember that a clergyman's daughter was regarded as eligible to marry the younger son of a peer, we arrive at some notion of the huge and amorphous character of this class.

Below the rank of 'gentleman', the class conventions of old England may best be illustrated by observing the way people married. The mother of William Lovett, the Chartist, was the daughter of a blacksmith, and she married the captain of a small trading-vessel. Lovett himself was a cabinet-maker, and he married a lady's maid.[22] Samuel Bamford, the Radical weaver of Middleton, was the grandson of a small farmer who married the daughter of a watch-and clockmaker; as such, she was considered 'something better in condition than was common in those days'. Bamford's father, a simple weaver, married a boot- and shoemaker's daughter. Bamford himself, a weaver's boy, was refused by the daughter of a small farmer's widow, the widow declaring that no man should marry her daughter who could not carry her away on his own horse. Bamford tells us of another farmer's daughter who spurned the suit of 'a common soldier', so that the poor fellow pined away and died. 'A common soldier', at that time, was apt to be regarded as the lowest of the low.[23]

3

The conventions of class, of property, and of family, did not prevent old England from being a remarkably organic type of society. Indeed, they were the surest prophylactics against the anarchical tendencies of a society of such virile individuality and informal government. Many factors were at work to neutralize any tendency towards the formation of a caste system, or even towards the development of acute class-consciousness. The greatest of these factors at that time, and indeed at all times in English history, is the plurality, one might almost say the ubiquity, of what is generally known as 'the middle class'. Rarely, if ever, synonymous with a 'bourgeoisie' of the continental type; shaded with a multitude of gradations within its hazy outlines; easy of access from below, and no less easy of exit from the top: it has served as an enormous shock-absorbing feather-bed or cushion between the 'classes' and the 'masses'. Common men are always springing into it, and uncommon men (and more especially women) are always springing out of it. Almost anyone might belong to it, at almost any time, from the younger son of a peer who has gone into trade, to the successful son of an artisan who has set up as a shopkeeper. A bridge, a buffer, a vestibule, an escalator: it has been all these things at different times, and often all of them at once. Its top level is always within sight of aristocracy; its lower levels are never far removed from the life of the labouring poor. In Regency England, Lord Eldon, the son of a Newcastle coal-merchant, presided over the House of Lords.* At the same time, James Mill, the son of a poor Scottish shoemaker, was the panegyrist of the middle class.

'There can be no doubt', wrote James Mill, in the year of Peterloo, 'that the middle rank ... gives to science, to art, and to legislation itself, their most distinguished ornaments, the chief source of all that has exalted and refined human nature ....' To him, Peterloo was only an unfortunate example of the sort of 'occasional turbulence which may be expected to afflict a manufacturing district, peculiarly unhappy from a very great deficiency of a middle rank' – a district where

the population almost wholly consists of rich manufacturers and poor workmen; with whose minds no pains are taken by anybody; with

* Haydon claims to have met a man in the King's Bench prison who had been committed for contempt of court by the Chancellor: the man had referred to his Lordship's ancestors as 'coal-heavers'.

whose afflictions there is no virtuous family of the middle rank to sympathize; whose children have no good example of such a family to see and admire. . . .

Mill thought that the universalizing of the opinions and values of the middle class was England's surest safeguard against revolution. It was our peculiar good fortune that

the opinions of that class of the people who are below the middle rank are formed, and their minds are directed, by that intelligent and virtuous rank who come most immediately in contact with them, who are in the constant habit of intimate communication with them, to whom they fly for advice and assistance in all their numerous difficulties, upon whom they feel an immediate and daily dependence, in health and in sickness, in infancy and in old age; to whom their children look up as models for their imitation, whose opinions they hear daily repeated, and account it their honour to adopt.[24]

Mill was right. The universalizing of the values of the middle class was undoubtedly to prove the key to the peaceable evolution of England's future. What he would not have understood, however, was the extent to which the older England had been preserved as an organic society by the homogeneity of outlook between aristocracy and people in a predominantly rural civilization. While it is more than doubtful whether the 'Tory democracy' which Disraeli loved to discern in the older English society had ever existed, it is still certain that the classes were not strangers to each other. 'Gentlemen then lived as they ought to live', says Bamford, who knew the old England as well as any man who has left us a record of it; 'in kindness with their tenants; in openhanded charity towards the poor; and in hospitality towards all friendly comers. . . . The gentleman transacted his own business, he met his farmer or labourer face to face.'[25] Even if this exordium requires some modification where business was concerned, it was certainly no exaggeration as regards its rival – and equal – sport. To turn out to hunt the hare was a normal part of the routine of life in a rural society, and there was a real democracy of the hunting-field. There was, likewise, the rough democracy of the prize-ring. In the days of 'the Noble Art', before boxing became a commercialized spectacle,* it was always open to the son of a belted earl to prove himself as good a man as the son of a coal-heaver, and he often did. Great country gentlemen like Thomas Coke of Holkham or William Windham of Felbrigg never missed an opportunity to attend a 'milling-match' or a cock-fight. And, like the great Duke of Bridgwater among his canal 'navigators', they were content to speak the dialect of the crowd. It was rarely that the gentlemen of England lacked 'the common touch'. These encounters of the classes and the masses are none the less important as 'organic filaments' (to use Carlyle's phrase) because they have been sentimentalized by later generations.

Men are never wholly romantic and absurd when they talk of a departed Golden Age. In the early nineteenth century, they talked of such an age so frequently and with such nostalgic ardour, that no member of a 'useful-knowledge society' need hope now to stop their mouths with a figure in arithmetic. Whatever degree of exaggeration there may be in their well-known portraits of the virtues of a vanished race of gentlemen, there can be no doubt that there was more sense of social responsibility, more genuine understanding and sympathy for the labourer, more steady human contact with the daily lives and daily needs of the masses, on the part of the gentry of the older England than could ever be expected of the men who, whatever their intentions, acquired authority over the English countryside in the age of Pitt and Napoleon. Cobbett pitied

the shallow fool who cannot duly estimate the difference between a resident *native* gentry, attached to the soil, known to every farmer and labourer from their childhood, frequently mixing with them in those pursuits where all artificial distinctions are lost ... and a gentry only now-and-then residing, having no relish for country-delights, foreign in their manners, distant and haughty in their behaviour, looking to the soil only for its rents ...[26]

When one of them went to the country, 'they looked upon it that they were to begin a sort of warfare against everything around them ...'[27]

* That great authority, George Borrow, was already deploring the commercial exploitation of the Noble Art by Jewish business men when he wrote *Lavengro* in 1851. See ch. XXVI.

Chapter 3

OLD ENGLAND:
THE PEOPLE IN THE LANDSCAPE

> The thing I want to see is not Redbook Lists, and
> Court Calendars, and Parliamentary Registers, but
> the LIFE OF MAN IN ENGLAND: what men did,
> thought, suffered, enjoyed: the form, especially the
> spirit, of their terrestrial existence, its outward en-
> vironment, its inward principle . . .
>
> CARLYLE: *Boswell's Johnson*, 1832

I

ALMOST in that very hour, when Thomas Carlyle's passionate
imagination was striving to recapture the forgotten lives of forgotten men, the busy pens of William Cobbett, Samuel Bamford
and William Lovett were engaged in piercing the blanket of old
night for the enlightenment of all future generations. With these
men, a world became vocal, the world of the poor.

It is true, of course, that when a working man sits down to write
his autobiography, he has generally ceased to be a working man.
Often, indeed, he is much concerned to proclaim his difference
from the class which bred him. Nevertheless, allowing for the
arrière-pensée, the concern for the success-story, or the latter-day
repentance, we can still avail ourselves of a great deal of unique
documentation, first hand evidence which is lacking for any earlier
age in our history. These three men divide the map of England
between them. Cobbett was of the south and east, the home counties, the countryside; Lovett was of the west country, the sea-
faring population; Bamford of the industrial north. All three
require careful handling as sources of evidence for the life of the
poor. With Cobbett, as we have seen, we are dealing with a man
who escaped early from 'the plough's-tail' and became a much-
travelled and highly successful journalist. He was a liar very often,
and a bully always. Bamford, on the other hand, was something
of a snob. He never allows us to forget that he might have been

Squire Bamford of Bamford Hall, and he is forever asking us to admire his literary abilities and to appreciate all those things which marked him off from the common run of his fellows. He wrote in his respectable old age, when he was prepared to serve – along with Louis Napoleon – as a Special Constable among the Chartists. As for Lovett, although he is less priggish than Bamford and less bombastic than Cobbett, his thirst for self-improvement and for the legitimate glories of leadership set him apart from the average working man of his time.

They take us into a world where hardship was expected and accepted like inclement weather, a world where physical violence was a commonplace of daily living. There was the violent exertion demanded by the daily task; there was the violent, even savage, indulgence in sport, horse-play, or public riot; there was the universal proximity of violent and sudden death. Even to be born into the world of the poor was a hazardous adventure. As soon as you were born you were very likely to die. If you were born in London between the years 1770 and 1789, you had slightly less than an even chance of ever reaching the age of five. The men of the Spa Fields Riots and of Peterloo were the children of this time of appalling infant mortality. They can have had few illusions about the ease and security of life on this earth. They had known death as the close neighbour of their earliest years. Both Lovett and Bamford tell us of the ravages of the smallpox in their childhood. To Lovett, the pock-marked faces of his school-fellows had seemed the normal physiognomy of infancy. Bamford lost his mother, his grandfather, an uncle, a sister and a brother with typhus in the course of a few weeks.

Having avoided death in infancy, the child attended it as a public spectacle. Parents took their children to public executions as a moral entertainment, improving the occasion by a homily upon the wages of sin. Young Bamford confesses to having been deeply impressed by the moral lesson afforded by the execution of 'that unfortunate youth', George Russell, on Newton Heath. On the other hand, George Combe, the phrenologist, says of a similar occasion in his childhood: 'neither in myself ... nor in the other spectators, so far as I could discover by their talk, did this spectacle excite one thought of a nature calculated to deter us from crime'.

41

Indeed, it was a well-known fact that more pockets were picked at the public execution of a pickpocket than at any other time. Nevertheless, the 'Dying Speeches' of condemned criminals were hawked about as moral tracts. The pillory, flogging at the cart-tail, the ducking of scolds and witches, were likewise regarded as 'improving occasions', while suicides were still buried at the cross-roads, with a stake through the heart to prevent the Devil from flying away with them.* Indeed, the men and women of Regency England had lived their infant years very close to the brutal, colourful world of the eighteenth century. The child Samuel Bamford listened to the talk of villagers who professed to have seen Dick Turpin at his boozing-ken at Middleton. His grandfather had marched out with the Young Pretender in 1745, and Walter Scott's uncle saw the executions at Carlisle after the battle of Culloden. Both the Radical and the Tory had heard the story of 'the Good Old Cause' from the lips of those who had seen its end. The one drew from it the conviction that a rebel was a fine fellow; the other that 'the Cavalier creed was the more gentlemanlike persuasion of the two.' Both imbibed something of the eighteenth-century taste for action and faction. The gallows, outlaws, and old rebellion lay in the near background of the popular mind long into the nineteenth century. Thus, when the desperate days came for Radical politicians after Waterloo, there was still a residue of blood-and-thunder men in the ranks of the working-class reformers, men who still associated active politics with the heroic gesture of snatching up a sword or a pike, and rushing into the van of Liberty as they imagined their fathers to have done before them. Not everyone condemned Arthur Thistlewood, whose politics consisted of cutting off the heads of Cabinet Ministers. 'Oh, there was something in those fellows!' George Borrow sighed, when he compared them with the Radicals of 1832.[1] Borrow lived much of his life very close to the old world of swords, bare fists and hot blood. No one would pretend that Borrow was representative of the working class of his time, but the world that Borrow knew and loved was still alive, and very near to the surface of popular memory.

The home, the school, the church or the chapel effected some

* Cobbett cruelly prophesied that this practice would go out of fashion when Castlereagh took his own life in 1822.

softening of the hard, vigorous lines of working-class life. The actual physical environment of the workman's cottage, however, was stark enough. Most labourers lived in tiny dens of daub and timber, beneath thatched roofs, and behind close-shut windows. The floor was often a foot or two below the level of the street. Diet was plain and monotonous; barley-bread, potatoes, a little pork on Sundays, plenty of beer, and very little tea. Scarcity of bread was common enough. Famine was a crisis that the mass of the people were accustomed to in an age when England normally depended upon her own harvests for the staff of life. In these cramped quarters, close to the margin of subsistence, the child was early put to work upon 'the little labours and cares' of the cottage industry or the neighbouring fields. Schooling began, and often ended, in the home; but illiteracy was a good deal less common than the champions of public and state-provided education sometimes maintain. Most children of the poor attended for some period of their infancy at one of the tiny dame-schools that existed in almost every village and hamlet. Nor were the ancient Grammar Schools by any means beyond the reach of the poor man's child. To learn to write and to cypher, however, was 'thought at that time to be all the education required for poor people', William Lovett tells us.

The most significant feature of the education of the children of all classes in the community, however, was its predominantly religious character. The child came at education through religion. The masters of the free Grammar Schools were nearly always clerks in Holy Orders. The classes were often denominated 'Higher Bible', 'Lower Bible', and 'Testament'. The artisan's child learnt to read through the Bible: it was the cheapest and most accessible book to be had.* Outside the Anglican Church, the children re-received instruction at the hands of Sunday School teachers. The Arminian Wesleyans undertook to teach writing on Sundays, between the services. Bamford gives us a vivid picture of the sons and daughters of the Lancashire colliers and weavers trooping in from the distant villages to avail themselves of the Sabbath lessons

---

* Since the foundation of the Society for Promoting Christian Knowledge in 1698. The Society is said to have rejoiced in the slogan:
'The Devil trembles when he sees,
Bibles sold as cheap as these.'

at Middleton Chapel.[2] This use of the books of the Christian religion, and the premises of Christian dogma, as the vehicles of secular instruction, served to impress the tenets of Christianity upon the minds of the people as the primary conditions of human existence. Religious unbelief was common enough among the aristocracy. Among the mass of the people, the village atheist was pointed out as a local monstrosity.

Politically, the consequences of this religious background of the working-class child were profound. There were always people like Cobbett, with his attacks on 'the Saints' as conspiring to 'keep the poor from cutting the throats of the rich ... to starve without making a noise'. Religion as 'the opium of the people' was a gibe thirty years before Charles Kingsley, and a hundred years before Lenin. But there is another side of the picture. In a thousand little Bethels up and down England, the working man was drawing his own conclusions from the reading of the Scriptures. How the process worked out depended upon the sect, and upon the individual. The original Methodists, organized by the Tory autocrat, John Wesley, were generally Tories in politics. Those of the New Connexion, who broke away in order to govern their affairs more democratically, were often Radicals. Everywhere, self-organization in Chapel communities afforded an elementary training in self-government. The 'Chapel classes' with their travelling preachers readily became the model for Hampden Reform Clubs and travelling 'Delegates'. The prim respectability of Radicals like Zachariah Coleman* was not the achievement of an opium-peddling clergy making converts for the Tory party, but the typical product of an ethos created by earnest, callow, decent-living, dissenting Christians for themselves. And anyway, as Bamford remarked, 'there was no religion in the world that could ever make a bobbin-winder content with his lot.' Yet, one thing is certain: the religious background of working-class life made it inevitable, when the time came, that the English working-class movement should be an essentially moralistic movement. And this fact took the edge off the sword-and-dagger tradition where it survived the departure of the eighteenth century, with its Jacobites and its Lord Gordons.

* The hero of Mark Rutherford's novel, *The Revolution in Tanner's Lane*, which gives a valuable picture of English radicalism at this time.

Religion, however, did nothing to undermine the strength of popular superstition. The lives of the poor were still neighboured by a whole phantasmagoria of ghosts, boggarts and witches. After the Bible, cheap reading-matter comprised such universally popular works as *The Seven Champions of Christendom*, *The History of Friar Bacon* and *The Arabian Nights*. Lovett says of a west country town, as late as 1810,

there was only one book-seller ... and with the exception of Prayer-Books, spelling-books and a few religious works, the only books in circulation for the masses were a few story-books and romances, filled with absurdities about giants, spirits, goblins, and supernatural horrors.[3]

Lovett's scorn for such things was a late development. He admits that 'it was many years after I came to London before I became a sceptic in ghosts.' Bamford fully appreciated the tremendous part played by boggarts, witches and clap-cans in the lives of ordinary men and women. The effect of all this on the 'minds and manners of the rural population of the period' seemed to him more important than was commonly supposed.[4] He hints that simple folk tended to extend such superstition to the established authorities in Church and State, so that the parson and the magistrate were liable to be included in the category of the supernaturally powerful. It was certainly a propitious omen to be blessed by the right hand of the Bishop at confirmation; it was regarded as a wise precaution to seek the parson's permission to work on the Sabbath; and the efficacy of being 'touched for the King's evil' was believed in until the reign of Queen Victoria.

The established authorities in Church and State were still considered by most people to exercise their powers by much the same right as the sun shines or the clouds bring rain. The use of force, even brutally, on the part of authority, struck few people as a matter for comment. When the press-gang appeared on the horizon, there was rarely anything like a common resistance, only a cry of 'sauve qui peut', in its English equivalent. Lovett writes of the common spectacle of eligible young men running away to hide for the day in the woods. Sometimes, he tells us, 'the authorities arranged for a troop of Light Horse to be at hand to cut off their retreat. ... Then might the soldiers be seen, with drawn swords, riding down the poor fishermen, often through fields of standing corn where they had sought to hide themselves.'[5] Likewise the stout-hearted young Bamford, walking from London to Lancashire, went in fear of the press-gang at every town. When at last they came up with him, he told them that he was a free-born subject with a right to walk the highway without a pass. At this, 'they looked at each other, and then at me .... They had no idea of free-born subjects.'[6] It was, indeed, the common habit to round up the people like cattle. Peterloo was in an ancient tradition. The people who endured the rule of Castlereagh came of a stock which knew familiarly the menace of the press-gang, the gallows and the lash. They had lived in a world where man-made violence ranked with the fell forces of nature. It was some measure of the change of sentiment, and the growth of a more widespread critical temper, among the people of Regency England, that Peterloo was condemned as an outrage by men and women who in their childhood and youth had watched with comparative passivity the many-sided violence of authority thirty years before.

As for 'government' itself, that distant abstraction which wielded the fitfully harsh instruments of authority, who can now imagine what the word may, or may not, have conjured up in the minds of common men before the invention of photography? The tremendous sense of shock which such men experienced when actually brought face to face with England's governors in their human flesh and blood is conveyed to us by Samuel Bamford, whose political education was carried a long step further, at public expense, when he was taken before the Privy Council for interrogation in 1817. Lord Castlereagh turned out to be 'a good-looking person in a plum-coloured coat, with a gold ring on the small finger of his left hand, on which he sometimes leaned his head as he eyed me over . . . .' Lord Sidmouth, the putative father of the Government's secret intelligence system, had deep-set, friendly eyes. 'His manner was affable, and much more encouraging to freedom of speech than I had expected.' Bamford discovered, too, that the Lords of the Council were even capable of laughter. 'Quite a merry set of gentlemen', he found them. He went away with the feeling that this kind of meeting should have occurred more often. If only governors and governed 'could have known each other better beforehand', he reflected, 'their feelings, ideas, and interests – there would have been no Six Acts on the one hand, or Spa Fields and Manchester meetings on the other.'[7]

Bamford's rather too comfortable reflection is one of his over-frequent *arrières-pensées*. Moreover, it overlooks the important fact that most Englishmen met 'government' not in the Lords of the Council, but in the Lord of the Manor. When Jeremiah Brandreth, 'the Nottingham Captain', arrived in the Derbyshire village of South Wingfield one day in June 1817, to lead out the local revolutionaries to overturn the Government, nobody mentioned Lord Castlereagh. Instead, an old woman tapped him on the shoulder and said: 'We have a magistrate here, my man.'

2

Properly speaking, the mass of the labouring population had no political standing, as such, in the old England. 'Of the labouring classes, who in all countries form the great majority of the inhabitants,' Coleridge was content to say, when addressing his fellow countrymen on the public discontents, as late as 1816, 'they are not sought for in public counsel, nor need they be found where politic sentences are spoken. It is enough if every one is wise in the working of his own craft: so best will they maintain the state of the world.'[8] They might be said to be part of the Third Estate of the Realm, 'the Commons', in so far as their interests were bound up with one or other of the quite tangible and substantial 'interests' of society – the landed, the commercial, the professional, and so on. But there was no separate or distinct 'labour' interest. Labour, as such, had no 'constitutional presence'. It was certainly not identical with 'the people'. That term was reserved for the comparatively small and select part of the population which possessed a certain degree of property and education. The rest, it was supposed, existed rather to be governed than to take part in government, and was variously named 'the populace', 'the mobility', or (by Burke on an unfortunate occasion) 'the swinish multitude'. Burke, indeed, accurately defined the eighteenth-century situation when he wrote:

47

Those who, in any *political* view, are to be called the people are of adult age, not declining in life, of tolerable leisure for such discussions, and of some means of information, above menial dependence: i.e. about 400,000. This is the British public; and it is a public very numerous. The rest, when feeble, are the objects of protection; when strong, the means of force.[9]

Much the most important element in this 'public' was the aristocracy, great and small. It was never a closed circle, jealously guarding its quarterings or its blood. Blood has never been ennobled in England, and quarterings have generally been attainable at a price. Constantly refreshed by intermarriage with, and recruitment from, other sections of society, it was (and, where it survives, it still is) what Matthew Arnold called it – the most just and sympathetic, the least impertinent and frivolous aristocracy in the world.[10] Its most singular characteristic was perhaps its preference for the concrete and the tangible, its perennial distrust of ideas. For, after all, the aristocracy, self-based upon its own substantial wealth, scarcely needed to argue. It shone by its own light. It was not created by 'the State'. Indeed, if it was a question of which came first, the State had been made by the aristocracy. The State existed by their grace, in so far as it existed at all.* Not for them the pompous refinements of 'High-state doctrine'. Only a foreign *parvenu* like Burke (an Irishman dependent upon the bounty of the Marquess of Rockingham) would talk about the 'sanctity' of the State, its constitution, or its institutions. The aristocracy, who ruled the State, and made its insitutions work, and used its offices as almshouses for their needy friends and relations – the aristocracy had no such illusions. They might well have said: 'L'État? C'est nous.' Men who use the institutions of their country with such proprietorial familiarity are not apt to harbour illusions about their sanctity. And these gentlemen of the eighteenth century in England sometimes behaved like very proprietorial lords indeed. As late as 1818, when the upstart lawyer, Henry Brougham, ventured to contest a Westmoreland election, the Lowthers concentrated troops from every part of the

* A debatable question among German philosophers since Hegel: e.g. Oswald Spengler – 'In England, the island replaces the organized state. A country without a state were only possible under this condition.'

county at the polling-booths, brought coach-loads of sailors and carpenters from Liverpool 'to keep the peace' at five shillings a day, and marched out two hundred special constables in arms.[11]

Two important distinctions must be borne in mind in any discussion of the aristocracy in the reign of George III. First, there is the distinction which Cobbett was never tired of making, between the old 'native' aristocracy and the newly enriched families who were coming to the old houses of England in ever-increasing numbers as the growth of large-scale industry shifted the balance of wealth. Shelley, who belonged to the old aristocracy himself, always insisted upon the distinction between 'the Corinthian capital of polished society' and 'the creeping weeds which deface the rich tracery of its sculpture'.[12] The second distinction is between the small group of hereditary peers who comprised the nobility, and whose political activities were centred in the House of Lords and in the Lord-Lieutenancies of the Counties; and the very much larger body of the lower aristocracy, loosely described as 'the country gentlemen' or 'the landed gentry'.

There has never been in England an isolated and exclusive 'caste' of noblemen equivalent to the *grands seigneurs* of France. The younger sons and brothers of noblemen were commoners, and frequently engaged in trade or lived as plain country gentlemen. Many a wearer of a coronet had himself lived the life of an ordinary country gentleman before his succession to the peerage and the ancestral estates. Even so, the education of the eldest son of a peer tended to take a peculiar and strictly predestined course. Conscious that his destiny ultimately lay in the high places of the political world of courts and cabinets and embassies, he was often reared in a more sophisticated and cosmopolitan atmosphere than his younger brother of the Quarter Sessions and the Yeomanry. When, and if, he went to the University he would wear the gold-laced gown and the gold-tasselled cap of the Fellow Commoner. He would spend rather less of his time than his brothers in scrambling about the countryside with the sons of keepers and tenant farmers. He would learn rather earlier how to drink his wine, wear his lace, and enter a drawing-room. When he went out riding, he had a pony with silver bells, and a serving-man running behind. Certainly he would pass more youthfully, and more splendidly attended, beyond sight of the village steeple to see the best society of Europe on the Grand Tour. Thereafter, the running was fairly smooth to the House of Lords and the Grand Jury, and all the business of mortgages, heiresses and the beautifying of parks and mansions. In their prime, and at their best, these men were a unique breed, great arbiters of quality in all the outward things of life, great patrons of letters and the arts. Haydon, the painter, staying at Petworth with Lord Egremont, has left a word-portrait of the spacious, liberal life of the great house,[13] to which only Turner was to do justice in paint. The very flies seemed to know there was room for their existence in that world within a world, where everything was so 'solid, liberal, rich and English'. There were the guests accorded perfect freedom, the happy children, the sleek spaniels feeding on cakes and comfits from his lordship's own hand .... 'There is nothing like 'em when they add intelligence to breeding,' Haydon concluded. And they often did.

They were, however, far less remarkable than their younger brothers of the landed gentry, if only because they were far less numerous and far more remote from the world of primary production.* The English country gentlemen were indeed perhaps the most remarkable class of men that any society has ever produced anywhere in the world. They were the men who governed England where England mostly lived : in market town and village and hamlet. In the House of Commons they formed a body of independent members whose votes were courted by Ministry and Opposition alike. But it was on the countryside that their greatest influence was exercised, where they served as Captains of the Yeomanry and Justices of the Peace.

> God bless the squire and his relations
> Who keep us in our proper stations ...

is something more than a cynical description of a bygone social phenomenon. Squire and his relations really did preside as the stewards of that divinity which had been pleased to ordain the just and proper order of society. Squire dispensed the law because, it was presumed, he knew what the law was : often, indeed, he had

---

* There were great exceptions, however : few men of the eighteenth century were nearer to 'primary production' than the Duke of Bridgwater.

helped to make it. He told the county freeholders how to vote because, it was presumed, he knew what was best for the country –
which meant the countryside. Anyway, he dispensed the loaves
and fishes. Most of the people on his land depended upon him, for
their cottages, for their employment, for their relief in times of
distress, and for the custom which he and his family brought to
their shops or workshops .... No doubt he shared the outlook of
the governing class, but he also shared the outlook of the governed.
There was no isolation about his life. Every day brought him close
to the common life of common people. He was unlikely to be
troubled by any such mystic entity as 'the mob': he knew too
much about Tom and Dick and Harry. He had his prejudices in
plenty, but he was never far from ordinary humanity in his
capacity of magistrate, landlord and local oracle.

Growing up in some commodious old house bordered by its elms
and hollies and ancient turf, alive with the bustling familiarities
of grooms and servants, he was learning the business of his ancestors from his earliest days. He got his formal education at the
hands of a private tutor or at a public school. Sometimes, but not as
often as might be supposed, he went on to the University. In the
eighteenth century, the parents of most upper-class young men
would have agreed with Cobbett who called the universities 'dens
of dunces', or with the aunt of Thomas Coke who called them 'dens
of vice' and paid her nephew £500 a year on condition that he went
on the Grand Tour instead. The Grand Tour, however, was a fabu-
lously expensive form of education. Most sons of country gentlemen passed straight from private tutor and public school into the
active life of the countryside, riding over the estate, riding to
hounds and riding to market. Riding to hounds, in pursuit of
the fox rather than the hare, was regarded as something more
than a sport. It was held to be an education in those qualities of
courage and hardihood which were expected of an English country
gentleman.

The manly amusement of fox-hunting [wrote Eardley-Wilmot, one
of its greatest exponents] is the best corrective to those habits of luxury
and those concomitants of wealth which would otherwise render our
aristocracy effeminate and degenerate; it serves to retain the moral influence of the higher over the lower classes of society, and is one of the

strongest preservatives of that national spirit by which we are led to cherish above all things a life of active energy, independence, and freedom.[14]

It was generally felt among the English squires that the battle of Waterloo was won on the hunting-fields of Leicestershire:

> Thus trained, my masters, you would meet the foe,
> Furious to battle as to covert go.
> A cavalry already formed the French to rout,
> And 'Tally-ho!' your frantic war-whoop, shout!

Thus born and bred, the country gentlemen brought to the tasks of government both the merits and the defects of their upbringing. The merits were those of courage, vitality and 'the common touch'. If the country gentleman became convinced of the necessity of Radical reform – as did, for example, Sir Francis Burdett – he went in for reform with all his might, prepared to face the consequences of his convictions with all the arrogant fearlessness of his kind. In any case, and whatever his politics, he carried the bold manners of the hunting-field and the prize-ring into the arena of public life. He was always a fighting politician. The gentlemen, Bamford noted, 'were too prone to lay on hard when they got the upper hand'.[15] He might have added that it was their habit to do the same when they were at a disadvantage, too. Cobbett never forgave Mr Thomas Assheton-Smith for hanging two poachers, but it was this same Mr Assheton-Smith who won the heart of the mob that tried to howl him down on the hustings at Nottingham with the cry of 'No fox-hunting M.P.!' by offering to fight any man of them with his bare fists. When, three years after Waterloo, Mr Assheton-Smith was beaten in a stand-up fight in the street by a coal-heaver, the victor went home in great 'fear of arrest for striking a gentleman'. So far as Mr Assheton-Smith was concerned, he need not have troubled his head about that.[16]

The quality of the justice and administration dispensed by this race of men in their capacities as landlords and justices of the peace, was very much what might be expected. It was always forthright and empirical; it was humane, except where the sanctity of property had been infringed, and especially where it had been infringed by poachers; it was energetic, except where the law was inimical to the interests of country gentlemen. The principal weakness of the old system of amateur government was that it gave over-much scope to the vagaries and prejudices of the individual magistrate; although it must be admitted that much of its strength and virtue resided in the scope it left for the free play of personality. If anyone still believes that the country houses of old England were occupied by the ruthless minions of an aristocratic oligarchy, he should dip into the journals of Sir Robert Heron.[17] Heron was a Lincolnshire squire, a Whig, a Member of Parliament, a Justice of the Peace, and a busy landlord. The range of his interests and sympathies is astonishing. On alternate pages of his journal, we find him occupied with the nurture of pea-fowl, the iniquities of the Holy Alliance and Lord Castlereagh, a pair of kangaroos given to him by Lord Bath, the evils of the Poor Law Bill of 1796, and the death of the 'remarkable large gold-fish at Ponton'. In 1814, Sir Robert ensured good gardens and pasture for one cow to all his labourers, while Lady Heron employed the women of decent character in 'our four villages' in spinning. He advances loans to his labourers with the entry: 'Why do men so frequently complain of the ingratitude of the labouring class and of servants?' Like all his race, however, Sir Robert believed himself to be indispensable. 'The people of England have never acted, and never will act, with permanent vigour and resolution,' he confided to his journal, 'unless under the guidance of men of rank and consequence.'[18]

This is the prevailing prejudice of the country gentleman, Whig or Tory. He might believe, as Heron believed, that the Government of the day was dishonest and inane in fearing an imminent revolution, but he retained the fundamental attribute of the politics of his class: a constitutional inability to conceive of 'the people' acting alone. That is why, despite the many contacts which he enjoyed with the common life of the people as landlord, magistrate and local oracle, he was to remain an exponent of the values of old England longer perhaps than anyone else in the community. No class was so strongly tied to the old order and its values. The great nobleman might own the soil, but he rarely lived with, and like, the people of the soil; he might fancy that he governed the state, but he certainly did not govern the village: he might know Man, but he had fewer opportunities to know men. Likewise, the yeoman farmer lived and died upon his own ground, but he commanded no authoritative share in the political and administrative life of the county. Neither the middle classes nor the labourers possessed those roots in the very fibre of England which long generations of ownership and public responsibility alone can give. The country gentleman lived on his land and by his land, he hunted over it, and he was buried beneath it. Land was the condition of his thought, and of all his feelings. His politics were derived from its needs, his patriotism sprang from his passion to defend what was his own. He might see, as Sir Robert Heron saw, that both Italy and Germany were to become great united states; but he could not see that there would ever be a case for the free importation of foreign corn. Those who imagined the possibility of such a thing were described by Sir Robert as 'utterly incapable of understanding the question'. For the price of home-grown corn was more than an economic question. It was the foundation-stone of a way of life, a civilization, even of the Constitution. 'If landed property has not predominant influence', Lord Redesdale wrote to the Home Secretary, in 1816, 'the British Constitution, which is founded on the predominance of landed property, cannot stand.'[19]

3

The habit of hypostasizing the institutions of one's own day is almost as common as the habit of mistaking contemporary prejudices for eternal verities. It was particularly common among the landed gentlemen of the eighteenth century. Lord Redesdale and his kind habitually spoke of 'the British Constitution' as if it were a fixed and objective reality, instead of the name for a highly plastic garment which had adapted itself to the changing shape of the body politic, and which would continue to do so, more or less readily, as the body politic itself was transformed by changes in the structure of society. Edmund Burke was wiser in his generation. 'A state without the means of some change', he declared, 'is without the means of its conservation.' He likened the constitutional policy of his country to 'the pattern of nature', and the nature of the world itself, wherein a permanent body is composed of transient parts, so that 'the whole, at one time, is never old, or middle-aged, or young, but, in a condition of unchangeable constancy, moves on through the varied tenor of perpetual decay, fall, renovation, and progression.'[20]

Old England had its 'growing points', areas of society where the future was already in the bud. Revolutions begin with the misfits, and they take an evolutionary form so long as the misfits are able to believe that the old order of things can be made to accommodate itself to their needs. A veritable revolution took place in England between the middle of the eighteenth and the middle of the nineteenth century, but the men and classes of men who provided its impulse were never driven to despair by the inflexibility of the *status quo*. John Wesley was a misfit in the English Church, but he was able to make that Church fit for the ministrations of a pious and enthusiastic clergy. Jeremy Bentham could not bring himself to practise the law as it existed in the age of Lord Mansfield, and for sixty years brought to bear all the energies of his ruthlessly rational mind upon the task of transforming not only the judicial, but the legislative and administrative, life of England. Sir Francis Burdett found himself unable to stomach the tepid reformism of the Whigs, and spent his whole life in trying to persuade the House of Commons to reform itself – which it eventually did. Each of these three men, the priest, the lawyer and the squire, could have lived highly respectable and comfortable lives within the old order of things. They had nothing to lose, and everything to gain, by acceptance. Instead, they accepted the role of rebels on behalf of the future, growing-points of the new society which was coming to birth within the old.

There was, moreover, a whole section of society which accepted this role. The prosperous Dissenters had nothing to lose and everything to gain by the transformation of society. Excluded from political life within the traditional institutions, and from the leading positions in many of the professions, by the antique survivals of seventeenth-century religious intolerance, they had taken to business and to science. There they flourished exceedingly by reason of their utilitarian virtues of orderly and well-regulated living. With their excellent educational institutions, their social clannishness, they formed almost a state within the state.[21] For them, the traditional sanctities of English institutions had little meaning, save as oppressive relics of a past which had persecuted dissent. For them, 'Church and State' meant Conventicle Acts, Five Mile Acts, and Acts of Uniformity. This, together with their strongly utilitarian cast of mind, made the Protestant Dissenters one of the most influential elements in the movement for constitutional reform. The alliance of dissenting religion and reformist politics, at the very heart of the middle class, did more than anything else to ensure a peaceful and positive transition in the difficult and dangerous years which brought the new England to birth from the old.

Chapter 4

THE MELTING-POT

> The anomalous occasions and stupendous events of
> the contest had aroused us like the blast of a trum-
> pet from the clouds; and as many as were capable
> of thinking were roused to thought.
>
> COLERIDGE, 1817

> The public resemble one hardly roused from a
> trance: – each conscious of his past slumber, but
> not completely recovered from its effects, although
> fully sensible that it is time to rise, – some do not
> like to move – others wish they were up, but take
> no steps to put on their clothes, – others sit on the
> bed-side and in the hurry to dress, put their gar-
> ments on wrong.
>
> Black Dwarf, 1817

WHEN peace came to England, and to Europe, in 1815, thought-
ful men realized that its coming meant a good deal more than the
mere cessation of war. The poets, always sensitive registers of im-
pending change in the body politic, were quick to cry the change
in the political atmosphere. To Southey, the change from war to
peace seemed like 'a change in life itself'. To Coleridge, it heralded
the breakdown of that artificial union of interests which had been
precariously maintained during the desperate struggle against the
enemies of national survival. He marvelled, however, that such
dread compulsion should have been necessary to preserve a society
which possessed so many of the influences which make for a normally organic type of life. An island power with an expanding
commerce, 'the inter-dependent hierarchy of classes ... the pressure
of ranks on each other ... the inter-dependence, the arterial or
nerve-like net-work of property' – surely a people thus blessed by
Providence and thus fortified by its own endeavours might have
been expected to enjoy a high degree of unity without the stimulus
of peril from beyond its borders?[1] Yet, at the moment when Coleridge was writing, England seemed nearer to revolutionary up-

heaval and civil war than at any time since the seventeenth century.

Coleridge was a philosopher, and he laid the blame for this perilous situation upon the prevalence of a false philosophy. At the darkest hour of England's post-war agony, when other anxious citizens were recommending measures to restrict the Radical press, to arm property owners against machine-wrecking workmen, or to secure the loyalty of the army by issuing belatedly a series of 'Victory-medals', the philosopher of Highgate Hill wrote to the Prime Minister recommending the abandonment of the philosophy of Locke and a return to the philosophy of Plato. 'As long as the principles of our gentry and clergy are grounded in a false philosophy', he declared, not all the Sunday schools in the world could preclude schism and Jacobinism in the middle and lower classes. 'The predominant philosophy is the keynote . . . .'[2] Of course, he was right, but the suggestion was scarcely helpful at a moment when mobs were rioting in Spa Fields and the men of South Derbyshire were marching out to overturn Lord Liverpool and his colleagues with pikes and shot-guns. It says something for the philosophic calm of the Prime Minister that he took the trouble to endorse Mr Coleridge's highly abstruse letter with a fair summary of its contents and a modest note: 'At least, I believe this is Mr Coleridge's meaning, but I cannot well understand him.'

The predominant philosophy, which Coleridge called 'the keynote', was the philosophy of individualism which had been predominant in England since John Locke and which had recently found its fashionable restatement in the works of Jeremy Bentham. If every individual pursued a policy of enlightened self-interest, ran the argument, society as a whole would attain the maximum of happiness and the minimum of misery. In all cases, the individual was the best judge of his own interests. Government and laws were necessary evils. Their activities should be sharply circumscribed, and constantly judged by the test of utility in terms of the greatest happiness of the greatest number. This, the fashionable gospel of Utilitarianism, had been derived by Jeremy Bentham from Helvetius and the *Philosophes* of the eighteenth century. It took root in England with great rapidity for a number of highly practical reasons. In the first place, the doctrine derived immense force from historic fact. It was only too easy to argue that English government in the eighteenth century was too corrupt to be entrusted with any more business than was absolutely necessary. Nor was it difficult to show that when government did concern itself with anything but the minimal affairs of state, it produced disastrous results: witness the policy which lost the American colonies. Again, the theory provided a perfect theoretical justification of contemporary practice. It seemed to justify the ways of men to God. It enabled men who were trampling their way to industrial power over the bodies of enslaved women and children to identify their self-interest with the public weal. It did, indeed, cover a multitude of sins.

Finally, to repudiate government interference was natural to men who did not control that government. The English parliament was still mainly composed of men who represented the landed interest. In 1815 it erected a Corn Law to keep up the price of bread, with the result that the artisan demanded higher wages. By 1818 it was listening with some respect to proposals to shorten the hours of labour of children in cotton mills. In short, it seemed that an assembly of agriculturists was moved by spite and jealousy to ruin British industry. What more natural than that British industrialists – indeed, the middle classes in general – should resent and distrust government?

It must not be supposed, however, that dislike of governmental interference was confined to the 'excluded' interests in English society: those who found no place within the pale of the Constitution. It was equally the attitude of those who monopolized the government of the state. The counterpart of Benthamite individualism in the sphere of political economy was the *laissez-faire* doctrine which seemed to attain to the status of Holy Writ in Adam Smith's *Wealth of Nations*. It is hardly too much to say that the Younger Pitt had made the political economy of Adam Smith the official doctrine of the Tory Party, and in this, as in so much else, Lord Liverpool and his colleagues were faithful disciples of their master. Not only did Henry Addington compose an ode to the author of the *Wealth of Nations*; he lost no opportunity of absolving himself and his colleagues from all responsibility for the economic and social distress of the post-war years by attributing it to the inscrutable decrees of Providence. 'Man cannot create abundance where Providence has inflicted scarcity', he wrote, on taking office as Home Secretary in 1812. Again, in the dark and dangerous year 1817, he reminded his countrymen: 'The alleviation of the difficulties is not to be looked for from the intervention of the Government and Parliament.'[3] Divine Providence and Adam Smith were to serve as Lord Sidmouth's most cherished alibi for more than ten years.

Lord Liverpool himself was, as we shall see presently, capable of a somewhat more flexible application of the *laissez-faire* doctrine. Nevertheless, he stood firmly by the wise and salutary character of the doctrine in all ordinary circumstances. Even when defending the breach of principle embodied in the Corn Law of 1815, he maintained its general validity: 'The general principle, supposing all nations, or at least the most considerable nations, to act upon it, was that in these cases the Legislature ought not to interfere, but should leave everything to find its own level.'[4] Again, in replying to the proposal of a noble Lord in the critical year 1819 that state aid should be given to commercial undertakings in distressed areas, he said: 'I am satisfied that government or parliament never meddle with these matters at all but they do harm, more or less.' He went on to insist that the people ought to be taught that 'the evils inseparable from the state of things should not be charged on any government; and, on enquiry, it would be found that by far the greater part of the miseries of which human nature complained were at all times and in all countries beyond the control of human legislation.'[5] Lord Liverpool was fond of quoting a certain couplet from Samuel Johnson:

> How small, of all the ills that men endure,
> The part which Kings or States can cause or cure.

This, then, was the orthodoxy of the day, and it amounted – as Thomas Carlyle was to point out – to 'an abdication on the part of governors'. But it should never be forgotten, as Carlyle also pointed out, that the cry of 'Let us alone' was less a criticism of all government than a symptom of men's distrust of a certain kind of government. What men most often meant by it was, 'let us alone of *your* government.'[6] John Stuart Mill put it more historically when he declared that the *laissez-faire* doctrine was the offspring of 'the manifest selfishness and incompetence of modern governments'.[7]

Whatever it meant, however, and from whatever motives it sprang, it was an affront to the principles of social cohesion. And the interesting thing about the age and the society in which this anarchic doctrine flourished is, that hardly anyone cared. The notion that English society might fall to pieces under the impact of such powerful centripetal forces in thought and action scarcely occurred to anyone in Regency England. An island people, guarded by a strong navy, proud of its antique constitution – a constitution under whose aegis Britain had survived the revolutionary storm which had swept Europe for more than twenty years – a people full of enterprise and vitality, and serenely confident in its expanding economy: could such a people not afford a little anarchy – more especially when it was presided over by an English Providence and Adam Smith? Less than a generation later there were to be plenty of prophets to cry the need of social integration: Carlyle with his gospel of heroic leadership; Disraeli with his warnings of 'the Two Nations'; Young England with its plea for alliance of Monarch, Aristocracy and Multitude; and Marx following on with his gospel of class-war as the way of salvation. The England of the Regency was content to leave such prophecies and prognostications to the lonely visionary of Highgate Hill. Now was the day and now the hour of a universal and enlightened individualism. Young Mr Weller, already polishing boots at the *White Hart*, spoke for the *zeitgeist*: 'Every man for hisself, and God for all of us, as the elephant said when he danced among the chickens.'

This sublime mood, however, was not one of complacency in the face of the world as at present constituted. Government might be ardently requested to let things alone, but everyone else was busy with schemes for improving the world at the earliest possible moment. The long war had laid a frozen hand upon the stream of universal improvement which had been flowing ever faster and more energetically since the scientific renaissance of the seventeenth century. Eighteenth-century England, at least until the outbreak of the war with Revolutionary France, had been persuaded that everything could be improved, from the making of laws to the making of stockings. The breed of sheep, the utility of commons, the navigability of rivers, the manufacture of hosiery and lace and cheap cotton shirts: all these things, and many more, had come under the dominion of human ingenuity and inventiveness. Society itself, in its laws and customs and institutions, had been subjected to inspection and suggestion. The dire necessity to repel the forces of improvement when they came in the shape of French bayonets had discredited the notion of the necessary nature of improvement for a time, but once Napoleon – the arch-improver with a bayonet – was safely lodged in St Helena, the tide began to flow again with an impetus all the greater for the temporary dam. In Regency England, it may safely be said, everyone had a 'plan', and everyone talked about it, wrote about it, agitated his fellow men about it, day and night, without ceasing. Never since the hot days of the Commonwealth had England known such intensity and diversity of thought.

There was old Major Cartwright, who had been preaching parliamentary reform since 1776, and was now dashing about the industrial districts with a box of petitions and the gospel: 'Petition for a reform of the House of Commons, and all else shall be added unto you.' There was William Cobbett carrying a motion at a farmers' meeting in Hampshire: 'That this meeting have a firm conviction that it is in the House of Commons as at present constituted that exists the great and efficient cause of the profligacy of manners amongst so many in high life ....'[8] There was, on the other hand, Robert Southey – Byron's 'Bob Southey, the Poet' – who thought parliamentary reform important only as 'depriving the anarchists of the only topics which give a shadow of plausibility to their harangues'. Southey advocated, instead, an increase in the workman's spending-power, a cheaper system of justice, the inclusion of Dissenters in the Church of England, an improvement in the condition of women. 'The present Ministry,' he declared, 'is deficient in everything but good intentions ....'[9] Jeremy Bentham described Robert Southey as 'an ultra-servile sack-guzzler'.* The only way to cure man's complaints, Bentham held, was to measure every law by the slide-rule of the Felicific Calculus, as constructed

* Presumably because the Poet Laureate traditionally received payment in kind – and partly in sack.

by Jeremy Bentham, thereby ensuring the Greatest Happiness of the Greatest Number. Thomas Malthus, however, considered it to be entirely a matter of over-population, and that checks on its increase should be encouraged – more especially among the poor. Southey, looking at his son and three daughters, reflected 'what a fit thing it would be that Malthus should be hanged'.[10] Shelley took it for granted that 'Parson' Malthus, being a priest, must also be a eunuch and a tyrant. 'He has the hardened insolence to propose as a remedy that the poor should be compelled ... to abstain from sexual intercourse, while the rich are to be permitted to add as many mouths to consume the product of the labours of the poor as they please ....'[11]

Coleridge had come to the conclusion that all the ills of society were the consequence of 'the over-balance of the commercial spirit', and that society could only be saved by making the Bible the statesman's manual.[12] At almost the same moment, in 1817, Robert Owen was addressing a public meeting on the social poison known as 'religion'. He delivered himself thus:

My friends, I tell you that hitherto you have been prevented from ever knowing what happiness really is, solely in consequence of the errors – gross errors – that have been combined with the fundamental notions of every religion that has hitherto been taught to men. And, in consequence, they have made men the most inconsistent and the most miserable beings in existence.[13]

Owen proposed to leave the Christian Paradise of the hereafter severely alone and to concentrate on founding the New Jerusalem here and now. In his *New View of Society*, published in 1814, he had stated with all the religious fervour of the agnostic his unswerving confidence in the infinite perfectibility of man through the improvement of man's environment. By 1817 he was prepared to save humanity at £80 per head through a system of cooperative industry. It is characteristic of his time that while Lord Sidmouth circulated his schemes to the crowned heads of Europe, he encountered his strongest opponents among his fellow Radicals. William Cobbett dismissed Owen's plan as 'a species of Monkery'.

Owen was not alone in scenting the advent of the millenium through a 'plan'. The Society of Spencean Philanthropists were advocating the adoption of the 'Glorious Plan' of Thomas Spence,[14] a poor but earnest Newcastle schoolmaster, for the equal division of the land between the parishes of England. Thus would be cured 'the poor man's poverty and the rich man's gout'. In the meantime, the Spenceans employed their time in chalking the legend: SPENCE'S PLAN on every wall in London and in hailing the approaching millenium at their convivial meetings with the anthem:

> This reign of Plenty, Peace and Love
> The Good have long fore-told,
> A blest Millenium will prove
> To mankind young and old.
> No more distress, all happiness,
> From Landlords once set free,
> The bells shall ring, we'll dance and sing
> On Spence's Jubilee.

The *Black Dwarf*, an ultra-radical journal, declared in March 1817 that the lower classes were fully aware of the folly of the Spencean system. 'They know that scarce a man of common sense entertains any disposition to listen to such romantic schemes.'[15] The *Black Dwarf* had its own ideas on what a man of common sense should, or should not, believe. In the previous February, the editor had apologized for the omission, owing to its late arrival, of 'The Song of a Patriot: showing compendiously how to rectify all the Political Evils of this, or any other Nation, without Violence or Injustice'.[16]

Thus they went at it, writing, talking, plan and counter-plan, blast and counter-blast. The melting-pot of Regency England bubbled to the brim. No attempt will be made here to separate out the constituent ingredients of this astonishing brew. Our purpose is merely to illustrate their variety, although we shall later make some attempt to follow the consequences of those opinions which had effect on political action. Here it is sufficient to say that it was in this fierce cauldron that the mental conventions of Old England went through the ordeal of fire. When they emerged, they bore the stamp of those conventions which, for want of a better word, we call 'modern'.

Chapter 5

CHALLENGE TO MONOPOLISTS

> At the date of Waterloo there did not exist in Eng-
> land, outside the landed class, five hundred persons
> whose incomes exceeded £5,000 a year. Now such a
> small, cohesive class, having 'the monopoly of
> varied experience', united by subtle similarities of
> taste, behaviour and judgment, and with constant
> opportunities for meeting each other, makes a very
> enviable society, especially when it is unchallenged.
> There is a delicious *chez-soi* feeling when any who
> belong to it meet together, and this feeling is inten-
> sified when they are conscious that they are descried
> and gaped at by those outside ...
>
> PHILO-FILMER: Encomiastic Advice, 1792

> Shall those who drudge from morn till night
> Pretend to talk of wrong and right?
> No, no, the sweat which toil produces,
> Exhausts the intellectual juices.
>
> PHILO-FILMER: *Encomiastic Advice*, 1793

WHEN the values of an ancient society are in the melting-pot,
as the values of Old England were in the days of the Regency, it is
necessary to discount a good deal of talk about 'national decadence'.
There is, of course, a widespread conviction in such a society that
things are not what they used to be. It may safely be maintained
that they never were. We can at any rate set aside the inevitable
complaints of those who automatically interpreted social changes
in terms of their own threatened interests. For example there was
the man of fashion who read the decadence of the age in terms of
'trowsers and turned-down collars, slang and impudence'. And
there was the crusted aristocrat who associated the troubled times
with the decline of the influence of crusted aristocrats. 'Many of
the old county families are gone,' sighed Lord Redesdale; 'and I
have not a doubt that the destruction of their hereditary influence

has greatly contributed to the present insubordination.'[1] On the other hand, those wide-eyed observers of the human comedy – the poets and novelists – were scarcely less alarmed than the men of property and breeding. It was in 1817 that Coleridge made his great appeal for the re-education of the governing class, the intellectually debilitated leaders of an intellectually paralysed public. Robert Southey had observed nearly ten years earlier: 'The middle classes are veneered instead of being heart of oak, and the higher ones are better classics and worse in every other possible point of view. Ours,' he concluded, 'is a degrading and dwarfing system of society.'[2] As for Sir Walter Scott, he declared himself to be less alarmed by the Radicals than by 'the vile and degrading spirit of *egoisme* so prevalent among the higher ranks, especially among the highest'.[3] He suspected that 'our coach-driving noblesse' would be seduced by any government which admitted champagne into the country duty-free. Shelley, too, had his quota of gloom and bitterness to bring to the social analysis of these years. The old aristocracy was supplanted by 'petty piddling slaves' of fundholders; the mass of the people were sunk in apathy and dejection; the very air was polluted with decay. 'Mourn, then, people of England', he cried; 'clothe yourselves in solemn black. Let the bells be tolled. Think on mortality and change. . . . We move about in a dungeon more pestilential than damp and narrow walls, because the earth is its floor and the heavens are its roof.'[4] Even the sane and sober Henry Crabb Robinson feared that the sun of England's glory had set in 1801.

What was really happening, however, was not a process of national decadence but a process of social and intellectual displacement. Privileged minorities were being challenged in their possession of age-old prerogatives. The idea was abroad that anyone and everyone had the right to go anywhere or to become anything by the passport of his own energies, talents or superior cunning. The whole social order of Old England was in flux, and the whole complex of ideas and conventions that had maintained it was being contested on every side. The very tempo of life was changing. Ease and insouciance were in flight before hurrying hordes of men who were putting a premium upon enterprise, speed, economy and efficiency. Above all things, these men were declaring war upon waste: waste of land, waste of money, waste of time, even waste of words. The war had been an immense stimulus to economy of all kinds. Landlords had put an end to the 'waste' of common-land. Waste of time was fast becoming synonymous with immorality. The passion for improving the shining hour, which was to become so characteristic of the Victorian Age, was already sending a tremor through society. To 'get on', to rise in the world by dint of more or less honest labour, to 'improve' oneself : these were becoming the common concern of common people as never before. No doubt there had always been a certain number of potential pupils of Samuel Smiles, but now they begin to swarm from the earth, shoving aside the idle, tea-drinking, gossiping old vagrants whom Haydon had loved, forging their way to name and fame in a world of infinite possibilities. We feel, in fact, that it was becoming increasingly impossible for Dr Burney to be carried back to Calais.

Consider the astonishing number of young men who were arriving in London at this time in hot pursuit of their fortunes. Haydon himself was an early arrival. There, too, was young William Lovett, the west-country fisher-lad, all agape. Thomas Bewick, genius of the wood-cuts, has told us of the wild excitement with which he climbed into the Highflyer at Darlington, bound for the mysterious and far-off haven of his youthful dreams. It was a great adventure, this going to London, 'especially when a journey of three long days and nights by a stage-coach lay between me and my haven of bliss'.[5] And there is Robert Owen, perhaps the most remarkable highflyer of them all, the self-made man of the Industrial Revolution *par excellence*. The saddler's son from Wales arrives in London at the age of ten with forty shillings in his pocket. He goes as a shop-assistant in High Holborn and at London Bridge for £25 a year. At eighteen, he decides to go into business for himself, and, borrowing £200 from his brother, sets up in the manufacture of spinning mules after the unpatented designs of Samuel Crompton. His first year's profit came to £300. At the age of twenty-eight he marries the daughter of a wealthy Scottish textile manufacturer, and finally buys up his father-in-law's mills for £60,000. By the end of the Napoleonic Wars he was one of the wealthiest men in the United Kingdom and ready to devote himself to the cause of utopian socialism.

It is doubtful whether such scope for the will-to-power in man had ever existed before, or whether it will ever exist again. The conditions of the time, social, political, economic, were ideal for its purposes. There was no compulsory education to keep the poor boy out of industry until he was fourteen: Robert Owen and his kind had some four years' start of their latter-day exemplars. Government was scarcely aware of the industrial problem, and it was perfectly easy to get in before government awoke and began to make rules for the game. There was no rigid system of patents to prevent an enterprising young man from picking any brains he chose. The regimentation of working-class youth by State and trade union was still far away. In this haphazard, chaotic, semi-medieval, semi-modern order of society, the quick-witted could snatch at his opportunity and wax fat on the proceeds in early middle age. This was not a matter of a small number of unscrupulous and cunning men setting to work to enslave their fellows. It was a matter of a large number of men letting loose the life within them into a new field of adventure.

It was men like Robert Owen, men who made fortunes and lent them to other men or to the Government, who effected the first breach in the walls which guarded the preserves of ancient privilege where dwelt the monopolist of 'varied experience', a breach through which were to pour 'the swinish multitude' of mill and factory and mine in the subsequent century of torrential invasion. In Regency England, however, the vanguard of this rough-shod regiment came in for the withering scorn of almost every social critic, Tory and Radical alike. To Shelley they were 'a set of pelting wretches ... petty, piddling slaves', supplanting the old, native aristocracy. To Cobbett they were the scum of the cities, the very dregs of society. When they came upon the land, seeking to disinfect the spoils of the counting-house and the stock exchange by investments in broad acres and country houses, Cobbett hooted with derision at the shallow fools 'who cannot duly estimate the difference between a resident *native* gentry, attached to the soil ... and a gentry only now and then residing at all ....' Nor was the phenomenon confined to a change of personnel. It involved a disaster to the standards of taste. Cobbett was a man of taste, at least in the sense that he knew the cheap, the nasty and the pretentious when he saw them. These gentlemen from the City of London were going in for mock-Gothic architecture. 'Of all the ridiculous things I ever saw in my life', Cobbett declared, after seeing Mr Montagu's new place down in Hampshire, 'this place is the most ridiculous. The house looks like a sort of church. . . . I do not know who this gentleman is. I suppose he is some honest person from the Change or its neighbourhood; and that these Gothic arches are to denote the antiquity of his origin.'[6] It was indeed unfortunate that the invasion of the countryside by the manufacturer and the financier in these years should have coincided with the fashion for 'the Gothic', which formed so prominent a part of the Romantic Revival. The same movement which gave to the world the novels of Sir Walter Scott, the loveliness of Coleridge's *Christabel,* and (at a second remove) the dark splendours of *Wuthering Heights,* also broke the fine neo-classical façade of Regency architecture with unseemly outcrops of 'the Gothic' after the style of Mr Montagu's place down in Hampshire.

It was this kind of assault upon contemporary canons of taste which provoked some of the bitterest reaction of opinion on the part of the 'monopolists of varied experience'. The political challenge could be resisted at a centre. The old House of Commons was, it seemed for long, an impregnable citadel beneath whose walls the enemy could be destroyed in detail. So secure were its defenders that they might even from time to time admit some carefully selected leaders of the besieging forces, once they had wiped their feet and given up their weapons. But the challenge to established taste could not be countered in this way. It was ubiquitous. Anyone with enough money could build himself a sham-Gothic mansion, just as anyone could wear trousers and turned-down collars, or buy the vulgar outpourings of the Cockney School of poetry. And from the point of view of the self-appointed guardians of traditional standards, all these things were one thing. There was an inner connexion between sedition and infidelity on the one hand, and the breakdown of standards in manners, morals, dress and reading-habits on the other. It is noticeable that when a gentleman like Sir Thomas Hammond upheld knee-breeches and tight pantaloons because they 'contributed perhaps to forbid slovenliness of step and maintain a certain elegance and grace', he was thinking in terms of morals as well as manners. Trousers and turned-down collars encouraged 'fast talk and slang'. It was true that the war had made it patriotic to forgo the expenditure of starch and flour on powdering wigs and laundering cravats and ruffles. But this did not preclude the charge that the fashion for wearing your own hair instead of someone else's, and for wearing an open-necked shirt and no ruffles at all, was associated with the loose morals of unruly young men like Lord Byron, Mr Keats and Mr Shelley, and the whole seditious train which proposed to follow Jean Jacques Rousseau 'back to nature'. It was noticed, too, that the white top-hat affected by Radical demagogues like Orator Hunt was first-cousin to the head-gear of the French Jacobins. How this symbol of subversive principles ever became transformed into the chimney-pot hat of the Victorians has never been satisfactorily explained.

As for the reading habits of the age, they were undergoing the same process of corruption. There was no longer a small enclave of cultivated people, all sharing the same tastes, all reading the same books and journals, all speaking the same intellectual language. There was now not one 'public'; there were many. Indeed, the traditional 'public' now began to appear so small and select that it began to merit the name 'private', when compared with the truly numerical 'public' which now demanded to sit down at what Coleridge called 'the two public ordinaries of literature, the circulating libraries and the periodical press'. Indeed, to Coleridge it seemed likely that the growth of this literary phenomenon, 'a public', would be the end of true literature[7] – as distinct from the inferior pabulum demanded for the satisfaction of the appetite for 'desultory reading'. The diehards of literature insisted that it was this wretched 'public' which provided a market for the mawkish productions of the Cockney School of poetry led by Leigh Hunt and Keats. Indeed, in 1817 the monopolists founded *Blackwood's Magazine* for the especial purpose of defending the citadel of tradition on its literary rampart, a defence that was conducted by J. G. Lockhart with almost unbelievable vituperation. Here again, the inner connexion between form and matter, manners and morals, was predicated. The Cockney School were not merely charged with writing bad poetry, but with undermining family affection and the established religion. A plague of wickedness and corruption was supposed to be spreading over England from Leigh Hunt's parlour in the Vale of Health at Hampstead.*

There were, however, some wise and humane spirits among the defenders of the beleaguered citadel who were ready to hold out a helping hand to the invaders, men who understood the historic inevitability of the contest, and who believed with Burke that 'if a great change is to be made in human affairs, the minds of men will be fitted to it ...' Indeed, that the minds of men *must* be fitted to it. In the autumn of 1817, at the very time when *Blackwood's* chose to wield the sledge-hammer, Coleridge drew up a prospectus for a course of lectures. His purpose was to convey those 'rules and principles of sound judgment' which his listeners would otherwise be unable to attain 'without that quality of time and attention which can be reasonably expected, or even wisely desired, of men engaged in business and the active duties of the world'. He wanted to show 'how moderate a number of volumes, if only they be judiciously chosen, would suffice for the attainment of every wise and desirable purpose'. Here it is that we come upon one of the earliest proposals for 'an Outline of Culture'. Coleridge proposed to follow up this course with 'an outline history of the Dark Ages, 700 to 1400', a series on 'Great Men of Letters', and finally 'a few easy rules for the attainment of a manly, unaffected and pure language ... whether for the purpose of writing, oratory, or conversation'.[8] Whether the lectures were ever really 'popular' remains doubtful. Henry Crabb Robinson tells us that the audience was composed 'generally of superior looking persons, in physiognomy rather than in dress'. Many of them were law-students from the Temple.[9]

Two years later, we find the plague-spreader of Hampstead Heath, Leigh Hunt, founding the ancestor of those tuppenny journals of cultural snippets which were presently to flood the bookstalls of the English-speaking world. It was called the *Indicator*, or *Knowledge for All*, and was deliberately aimed at that hypothetical being, 'the Common Reader'. In 1827, Henry Brougham founded the

---

* History does not repeat itself, but the feuds of literary critics and creative artists seem to repeat themselves in every century. It was the Vale of Health at Hampstead that was imagined to harbour the plague-centre associated with the names of D. H. Lawrence, Mr Middleton Murry, and their circle just a hundred years after Leigh Hunt and the Cockney School ...

Society for the Diffusion of Useful Knowledge,[10] which put forth sixpenny text-books on every conceivable subject. Thomas Love Peacock was to ridicule the endeavours of 'the Steam-Intellect Society', and Henry Brougham was indeed a vain and demagogic patron of the people. Nevertheless, it is doubtful whether anyone in that difficult and dangerous age of transition did more to ease the passage of the once-excluded masses of English working men into the charmed circle of literacy. Not only must we take account of his *Penny Magazine* and *Penny Encyclopedia* and *Library of Entertaining Knowledge*; we must attribute largely to him the successful launching of the Mechanics Institutions in the eighteen-twenties. Among the members of the London Institution we discover William Lovett, the west-country lad, whom we last saw among the eager arrivals in the capital. Here is a man whose ancestors had for generations dwelt very definitely outside the pale of 'varied experience'. Young Lovett, living in these times of transition, finds himself inside. We shall never know with what wonder and exaltation he, and many like him, now looked around them: verily like stout Cortez on his peak in Darien. But the peak is in London, somewhere near St Paul's Cathedral. The lecture is over, the mechanics disperse into the dark lanes of the City. But William Lovett remains. He cannot go home. Not yet. For hours he walks in the moonlight with the lecturer, Sir Richard Phillips, through Newgate Street and Old Bailey and St Paul's churchyard, Sir Richard demonstrating his scientific theories by chalking diagrams on walls and window-shutters.[11] No doubt the citizenry abed heard their passing footfalls, their muttered discourse, the quiet squeak of Sir Richard's chalk. Dogberry, on his round with staff and lantern, might hesitate for a moment in the midst of his age-long message: 'Twelve of the clock, and a fine night . . . .' Did he perhaps wonder whether all was as well as he declared it to be? The city merchant, passing to his house of business next morning, and seeing the chalk-marks on walls and shutters, probably put them down to the seditious Spenceans. Had Lord Sidmouth seen them, he must have been more convinced than ever that the long-awaited revolution was at hand. And Lord Sidmouth would have been right. A silent social revolution was going on under his Lordship's very nose.

By the early eighteen-twenties, London was fairly honeycombed with workmen's clubs and societies. The 'Liberals' met in Gerrard Street, Newport Market, to debate metaphysical questions: they also ran a library on weekly subscriptions. There were debates at Tom's Coffee-house in Holborn and at Lunt's Coffee-house on Clerkenwell Green. At Lunt's it was possible to hear some of the veteran Radicals of the nineties, like Richard Carlile and Gale Jones. To William Lovett these debates were a revelation. 'It was the first time that I had ever heard impromptu speaking, out of the pulpit', he tells us, 'my notions being that such speaking was a kind of inspiration from God.'[12] No less startling must this multifarious congregating of the 'lower orders', or the 'passive' element of society, have been to the minds of their superiors. Even the liberal Crabb Robinson was puzzled. Falling in with a master bricklayer, 'whose appearance was that of a very low person', he was astonished to find that his conversation was 'enlightened by those principles of political economy which are indeed becoming common. . . . He did not talk of the books of Adam Smith, but seemed embued with their spirit.' Mr Robinson went on his way marvelling that such ideas had 'alighted on the hod and trowel'.[13]

Others felt more misgivings. It was commonly held that if a working man could read, he would read only what was blasphemous and seditious. 'Everyone who reads at all', wrote a friend to Robert Southey in 1812, 'reads a Sunday newspaper, not the Bible.'[14] In that ever-critical year, 1817, we find the author of a pamphlet on *Constitutional Politics* attributing all the present discontents to the Sunday newspapers which the poor read in barber's shops, village ale-houses and benefit-clubs.[15] Yet we know, on good evidence, what the main body of working men were reading in that year of peril. They were reading Cobbett's *Political Register*, the 'tuppenny trash'. It was read on every cottage hearth in the manufacturing districts at this time, Bamford tells us, and its influence was wholly in the direction of law and order. We need not take too literally Bamford's assertion that the reduction of the price of this paper to twopence in the winter of 1816–17 put an end to the vogue for rioting,[16] but only those who had never seen a copy of the *Register* could possibly have deplored its influence.

As for the notion that the working man was turning from his

Bible to blasphemy, or that the mass of the people were tending towards irreligion, the association of radicalism in politics with atheism is a stock form of association in every age of popular politics. In the early days, when radicalism took its flavour from France, this kind of assumption was not unnatural. After all, Tom Paine had knelt with the leaders of the French National Convention before the Goddess of Reason. Nor had it been necessary to be a free-thinker in order to attract the attention of Church-and-King mobs in the nineties. Everyone knows what dastardly treatment was meted out to Dr Priestley, the Unitarian, when Birmingham exhibited its loyalty to Church and King in 1791. A Radical was likely to suffer either way, whether he were a pious Dissenter or an atheist.

That certain of the more picturesque Radical leaders were free-thinkers at least lent a semblance of justice to the reaction of outraged prejudice. Robert Owen's agnosticism was notorious, and probably did more to prevent the acceptance of his schemes of social amelioration than anything inherently impossible in their own nature. Unfortunately, it is easy to understand that well-meaning men should have mistaken the Church of England for the Christian religion. At a time when bishops expended their eloquence in opposing Factory Acts, the mistake was almost commendable. But unbelief was most common among the poets and journalists. The poets escaped the worst penalties of social stigmatism, partly because the English refuse to take poets seriously until they are dead, but mainly because the worst offenders were of aristocratic origin. So far as they suffered (one thinks especially of Shelley and Byron) it was less for the heterodoxy of their religious views than for the irregularity of their matrimonial affairs. The journalists, however, were very often men of obscure social origins, and they suffered frequently. Thomas Wooller of the Black Dwarf; Richard Carlile, errand-boy and factory hand, of the Republican; Sherwin, an ex-turnkey, of the Political Register; John Hunt, middle-class journalist, of the Examiner; William Hone, who defended his blasphemies in his Register with such skill in Court that Lord Chief Justice Ellenborough took to his bed and died: all underwent varying terms of imprisonment, generally for impious and profane libel.

It is significant, however, that the men who appealed with the greatest success to the people were neither atheists nor even free-thinkers. Of these, William Cobbett was by far the most influential, and Cobbett might best be described as the average English common-sense Christian. He disliked parsons in politics, Evangelicals who 'danced about with Tracts', tithes, and – above all – William Wilberforce. It is probable that his religious opinions, if they may be called opinions, were those of the great body of English working people of that day. Similarly, that other great character who really made contact with the common lives of common men, Major John Cartwright, thought of God as a god of common sense and common decency rather than as a philosophical abstraction. Richard Carlile, the militant atheist, took him to task for the semi-religious character of his appeal to the people, and the Major was prepared to admit that he was very much of a field-preacher. The Government did its best to equate sedition with blasphemy in the press prosecutions of these years, but the attempt was unconvincing to anyone lacking the will to believe.

Much more striking, and important, than the spread of unbelief amongst the people at this time, was the tendency in all parties and sects to measure religion in terms of its utility. Bentham himself seems to have been prepared to believe in God if it could be shown that He was a Utilitarian. Evangelical preachers, of whom the most popular was William Jay,[17]* were prepared at any rate to prove that religion was a social utility. Jay would pray for the early rising of a new servant, or for the safeguarding of his congregation against the acceptance or the giving of accommodation bills at a time of financial crisis. His sermons were immensely popular. Even Cobbett admired them : indeed, there is a good deal of Jay's utilitarian morality in Cobbett's *Advice to Young Men.*

Utility. The term might stand as the watchword of the advancing forces of social change in Regency England. By its measure – the characteristic measure of an age of rapid industrial and commercial expansion – the claims of the old monopolists in church, state and society were to be tested. 'What is the use of it?' Jeremy Bentham asked of all established ideas and institutions, and taught

* Jay's *Morning Exercise for the Closet for every day of the year* (1829) reached a tenth edition.

his age and generation to ask the same. Such a question, when posed to venerable authorities whose credentials had rarely been submitted to the mildest and most respectful examination, implied the arrival of a new mood in social and political thinking. It implied the intention to 'rationalize' politics, to set aside 'vague generalizations' in favour of 'political arithmetic', to make government a science, and a quantitative science at that. The new mood showed itself in a certain impatience with what old Major Cartwright called 'Burkism' – or 'never speaking on the Constitution ... but in trope or figure, in simile, metaphor, or mysterious allusion'.[18] Already in 1792, the Derby Society for Political Information had opened fire with An Address to the Friends of Free Inquiry and the General Good with the announcement: 'We refuse to approach the defects of good government with pious awe and trembling solicitude' – which was a quotation from Edmund Burke himself. Instead, the Derby Society proceeded to a practical analysis of current abuses, and a series of highly embarrassing questions. Why, for instance, are seven million people required to pay seventeen million pounds in taxation? Next year, a gentleman who called himself 'Philo-Filmer' put it on record that 'The movers of the Derby Address have been fed on Reading and Observation, put Facts above Words, and prefer naked Truth to beribboned Falsehood.'[19] Again, in 1809, Sir Francis Burdett, the Radical Baronet who represented Charles Fox's old constituency of Westminster, told the House of Commons that he was prepared to 'let others deal in whimsical speculations and whimsical mysterious notions of a constitution which eludes the grasp and soars above the conceptions of ordinary minds'.[20] The Radical member for Westminster declared himself ready to 'hold fast by that plain and substantial constitution adapted to the contemplations of common understandings, to be found in the statute-book and recognized by the common law of the land'. All the same, if it came to a matter of phantasy-hunting, we need look little further than at the behaviour of these Radical gentlemen who prided themselves so often upon their 'plain common sense'. It was Major Cartwright who recommended his nephew to hang the Bill of Rights in his bedroom at Oxford. It was Sir Francis Burdett who was arrested while teaching his son to read Magna Carta in the original.

Chapter 6

POLITICAL TRANSLATION

There never was a period in our history when the
representation of the people in parliament was less
unequal. That it was unequal in theory he would
admit, but that theoretic inequality he regarded as
one of the greatest advantages of our constitution.

LORD LIVERPOOL, reported in 1810

Equal representation – or Death !

From a banner at Peterloo, 1819

THE widespread agitation for parliamentary reform, which dominated the internal politics of Regency England, represents the
translation into political terms of those forces of change and challenge which we have examined in the last two chapters. The
unreformed House of Commons was an affront to the spirit of
rationalism in politics. Only by a travesty of logic could it face up
to the Benthamite criterion of Utility. Nor did it reflect in anything
but an infinitesimal degree the balance of economic forces in
society. Out of a House of Commons of nearly six hundred members, only slightly less than sixty were bankers, merchants or men
of business.

This state of things was not only tolerated but applauded by
many of the wisest and most responsible men of the age. Coleridge, Canning, Peel, Wellington, in addition to Liverpool, Castlereagh, Sidmouth and Eldon, believed it to be a true representation
of the people, susceptible of adjustment in minor points, perhaps,
but immune from fundamental alteration. The argument on which
they based their defence of the existing order, in so far as they
troubled to offer an intellectual statement of their case, may best
be described as that of 'Virtual Representation'. It rested upon the
ancient conception of the House of Commons as a 'deliberative'
assembly in which every member represented not only his own
constituents, but the interests of the whole nation. Edmund Burke

had given this doctrine its classic statement in his famous speech to the electors of Bristol in 1774.

> Parliament is not a *congress* of ambassadors from different and hostile interests ... but Parliament is a *deliberative* assembly of one nation, with *one* interest. ... You choose a member indeed; but when you have chosen him, he is not member of Bristol, but he is a member of *parliament*.

It is echoed time and again throughout the years of reformist agitation. Lord Liverpool himself, speaking against Grey's motion for reform in 1810, cited the authority of 'that enlightened statesman, Mr Burke' for the view that the House was intended, by its mode of election, to be 'instead of an assembly of deputies, an entire and perfect deliberative meeting'.[1] Lord Eldon, Sir Robert Inglis, Sir John Walsh, and many more, paraphrased Burke in attacking the reform proposals of 1831–2. Sir John Walsh put it: 'Parliament is the guardian of the interests, not the echo of the will, of the people. It is composed of representatives, not of delegates.'[2]

It is clear that this doctrine attaches more importance to the character of the House in session, as a deliberative and government-making body, than to the mode of its production by the constituencies. It attempts to turn the flank of its critics in the same manner that opponents of Proportional Representation employ at the present day. That is to say, it insists that what matters is not so much that every person and every opinion shall be quantitatively represented, as that the country as a whole gets a coherent and workable assembly. Indeed, it might be described as an essentially qualitative, rather than a quantitative, treatment of the problem. If it be argued, as it is often argued today, and was still more often argued a hundred and fifty years ago, that a large number of people cannot fairly be said to be represented by a member of their own choice, it is answered that there is a sense in which *every* member represents *everyone*, whether he was directly chosen by them or not. It is even possible to argue, as Disraeli was perhaps the last to argue at all convincingly, that representation has no necessary connexion with election. 'The principle of representation does not necessarily include election', Disraeli asserted, 'as there might be representation without election. ... The House of Lords

is the most eminent example of representation without election.'[3]
This, again, was only an echo of Burke, who insisted that 'The
King is the representative of the people; so are the Lords; so are the
Judges. They are all trustees for the people, as well as the
Commons.'[4]

'Virtual Representation', however, as the defenders of the unreformed House of Commons expounded it, depended for its feasi-
bility upon a certain structure of society. It depends upon the
internal division of society subsisting vertically rather than hori-
zontally; upon society conforming to a pattern of mutually dependent 'interests' rather than of mutually conflicting 'classes'.
Further than this, again, it depends upon government's taking
account of individual persons not as individual persons, but as
members of one or other of the component interests which make
up society. This is what Coleridge meant when he averred that
'Jack, Tom and Harry have no existence in the eye of the law,
except as included in some form or other of the PERMANENT
PROPERTY of the realm', and that a state which took account of
persons, as such, would be a tyranny – what he called a 'jacobin
state', and what we would call a 'totalitarian state'.[5] Persons should
therefore be represented in parliament only as components of the
particular 'interest' to which they belong: whether it be the
'landed', the 'commercial', the 'learned' or whatever. If those interests are represented fairly and adequately, 'the people' are represented 'virtually', even though many of them never cast a vote at
an election. William Paley, defending the eighteenth-century parliament, put it thus:

We have a House of Commons of 540 members, in which number
are to be found the most considerable landholders and merchants of the
kingdom; the heads of the army, the navy and the law; the occupiers
of the great offices of state; together with many private individuals
eminent for their knowledge, eloquence, or activity. Now if the country
be not safe in such hands, in whose may we confide its interests? ...
The different *interests* are actually represented, and of course the people
virtually.[6]

This theory had a good deal to be said for it, for so long as 'interests' rather than 'classes' were the dominant divisions within

society. It was one of the principal effects of the Industrial Revolution to put an end to that situation, to set a gulf between master and man, employer and employee, capital and labour. It would be ridiculous to suppose that it created classes; what it did was to make classes predominant over interests, to break up interests in favour of classes. It steadily became unreal to maintain that the landed interest, for example, was a coherent and united component of society, when the few people who owned the land regarded the many who worked on the land as wage-labourers, so many units of work which might be disposed of according to the market-price of corn, as factory hands were disposed of according to the market-price of cotton shirts. Not only did the Industrial Revolution replace the responsible relationships of the older economy with a series of relationships based upon a cash-nexus. It may be said to have created for the first time a 'universal individuality'. Society consisted of individuals, now, the atomized labour-units of an industrial world. If men – and women – were thus individualized vis-à-vis their employers, was it not to be expected that they would demand to be taken account of as individuals vis-à-vis the State, and more especially in the counsels of the State as represented by the House of Commons? The demand for universal suffrage was the translation into political language of the new social terminology of an atomized, because industrialized, society. It is scarcely to be wondered at that men and women thus turned loose, so to speak, into the wilderness of universalized individualism, should have demanded the political counterpart of their new social status the more persistently as it became apparent to them that only a House of Commons of their own direct choice was likely to interpose state-power on their behalf in their social distresses.

Thus, 'the people' became for the first time, in England, a legitimate political concept. It became so because it was already a living social fact. It could no longer be convincingly argued that they, the hewers of wood and drawers of water, found their political representation through their membership of some interest, landed, industrial, commercial, or whatever. They knew that it was not so, and they knew that the people who represented these interests in parliament were no longer to be relied upon to represent them. They demanded to have their own representatives, men experienced in their own situation and outlook. Their awakening to the possibility of this was slow and painful, indeed; for a century yet they were for the most part to find their champions within the ranks of the existing political parties. But they were already becoming aware of themselves as a distinctive political entity. They were reaching out beyond the bounds of the old interests, to which they were attached by the necessities of their labour, to an awareness of themselves as a 'class' – the same universal class, whatever form their employment might take. As yet, they rarely thought of themselves as 'the working class'. They preferred the term – 'the people'. For recognition of what had happened, however, we can best turn – as is so often the case in Regency England – to the watchful and sympathetic eye of the poet. Writing in the year of Peterloo, Shelley announced the invalidation of the doctrine of virtual representation thus: 'A fourth class therefore made its appearance in the nation, the unrepresented multitude.' This, in itself, might not have affected the representative character of the House of Commons, which,

though it had ceased to be a legal and actual, it might still have been a virtual Representation of the people. But universally the nation became multiplied into a denomination which had no constitutional presence in the state. This denomination had not existed before, or had existed only to a degree in which its interests were sensibly interwoven with that of those who enjoyed a constitutional presence . . .[7]

A constitutional presence . . . conformity to the logic of social change . . . the rationalizing of representation . . . such statements may reveal to the student of history the inner meaning of events, but they bear little apparent relation to the motives of men in action. Only slowly and painfully do men become aware of why they do the things they do, and it is the part of the historian to reveal not only the inner meaning of events but the outer semblance of activity in all its strange and often ambiguous complexity. Thus, when we turn to the origins of the movement for parliamentary reform, we find that it was not the concern of any such walking abstraction as 'the people', but of a number of aristocratic and middle-class individuals who thought in terms of reducing the opportunities for royal influence in politics or of increasing the political influence of certain kinds of Whigs and Dissenters. In 1780, Edmund Burke, as the spokesman of the highly aristocratic Rockingham Whigs, introduced a measure for 'Economical Reform', designed to remove a certain number of sinecure jobs which had for long been at the disposal of the Crown for the reward of faithful supporters of the royal policy; defeated at the time, the measure became law in a modified form two years later. In 1780, too, there was set on foot the great petitioning movement sponsored by the 'Yorkshire Association' for the same purpose. That year saw a widespread activity on the part of County Meetings – thoroughly traditional assemblies of the peers, M.P.s and freeholders of the counties – to bring pressure to bear on the Government for a reduction of corrupt influence, profligate expenditure, and general mismanagement of the nation's affairs. It was a protest on the part of the tax-payer against the mishandling of the nation's resources in the service of a policy which was losing the American colonies and reducing the country to a laughing-stock in Europe. It was high time, the Counties professed to believe, that 'the people' should intervene, although by 'the people' they can have meant little more than the propertied classes. The intervention of the Gordon Riots in the same year, however, damped down the movement, although it left behind it an important example of extra-parliamentary organization for future reformers.[8] The short-lived activities of Pitt as a parliamentary reformer in the years 1782–5 belong to the same tradition of reduction of royal influence rather than extension of the franchise. His schemes involved the buying out of certain decayed boroughs and the creation of new constituencies in the counties and in growing industrial districts. The outbreak of the French Revolution saw the indefinite postponement of his hopes.

With the French Revolution, parliamentary reform became a doctrine as distinct from an expedient. No longer was it simply a question of re-adjusting the constituency-system to the movements of population, or of reducing the opportunities for royal misgovernment in the interests of public economy and national self-respect. 'Economical reform', of course, remained a prominent issue, but suffrage-reform became an indispensable adjunct and an irrefragible principle. The abstract and ineluctable right of every man of adult years and sound mind to an equal share in choosing the governors of his country received the sanction of universal validity from the Declaration of the Rights of Man by the French. Some such right had always been implicit in the principle of 'no taxation without representation', although English constitutional ideas had never owned up to it.[9] The supposititious logic of this implication had been invoked by the American colonies in their resistance to the taxes imposed upon them by the government of George III, and wherever interest in and sympathy with the colonists were strong, the principle was to the fore. For example, it can be detected in the speech of John Wilkes, advocating reform of the franchise, in the House of Commons in 1776, when he made use of the ancient doctrine *Quod omnes tangit ab omnibus approbetur*, on behalf of mechanics and day-labourers. 'Some share therefore in the power of making those laws which deeply interest them ... should be reserved even to this inferior but most useful set of men.'[10]

In the early years of the French Revolution, however, the parliamentary reform movement in England was still largely monopolized by the 'men of rank and consequence'. Pure-minded noblemen, eccentric aristocrats – and some not quite so eccentric, middle-class intellectuals who thirsted for the reign of reason, indignant men of business who were tired of the mismanagement of their country's affairs by an obstinate king and a factious aristocracy, influential Dissenters who wished to open the door of the House of Commons to influential Dissenters: all these, and many more, were busy founding clubs to promote some brand or other of parliamentary reform. Many of them trifled with the question; to some it was a fashion, to others a fad, to some few a form of sport. There were young aristocrats who delighted to be known as 'furious democrats' as they delighted to be known as 'furious drivers'. One and all, it was a highly respectable cause, worthy the devotion of highly respectable men. The Society for Promoting Constitutional Information, which was founded in 1780 and reformed in 1791, had on its list of members no less than eighteen gentlemen of title, fourteen Members of Parliament, six doctors, four aldermen, and a clergyman. Likewise the London Revolution Society, whose conduct stung Edmund Burke to compose his *Reflec-*

tions on the Revolution, had four Doctors of Divinity on its committee, a peer for its chairman, and an entrance-fee of half a guinea. Most of these clubs contented themselves with restating the impeccable doctrines of John Locke, and with sending congratulations to the French National Assembly on the prospect of France's imitating the British Constitution – with a few necessary amendments in the matter of representation – and they did it all with the characteristic rhetoric of the eighteenth century. The provincial clubs in these early years bore much the same respectable and rhetorical features. After all, the Revolution in France was still led by aristocrats like Lafayette and Mirabeau.

The turning-point came on the night of 25 January 1792, when eight working men met at *The Bell Tavern*, in Exeter Street, Strand, and formally founded The London Corresponding Society for the Reform of Parliamentary Representation. Their leader was Thomas Hardy, a shoemaker of Westminster, and his intention was 'to form a society of another class of the people' – his own class, which consisted of poor men who were prepared to pay a subscription of a penny a week in the interests of the politics of bread. The Society soon had more than forty members, and sister societies sprang up in many provincial towns. The epithet 'Corresponding' indicates the significant feature of the movement: the sister clubs were to exchange 'constitutional information' by correspondence. Thus the whole corresponding movement was divided into groups of thirty members, each with its chairman and 'delegate', the function of the latter being to visit other groups and to represent the group in a 'convention'. A 'National Convention' met in Edinburgh in December 1792, and was attended by delegates from reform societies in Scotland. Hardy and his friends were planning a British Convention when he and several fellow members of the London Corresponding Society were arrested and put on trial for high treason in 1794. Their acquittal was greeted with widespread rejoicing. The Society persisted in its courageous but perfectly peaceable activities until Pitt suppressed it in 1799.

The London Corresponding Society is the parent of working-class reform politics in England. In both its aims and its organization it is the most significant phenomenon of its kind in this period of history. It was avowedly an organization of working men for working men. Its creed was the right of every capable adult person to the suffrage. But it was not content to argue the case for parliamentary reform on the basis of reason, economy and national self-respect. In its 'Address to the People', of August 1792, it promised the further blessings of 'taxes diminished, the necessaries of life more within the reach of the poor, youth better educated, prisons less crowded, old age better provided for, and sumptuous feasts, at the expense of the starving poor, less frequent ....'[11] There is here little parade of Virtue, Truth and Universal Liberty, after the rhetorical manner of its more expansive and expensive brothers. We have arrived at last at the politics of bread and cheese. Moreover, the Corresponding Society possessed a ubiquity which made it very difficult to suppress. Indeed, the head and front of its offence, in the eyes of Pitt and his colleagues, was its organization. Nothing could be further from the truth than Disraeli's remark that Pitt mistook disorganization for sedition. Nothing alarmed him more, in his dealing with the 'seditious' in the seventeen-nineties, than the organization of the Corresponding Society.

For, after all, it was incredible. Here were the 'passive', the politically unconscious, the excluded multitude – known to the monopolists of Pitt's world indifferently as 'the mobility', the 'populace', or (in the mouth of Burke) 'the swinish multitude' – taking upon themselves the title of 'the people',* and putting themselves into the posture of an organized political force. Pitt's political world understood, and approved, the traditional modes of extra-parliamentary activity as represented by the County Meetings. His own career as a reformer had been backed by such meetings, in 1780. It is true that some doubts had been expressed about the constitutionality of an *Association*, possibly nation-wide, of such meetings. Such an organization looked too much like an 'anti-parliament' or a 'convention', which latter name had revolutionary implications since 1688.[12] It is not difficult to imagine the shock administered to statesmen of Pitt's generation when these modes of political activity appeared in the earliest activities of the hitherto 'unpolitical' part of society.[13] But the group-and-delegate system, the multi-cellular organization, the convention of the

* What the eighteenth-century English statesman meant by 'the people' is best described by Burke's statement (see p. 48).

'anti-parliament', had come to stay in Radical politics. There is a slender but clear line of connexion between Thomas Hardy's Corresponding Society of the seventeen-nineties and the Chartist Movement of the eighteen-forties. Midway along this line we shall discover the Hampden Clubs and the *Crown and Anchor* meetings of the Regency.* The challenge to monopolists on the plane of politics had revealed its permanent features, in both spirit and form, from the day of its birth.

The monopolists could not understand it. Lord Liverpool, who was in so many respects the disciple of Mr Pitt, fully shared the disgust and astonishment of his great predecessor when he found himself in his turn confronted by this same phenomenon of the people adopting, and adapting, the political organizations of their betters. Reflecting upon the great popular meetings of 1819, of which Peterloo was only the most tragic in its consequences, he expressed reluctance at 'the necessity of coming to extremities' in dealing with such activities. He thought that it would be sufficient if such meetings were limited to those held 'under known constituted authorities'. These, he added, in a phrase which reveals the eighteenth-century squire blinking in the light of the nineteenth century, these were 'the only meetings, by the by, which ever took place fifty years ago'. To restrict the people to meetings held only in the parish where they resided would serve to restore the wholesome and beneficial influence of the gentry. 'In most cases,' he fondly imagined, 'the gentlemen who live in the parish would have influence enough to check those with whom they are so intimately connected, and whose actions in this respect could not be concealed from them.'[14] Lord Liverpool's mind worked still in terms of a parochial and rural society that was fast passing away. There was little that he did not know about the wealth-producing, and especially the tax-producing, value of a flourishing industrial and commercial society. But he seems never to have understood that an age and a generation had arisen that knew not squire.

* See chs. 11 and 12.

Chapter 7

THE GOVERNORS

It was not the young gentlemen's fault, but the fault of the Pa's and Ma's at home, and of the institutions of the country.

SAMUEL BAMFORD

THE men who, under the collective title of 'the Liverpool Administration', were called upon to preside over the destinies of England at this time of challenge and change, and whose names are forever associated with the government of Regency England, were very much men of the old England that was passing away. For the most part, they belonged to the inner circle of the 'monopolists of varied experience', the aristocratic defenders of a threatened order. They were not, however, the sons of ancient noble families. Lord Liverpool himself was the son of the first Earl of Liverpool, and did not succeed to the title until 1808. Lord Castlereagh was the son of the first Marquess of Londonderry, and never succeeded to the English peerage. Lord Sidmouth was the son of a medical practitioner, and himself became the first Viscount Sidmouth in 1805. Similarly, Lord Eldon, the son of a coal-merchant, was the first Earl of that name. With the exception of the last-named, all these men spent a considerable amount of their time in the House of Commons; Castlereagh died a member. None of them, again with the exception of Eldon, could fairly be described as belonging to the plebeian aristocracy which Mr Pitt was supposed to have 'clutched from the counting-houses of Cornhill and caught in the alleys of Lombard Street'. The Jenkinsons, the Stewarts and the Addingtons came rather from the squirearchy, that most typical and amorphous class of old England : the country gentlemen.

Their common father was the eighteenth century. They all lived the first thirty years of their lives within the temporal bounds of the classic age. Two of them, Eldon and Sidmouth, were born before George III became King; the youngest of them, Castlereagh, was a man of nineteen when the French Revolution broke out. They grew up in the days of duelling and highwaymen. Henry Addington, later Viscount Sidmouth, saw Pitt fight Tierney on Wimbledon Common, early one morning in 1798. Close by, the rotting carcase of Jemmy Abershaw, the highwayman, swung on its gibbet. Castlereagh met Canning on Putney Heath in 1809. The Duke of Wellington fought Lord Winchilsea, at Battersea, in 1829. When Arthur Thistlewood, the down-at-heel Radical, challenged Lord Sidmouth to a duel with sword or pistol in 1818, however, he was sentenced to a year's imprisonment in Horsham Gaol for attempting a breach of the peace. Thistlewood, after all, was described by George Borrow, as 'one of the excellent swordsmen of Europe', and Borrow was an authority on all forms of battle, murder and sudden death. Some sense of the strange juxtaposition of the old world and the new, within the lifetime of these men, may be gained when we remember that one member of the Liverpool Administration was relieved of his watch by a gentleman of the road, and another was run over by a railway-train.*

So much for their temporal span. Geographically, their life-experience was limited by the boundaries of the rural old England. Only one of the leaders of the Liverpool Administration came from England north of the Trent: the industrial region from which so many of their problems as governors were to arise. The exception was Lord Eldon, and he might as well have been born and bred in the Court of Chancery for all that he knew of anything outside the four corners of the English Common Law.

No doubt can be entertained [wrote a contemporary of Lord Eldon], that it was in consequence of carrying the principle of non-intercourse with the world too far, that Lord Eldon was so long insensible to the necessity of altering the policy of our laws and institutions. He had no acquaintance with the state of the institutions of other countries, and he had no notion of the rapid improvements that were going forward in his own. His studies in modern literature were confined to the *Gentleman's Magazine* ...[1]

For the rest, Castlereagh grew up at Mount Stewart, among the

* Sidmouth, between Bromley and Lewisham, in 1786: Huskisson, on the Liverpool and Manchester railway, in 1830.

beechwoods of County Down, a lovely Anglo-Irish island of eighteenth-century culture in the rough sea of native Irishry;[2] Robert Jenkinson, the future Earl of Liverpool, lived his early life among the country gentry of Oxfordshire or in the parliamentary circle of his father's friends at Westminster; and Henry Addington, who also came of an old Oxfordshire family, spent his childhood in the fashionable quarter of London where Dr Addington did very well out of the medicinal properties of port.

They came from an environment which had been supplying England with legislators for several centuries. They were the hereditary leaders of the people, those men of rank and consequence without whose guidance, according to Sir Robert Heron, the people of England were incapable of acting with permanent vigour and resolution. And yet, Sir Robert Heron and his friends of the squirearchy neither liked nor trusted them. For, although they belonged to the squirearchy by their roots, they were not squires, nor did they represent the outlook and interests of the landed gentry. Superimposed upon their landed origins, they possessed the wider outlook and interests of professional politicians. They had, with very few exceptions, come to the service of the state by the long and arduous road of public service, not by the mere possession of titles and estates. Their rank had served merely as the jumping-off place for their laborious course to the highest offices of the state. And in their progress they had made themselves into something other than, and more than, country gentlemen. No doubt they thought that the landed interest was the most important interest in the state, and they were right. But they did not glibly talk of 'the landed interest', nor were they willing to allow its claims to override the claims of manufacture and commerce. Lord Liverpool himself not only proposed to honour Arkwright and Boulton and Watt as among the greatest benefactors of their country, he professed an inability to draw any line of separation between the interests of agriculture and those of industry. In the debate on the Corn Bill of 1815, he stated that 'he wished carefully to guard against its being supposed that these interests were at all distinct from each other. On the contrary, he trusted he should be enabled to show ... that they were the same.'[3]

This was too much for the country gentlemen. 'Trade, manufacturers, and money are everything,' lamented Lord Redesdale. 'The landed proprietors are mere ciphers, they are of no consequence, either with ministers or with Opposition.'[4] And, indeed, the country gentlemen were to be called upon to witness some strange policies at the hands of this indispensable Tory government: liberalism abroad, and *laissez-faire* at home. The fact is that Lord Liverpool and his friends knew quite well, and welcomed without hesitation, the vast increase in the importance of trade and industry in the national economy. They recognized, without lamentation, what men like Lord Redesdale deplored when he said: 'We are rapidly becoming – if we are not become – a nation of shopkeepers.'[5] What they did not recognize was that a nation of shopkeepers could not continue to be governed by the social and administrative devices of a rural civilization. They understood and respected everything about the age of Arkwright except what it was doing to the minds and habits of the English people.

The striking thing about the careers of these men is their conformity to a pattern: the country house, the public school, the university, foreign travel, the pocket-borough, the legislature, the Cabinet. Robert Stewart, Viscount Castlereagh, goes to school at Armagh, in County Down, and thence to St John's College, Cambridge. His kinsman, Lord Camden, Lord Chancellor of England, advises him to 'look down among the pensioners' – the commoners of the College – where 'all the genius and capacity to be found in the world are produced'. There is no evidence that Robert Stewart took his advice. If he had looked down far enough, he might even have seen William Wordsworth. Instead, he associated with the Hon. Frederick Hervey, another Anglo-Irish aristocrat, and in 1789 he left Cambridge, without taking a degree, in order to enter the Irish Parliament as one of the Knights of the Shire for County Down. He was twenty-one. He was to hold supreme political authority in Ireland before he was thirty ....[6] Meanwhile, Robert Banks Jenkinson[7] was running a parallel course through Charterhouse, Christ Church, the Grand Tour and the pocket-borough of Appleby. At twenty-nine he held the valuable sinecure of Master of the Mint, and by the age of thirty-one he was in charge of the foreign policy of his country .... Some ten years earlier, his future

colleague, Henry Addington,[8] had made his way with similar
celerity through Winchester, Brasenose, and the close-borough of
Devizes, to become Speaker of the House of Commons at forty-
four .... Five years before Henry Addington went to Oxford, John
Scott, the future Earl of Eldon, and Lord Chancellor of England,
had proceeded thither by means of an Exhibition from Newcastle
Grammar School. At twenty-one, he eloped with a wealthy heiress;
at thirty-one he entered the House of Commons as member for the
pocket-borough of Woebley in Herefordshire; at forty-two he was
Attorney-General; and at fifty-six he was Lord Chancellor, an
office he was to occupy for more than twenty years. The Earl of
Eldon was not born in the purple; he reached the highest legal
eminence in England by means of a very long and arduous training. His colleagues of the Liverpool Administration had the start
of him; but they, too, arrived at high office only after an intensive,
if less lengthy, experience of the world of politics and administration.

Where Lord Eldon's future colleagues benefited by their early
aristocratic environment – the environment which ejected them,
so to speak, into the small and select world of the professional
politician – was in their experience of the cultivated life of the
governing classes of Europe, past and present. By their social intercourse, their classical studies, their mingling in the affairs of county
society, and their travels, they could be said to have acquired an
extensive knowledge of three things above all else: ancient Rome,
modern England south of the Trent, and 'that large place known
as "Abroad"'. Their knowledge of southern England came from
their quotidian activities as magistrates, landlords and officers of
the Yeomanry. We have seen how deep and extensive was the
knowledge of the class from which they came in all matters connected with the life of rural England. It was with scarcely any
sense of strangeness that they explored, at school and university,
the world of Horace and Virgil, Cicero and Caesar. Like Edward
Gibbon, who rode with their fathers as a Captain in the Hampshire
Militia, they adopted the more polished poets and statesmen of the
Roman world as honorary members of the English aristocracy,
recognizing in them and in their world the self-same ideals and
values of the classic mode. Young Robert Jenkinson, the future

Earl of Liverpool who was to rule the England of the machine-breakers and the Manchester mobs, spent his time at Charterhouse culling useful ideas of government from Greek and Roman history; and when in the fateful summer of 1789 he set out on a three-year tour of inspection of Europe, he took with him 'a small but well-chosen library' of the ancient writers. He went in search of history with Aeneas as his guide, and his head full of Cicero and Caesar: and he found the French Revolution. In Italy, he found the company of Virgil and Horace far more congenial than that of the modern Italians, who were dirty, lazy and altogether contemptible.

It had been the intention of Robert Jenkinson's father that his son should 'extend his general political knowledge by informing himself, on the spot, of the characteristics and resources of the different countries which he was to visit, and by cultivating an acquaintance with their leading men'. Robert, however, reported that 'among the higher ranks of people there are very few that are worth knowing.'[9] What a young man learns from foreign travel plainly depends upon what he brings to it in terms of sympathy and imagination. Robert Jenkinson brought only a tepid curiosity and a vast sense of the superiority of all things English. Having watched the fall of the Bastille, he seems to have been chiefly impressed by the part played by the women of Paris in the affair: 'how this matter will end', he wrote, as France continued to make history under his eyes, 'it seems more and more difficult every day to determine.'[10] On his return to England, however, the member for the pocket-borough of Appleby told the House of Commons, in a much admired maiden speech, that 'the strength and influence of France were at an end, so that we had no further dangers to apprehend from that once formidable rival.'[11] Presented with an unrivalled opportunity to study the French Revolution at Paris, he had preferred to take his opinions from the exiled members of the old order at Coblentz. Not that he found anything to admire in the *émigrés* on the Rhine. His hatred of Frenchmen was perfectly impartial. 'I have found in every place where I have been', he wrote, 'the most marked contempt for French of all descriptions, both aristocrats and democrats.'[12] The important thing was to prevent 'the incendiary lava' from passing the Straits of Dover. In a furious speech against Charles James Fox's motion to treat with the

National Convention, in December 1792, he showed himself a master of that Ciceronian terminology which Tory statesmen were to apply to France for the next ten years. 'Robbers and assassins', 'sanguinary ruffians', 'murderers and regicides whose hands are still reeking with the blood of a slaughtered monarch', these were but a sample of Robert Jenkinson's parliamentary epithets. When war with France broke in February 1793, he rejoiced that while it took 60,000 Frenchmen to defeat 17,000 Austrians at Jemappes ('with considerable difficulty'), a mere 1,500 Englishmen had cut to pieces 5,000 Frenchmen at Lincelles.

On the other hand, Robert Stewart, Viscount Castlereagh, arriving at his political majority in the more bracing air of northern Ireland, drank a toast with his fellow members of the Northern Whig Club at Belfast: 'To a happy establishment of the Gallic Constitution' – followed by another: 'To our Sovereign Lord – the People'. Little wonder that King George III once told Lady Fitzwilliam that Lord Castlereagh 'had formerly drunk to the rope that should hang the last King'. Robert Stewart, however, was too late for the taking of the Bastille, and instead we find him attending the debates of the National Assembly and deploring their 'tumultuous pedantry'. Nevertheless, he felt himself disposed to 'applaud the feeling which led the way to this unparalleled change', and he deplored the inability of the *émigrés* at Spa to recognize the fact that 'matters never could re-instated as they formerly were . . . .' He predicted that the Revolutionary armies would fight well, and, unlike Robert Jenkinson, he predicted a long war. In fact, his imaginative insight enabled him to realize that the *ancien régime* was over in Europe. The pity is that he never brought himself to admit that it was over in England. On his return from France, he eschewed the celebrations of the Belfast Whig Club on the anniversary of the fall of the Bastille, made a fierce speech against the Convention after the execution of Louis XVI, was sworn in as a Justice of the Peace, was gazetted Lieutenant-Colonel of the Londonderry Militia (Robert Jenkinson was gazetted Colonel of the Kentish Militia shortly afterwards), and accepted William Pitt's offer of the pocket-borough of Tregony in Cornwall. 'He is Pittized with a vengeance', wrote one who had known him as a lover of 'the cause of the people'.[13]

The third member of our Cabinet quartet, Henry Addington, seems never to have undertaken the tour of Europe. The nearest he came to observing revolution in the making was at Winchester school, where he witnessed one of those curious manifestations of aristocratic insubordination known as 'barring-out'. A pious letter of Mrs Addington at this time, however, would suggest that Henry took no part in it. Perhaps he already frowned upon 'disaffection'. Anyway, shortly afterwards his father removed him from all danger of infection, and he remained in the safe ecclesiastical hands of Dr Goodenough, the future Bishop of Carlisle, until he went up to Brasenose in 1774. There he read classics and took his bachelor's degree in 1778. Any experience that Henry Addington may have gained at this time, or indeed at any time, of the greater world beyond the home counties, he gained at second hand. His opinions likewise were intellectually adopted rather than proved upon his pulses in the world of the flesh and the devil. Burke, who appeared to him in the guise of a modern Demosthenes, taught him what to think of the French Revolution. Adam Smith taught him what to think of modern trade and commerce. Henry Addington, who wrote verses of the parish-magazine variety, addressed an Ode to the author of The Wealth of Nations. John Scott, Earl of Eldon, our fourth member of the Cabinet quartet, believed that it was incumbent upon a lawyer to live like a hermit and work like a horse. As we have seen, he scarcely put his nose outside the Court of Chancery once he had attained that dignified asylum. The single adventure of his life was his elopement with an heiress at the age of twenty-one. His idea of humour was to convert the ballad of Chevy Chase into the style of a Bill in Chancery.

Aside from their education in formal institutions and by foreign travel, these men owed most of all to the example of William Pitt. Indeed, the Liverpool Administration was in most respects the pale shadow of the great Administration by which the son of the great Chatham had ruled the England of their youth. They served their apprenticeship to politics in a world where Mr Pitt presided as the tutelary deity. When the Radical Black Dwarf called them 'apish Jupiters', the aspersion was intended to reflect upon their inadequacy to wield the thunderbolts of their great predecessor. Disraeli said that they inherited Pitt's errors without his genius: that they

exaggerated and caricatured his errors. Certain it is that they believed, at every turn, that they were imitating Mr Pitt, even when
they did not understand him. Pitt had been a reformer who found
himself compelled to resort to repression of reformism in face of
the threat of revolution and foreign invasion. His disciples forgot
his reformism and imitated his policy of repression. 'Like all weak
men, they had recourse to what they called strong measures, they
determined to put down the multitude. They thought they were
imitating Mr Pitt, because they mistook disorganization for sedition.'[14] Because Pitt had been compelled to postpone principle for
expediency at the great crisis of the French Revolution, his disciples
adopted expediency as a principle. It was said of Lord Liverpool
that the great secret of his policy was that he had none. A Frenchman went so far as to say that if Lord Liverpool had been present
at the creation of the world he would have said: 'Conservons-nous
le chaos.' Perhaps to turn expediency into a policy was the instinctive reaction of men of Lord Liverpool's social background. Disraeli
was not alone in detecting the secret of their unsuccess in their
distrust of principles, of ideas. Mr Keith Feiling has shown that
Lord Liverpool's characteristic defect was his 'unvarying neglect of
spiritual causes ... his original dread of ideas',[15] although it is
only fair to point out that he made an honest attempt to understand the most philosophical communication that can ever have
been addressed to a Prime Minister of England.*[16] Perhaps, however, we should remember Matthew Arnold's judgement upon all
aristocracies: that their absorption in the temporal and the tangible renders them inaccessible to ideas.[17]

Distrust of principle and devotion to expediency, however, may
have a certain short-term value in times of dire national peril. To
ride the whirlwind and control the storm has always been a more
likely activity in poetry than in politics, and in the great storms of
war and peace that smote Regency England the qualities of the
willow were perhaps more urgently called for than those of the
oak. Certainly Lord Liverpool and his colleagues were persuaded
that it was their duty to remain in office at the cost of concession
rather than to confront the forces of change with the rigidity of
unbending principle. It is not true that a practical man is a man

* Outlined on pp. 57-8.

who practises the blunders of his predecessors: he may also practise their wisdom. Nor is an open mind always equivalent to an
open drain, as the dogmatist would have us believe. *Pace* Disraeli,
and Mr Feiling, and Matthew Arnold, we might still ask ourselves
whether a more idealistic statesman than Lord Liverpool would
have interested himself in the millenarist plans of Robert Owen,
or whether he would have troubled to make head or tail of Coleridge's philosophical advice in the dark and dangerous year of 1817.
Of course, it is quite possible that the 'Arch-mediocrity' did not
know what he was doing. The puzzling Mr Coleridge and the in-
defatigable Mr Owen were only two of the great phantasmagoria
of prophets who hovered over the melting-pot of ideas which was
Regency England. Perhaps only a government of mediocre country
gentlemen under the presidency of an arch-mediocrity could have
contemplated such a scene *sans peur et sans reproche.*

Chapter 8

THE MIND OF THE GOVERNORS

I am grown as popular in 1821 as unpopular formerly, and, of the two, unpopularity is the more
convenient and gentlemanlike.

CASTLEREAGH

The very last who, in the strict sense of the word,
can be said to have governed England.

YONGE: *Life of Lord Liverpool*

WHEN Lord Liverpool took office, in June 1812, England was at
the climax of the war with France and on the brink of war with
the United States of America. Napoleon had devised his Continental System to close the European market to our manufacturers,
and the American Non-intercourse Act had closed the market for
a third of our textiles. In fact, it seemed that England was about
to stew in her own industrial juice. Certainly, she was nearer to
capitulation in 1812 than at any time during the war. Her exports
were down by 33⅓ per cent and her poor-law expenditure had
risen from four to six millions since the beginning of the century.
Prices were 87 per cent above pre-war level, and in August wheat
stood at 160s. a quarter: the quartern loaf cost 1s. 8d. The industrial north was in the hands of the machine-wreckers, a large part
of the army was abroad, and the Prime Minister had been assassinated in the precincts of the House of Commons. True, Spencer
Perceval was assassinated at the hands of a lunatic; the crime had
no political significance. But the manner of his death could hardly
be said to have lightened the gloomy prospect which faced the in-
coming Ministry. It was fortunate that Lord Liverpool put his faith
in a righteous Providence, for no other recipient of human confidence was very much in evidence. It was equally fortunate that he
was not a very imaginative man.

He proposed no comprehensive measures. The immediate task
was to win the war. He set about the problem with the assistance
of Lord Castlereagh at the Foreign Office and the Duke of Welling-

ton in the field, and in three more years the war was won. But neither at that time, nor for the rest of his fifteen years in office, did Lord Liverpool contemplate any far-reaching schemes of political or social reorganization. His record in domestic legislation is brief and uninspiring; a Factory Act in 1819, promoted by Robert Peel; a Truck Act in 1820; the resumption of cash payments in 1819–21, again promoted by Robert Peel – this time the son; the repeal of the Combination Laws in 1824, sponsored by Joseph Hume and Francis Place, and their restoration in a modified form in 1825, when the Prime Minister confessed that he had hardly been aware of the nature of the problem in repealing them. For the rest, Lord Liverpool believed that government interference in economic matters was nearly always disastrous. His measures were piecemeal and tentative, designed to check abuses wherever it was possible to do so without ingringing the sacred principle of 'freedom of contract'; to ameliorate distress without offending any important 'interest'; to preserve peace and order so that things might 'return to normal' of their own accord. In order to safeguard the landed interest in the post-war landslide of agricultural prices, he passed the Waterloo Corn Law. In order to mollify both the moneyed interest and the country gentlemen, he redeemed Pitt's pledge and withdrew the war-time Income Tax. Neither measure really promoted the well-being of the mass of the people. The Corn Law brought benefits to the farmer which his labourers did not share, and it certainly did not lower the price of bread for the industrial worker. The withdrawal of the Income Tax benefited the City and the moneyed men, while depriving the Government of revenue which might have enabled it to remit indirect taxation on the necessities of the nation.

Liverpool put his faith in something which he called 'the gradual effect of the general policy of the government'. It was as if he thought that by merely staying in office, year after year, balancing the budget, maintaining public order, reconciling interests, and cutting off a flagrant abuse where no one would be greatly offended, public confidence would be restored and things would 'get back to normal again'. Of course, in a painfully limited sense, he was right. England staggered along to the brink of revolution, looked over the edge, and staggered back again. The rich went on getting richer, and the poor mostly contrived to keep themselves alive. From the day the Government came into power, nobody believed that it could last for long. 'You have undertaken a most gigantic task', Wellington wrote to the Prime Minister from Spain; 'and I don't know how you will get through it.' Liverpool replied modestly: 'I can assure you I never sought the situation in which I find myself.'[1] It was true. Not the most ambitious politician would have sought to shoulder the burden which Liverpool took upon himself out of an hereditary sense of duty to his country in 1812. He was not even in the House of Commons; and the man best fitted to lead the Government's majority in that obstreperous assembly – George Canning – had declined to serve in the same Cabinet as his bitter rival, Lord Castlereagh. Castlereagh, of course, was indispensable for the conduct of foreign affairs, and Liverpool was obliged to depend upon him for the leadership of the Commons also: an unfortunate situation, since Castlereagh seemed to delight in rubbing the House up the wrong way. All that Liverpool could depend upon in the House of Commons, it seems, was the incompetence of the leaders of the Opposition. Lord Grey was in the Upper House; Ponsonby lacked fire; Brougham lacked breeding; Tierney lacked both. So the Whigs continued to make fools of themselves, to Lord Liverpool's profit. They were timid on the burning issue of parliamentary reform. They talked too much about the danger of standing armies in time of peace, and of the sorrows of Napoleon at St Helena. Meanwhile, Liverpool, who was a first-rate party manager, devoted most of his time to the task of keeping together his own difficult team until Divine Providence should see fit to hand out a halo for endurance under adversity.

In point of fact, the Liverpool Ministry survived, with shufflings and re-shufflings, for fifteen years. It survived Castlereagh's mishandling of the House of Commons in the debates on the repeal of the Income Tax in 1816: the occasion when that despiser of popularity made his ill-judged reference to the English people's 'ignorant opposition to taxation'. The Government was defeated by twenty-nine votes, and Liverpool wrote that 'the government certainly hangs by a thread'. The Prince Regent, however, assured the Prime Minister that he was 'true to the backbone', and the

Government stayed on.[2] It survived the admission of Wellington in 1818, and the widespread suspicion that it was proposed to set up military rule. It survived the threat of old Eldon to split the party on the resumption of cash payments in 1819–21. It survived the threat of a coalition between Canning and Brougham in 1821. It survived the storm of anger which followed Peterloo, the pelting fury of mobs roaring for Queen Caroline, the designs of Arthur Thistlewood to carry the Ministers' heads on pikes through the streets of London. Castlereagh died, Napoleon died, Queen Caroline died; Peel and Canning and Huskisson came in; Mr Pickwick set out on his travels; but the Liverpool Administration was still there, defeated in longevity only by the ministries of Walpole and Pitt. Then, one day in 1827, Lord Liverpool fell down under a stroke. As a feat of endurance, in an age of party warfare and public disorder such as later generations have not known, it was a remarkable achievement.

The Ministry that died with Lord Liverpool's paralytic stroke in 1827 was not the Ministry that came in with him in 1812, either in spirit or substance. The last seven years of its life saw the transformation of the Government from what was, not unjustly, called 'a reactionary caucus', to a Ministry of 'Liberal Toryism'. The passing of Lord Eldon's incubus, the death of Castlereagh, the retirement of Sidmouth, the entry into office of men like Peel, Huskisson and Canning, in the early twenties, marked the triumph of a forward-looking spirit in the leadership of the Tory Party which was to make possible its survival as a constructive force within the conditions of the new age that was dawning. Here, however, we are concerned with the first eight years, the years of the Regency, when the problems to be faced were those of war abroad and the threat of civil war at home. There is a unity about these years, a certain prevailing quality of mood and manner, which marks them off from the first decade of the century, when the internal tensions of English society were obscured by the necessities of the life-and-death struggle with victorious France, and the third decade of the century when those tensions were subdued by the prospect of peaceable reformism at the hands of Whigs and Tories alike. In the years 1812–20, with the slackening of the struggle with France, the cumulative challenge of profound social and economic problems at home, and the prevalence of a sense of hopelessness about the possibility of reformism at the hands of government itself, the dominant mood was one of fear among the governors and desperation among the governed. 'The years of un-rest' is but a pale, text-book title for this period of our history, which begins with the fierce clamour of the Luddites smashing machinery in the midlands and the north, and passes onward through the hunger-marching of the Blanketeers, the armed revolt of Jeremiah Brandreth and the Derbyshire men, the tragic clash of Peterloo, to the crazy St Bartholomew's Eve of the Cato Street Plot in 1820. It is the decade of sledge-hammers, pikes, home-made bombs and Oliver the Spy. It is the age of sabotage, sedition, spies, assassination-plots and suspended revolution.

We are concerned here with the mood of the governors; we shall concern ourselves at a later stage with the extent and quality of revolutionism in the country. In what spirit did this little group of country gentlemen, hereditary governors and 'routine statesmen', confront the problems of incipient revolution? Was Shelley wise in his generation when he likened them to a ghastly train of hypo-critical tyrants in *A Masque of Anarchy*? Were Mr and Mrs Ham-mond justified, a century later, in their assertion that 'probably no English government have ever been quite so near, in spirit and licence, to the atmosphere that we used to associate with the Tsar's government of Russia'?[3] The Hammonds wrote before the twentieth century had experienced the full rigours of the totali-tarian police-state. Perhaps, the nineteen-fifties are in a better position to answer these questions than were the nineteen-twenties – or the eighteen-twenties.

In the first place, we should remember that Lord Liverpool and his colleagues lost far less sleep over the dangers of revolution than might seem probable to the historian who spends laborious days among the packets marked 'Disturbances' in the Public Record Office. Alarmed they frequently were, but never haunted; anxious, but never panic-stricken. For long periods they indulged in amiable apathy towards the whole question. Certainly, the Home Office worked long hours; Lord Sidmouth was perhaps the hardest-worked member of the Cabinet. But the work of rat-catching and all that it entailed – the employment of spies, the interrogation of informers and state prisoners, the unending correspondence of local magistrates – these things held little attraction for the gentlemen of the Cabinet. Occasionally they sat in Privy Council and gazed with amused curiosity at a Radical weaver like Samuel Bamford or his friend 'Doctor' Healey. They listened to Sidmouth's reports on the temperature of the body politic, subscribed to his proposals to suspend the Habeas Corpus Act or to legislate for the control of public meetings or seditious literature. But all this was only a small and slightly repellent part of the preoccupations of the hereditary governors. Nobody who turns over the pages of the voluminous life and letters of Lord Liverpool is likely to imagine for one moment that he was much concerned with treason. Foreign affairs, quarrelling colleagues, the party majority, the military establishment, the Corn Law, the Property Tax, cash payments, the fate of Marshal Ney, the extravagance of the Prince Regent, the grant of a million pounds for building new churches in London : these are the headings of his daily agenda.

Nor is the impression to be gained from the parliamentary debates of the period very different. Measures like the Nottingham Peace Bill, and the Bill to make machine-breaking a capital crime, in 1812, were passed easily in a small House. The reports of Secret Committees of both Houses in 1817 and 1818, revealing plots for the 'total overthrow of all existing establishments and a division of the landed and extinction of funded property', excited little debate and were readily adopted. Even the suspension of the Habeas Corpus Act and the Additional Force Bills of 1817 failed to rally large numbers. The question of spies and *agents provocateurs* was before Parliament seven times in the years 1817 and 1818, sometimes with Oliver the Spy as the *pièce de résistance*. There was 'warm debate', but division-numbers rarely rose above two hundred in a House of Commons some three times that size. Even on Fazackerley's motion for inquiry into the conduct of spies, in February 1818, after a debate which produced from Grey Bennet the most sensational (and unreliable) account of Oliver's activities to which the House of Commons ever listened, only 163 members voted. The subject of this 'continental' and 'despotic' method of detecting crime interested the press and a radical section of the Whigs, but it can hardly be said to have crowded the House of Commons. It certainly never shook either the parliamentary majority or the self-esteem of the Liverpool Administration.

Within the contemporary perspective, as distinct from our own, the most important preoccupations of the Government in Regency England were finance and foreign affairs. The Prime Minister was traditionally First Lord of the Treasury, and attended to all questions concerned with both the raising and expenditure of revenue; the office of Chancellor of the Exchequer (at this time held by Vansittart, a comparative nonentity) was of quite subordinate importance. Liverpool was first and foremost, by both office and inclination, concerned with public finance and the finance-branches of trade, industry and commerce. It was his misfortune that he was obliged to entrust the leadership of the House of Commons to the only member of his Cabinet who might be said to have regarded such matters with a certain degree of contempt. Castlereagh had shown a fine disregard for economy in the launching of the ill-fated Walcheren expedition in 1809, and in his acceptance of the burden of fortifying the Flemish frontier in 1815. Grey, speaking for the Opposition, denounced this last as an example of 'careless indifference' in heaping 'most enormous burdens on the oppressed and deluded people of this country'. But Castlereagh's arrogance was notorious. In 1819, when defending the Government against Tierney's motion of 'No confidence', he coolly admitted that the Opposition's attack on the Government's financial policy was 'perfectly sound and warranted by facts', and then secured a crushing defeat of the motion by a brilliant defence of the Government's foreign policy.[4] His attitude of scornful indifference to anything outside the field of foreign policy earned for the Government a reputation for financial culpability which it certainly did not deserve on its record.

Foreign affairs were, of course, the Government's strong suit. It was strongest where the average Englishman was generally most apathetic or misinformed. The Prime Minister himself frequently remarked with surprise upon this apathy. 'It is quite astonishing', he wrote during the Congress of Vienna, 'how little interest is taken in what is going on at Vienna, except in so far as it is connected with expense.'[5] However, there was, as we have already seen, one other aspect of foreign policy which was always capable of stirring the people from their apathy. This was the suspicion that their government was hand-in-glove with the tyrants of the Holy Alliance, and that the spirit and methods of continental despotism were gaining ground here. We have seen how symptoms of this horrid tendency were detected in the hospitality accorded to the exiled Bourbons, in the lavish entertainment of continental Princes and Ministers in London at the end of the war, in the maintenance of a large standing army during the first years of the peace, in the participation of Castlereagh in European Congresses, in the admission of Wellington to the Cabinet in 1818, and in the 'massacre of Peterloo' in the following year. What justice was there in these suspicions? Was the Liverpool Administration really infected with the spirit of the Holy Alliance? Did they really aim, as Brougham suspected, 'to make the government of this country less free – and permanently so'?

In the first place, there is no reason whatever to suppose that they were in love with the House of Bourbon. They found Louis XVIII and the *émigrés* embarrassing guests, although they had to admit reluctantly that Louis was the only practicable alternative to Napoleon. The average Tory probably felt like Robert Southey: 'As for the Bourbons, I do not wish to see them restored unless there were no other means of effecting his [Napoleon's] overthrow ....They have been a detestable race.'[6]

As for the Holy Alliance, the fact that Castlereagh thought it 'a piece of sublime mysticism and nonsense', and that he was being steadily driven mad by his noble attempt to cooperate in a system of 'diplomacy by conference' while still standing firmly by the principle of national self-determination, could hardly be explained in simple day-to-day terms for the benefit of the parliamentary Opposition and the Radical press. The Government fully endorsed Castlereagh's opinions and policy. They had fought the war to restore the balance of power in Europe. The Foreign Secretary's farsighted genius had pledged them to a measure of conference with their late allies for the peaceful liquidation of future problems concerning the peace of Europe. Nor is it evident that, after twenty years of participation in the common life of Europe, they could have suddenly withdrawn into a policy of isolation. But for policing other people's Jacobins they had no inclination. They had their own Jacobins to police. It is true that Liverpool refused to intercede on behalf of Marshal Ney. Humanly the attitude was ungenerous; politically it was a blunder. It strengthened the suspicion that the Government subscribed to the vindictive policy of Legitimism. 'One can never feel that the King is secure upon his throne till he has dared to spill traitors' blood', Liverpool wrote of Louis XVIII. It was one of those things that are best left unsaid, and it was unlike Lord Liverpool to have said it.[7]

When Benjamin Robert Haydon looked back upon the long Tory regime in 1830, he reflected: 'The military vigour, the despotic feeling engendered by twenty-five years of furious war, rendered them unfit, perhaps, to guide the domestic policy of the country.'[8] Haydon was a Tory, but the attitude is simply English; and when the people became possessed of the power to change their governors by the ballot-box they were to act upon it. The rapidity with which war-winning governments have been swept from power in the first half of the twentieth century has kept pace steadily with the widening of the franchise. Nothing of the kind happened – or could have happened – under the conditions prevailing in the early nineteenth century, and the war-winning Tories brought to the problems of peace the mentality begotten by the harsh exigencies of war. 'Military vigour . . . despotic feeling . . . .' So Haydon described it. And it is true that these men had looked into the face of Napoleon. They had spent their youth and their middle years in the shadow of a cocked hat. They had lived their lives within the sound of guns and the tramp of marching men.

Superficially, of course, there must always be something ludicrous in ascribing military vigour or despotic feeling to Robert Jenkinson, with his long neck and his flickering eyelid. Nor had the military experience of any of the Ministers, with the exception of Castlereagh and Wellington, risen above the comic-opera level demanded by membership of the Yeomanry. Castlereagh had come near to danger and disfigurement during the Irish Rebellion of 1798, when he wrote to his wife: 'Scars, if not too deep and destructive of shape, are a soldier's most becoming adornment.' Wellington, the professional soldier, hated bloodshed as only a professional soldier can. However, it was not their experience of military habits that is important in its effect upon the mentality of the members of the Liverpool government. Of far greater importance was their prolonged concern with the details and the direction of a warlike foreign policy. They grew accustomed to think in terms of regiments. They handled far greater numbers of military effectives than any previous government in our history. Such men were unlikely to spend time deploring the existence of a standing army while Luddites created a reign of terror in Yorkshire and Napoleon was marching to Moscow with half a million men. It must have seemed to them, just then, that bayonets were the only things with which to hold together a crumbling world.

Lord Liverpool had defended the existence of a standing army during the war with the Revolution. He was inclined to think that altogether too much fuss was made about the question. 'As if a standing army had not been kept on foot for above a century,' he reflected, 'or as if any danger to the liberties of the nation had ever arisen from it.'[9]* As Secretary of State for War and the Colonies under Mr Perceval, he had handled unprecedented numbers of men and sums of money for warlike purposes. He calculated that the war had cost nearly three million in 1808 and over six million in 1810, exclusive of the cost of ordnance stores and transport. He reckoned on England having 50,000 men in the field in 1811. As Prime Minister during the last three years of the war, he was dealing in larger figures still. Vansittart's budget of February 1816 gave the total cost of the armed forces as £29,000,000. Wellington was in France with 30,000 men; there were 69,000 in the colonies; 25,000 each in England and Ireland: making a grand total of nearly 150,000. Liverpool defended this enormous establishment against the fierce criticism of the Whigs, who quoted the comparatively small numbers of the time of William III, by pointing out the greatly increased size of the Empire and the instability of the restored Bourbon regime in France. But it was the number of troops on foot in England – 25,000 – that caused alarm. The number continued large: there were 26,000 in 1817. Their purpose was obvious and unconcealed. They were stationed in the manufacturing districts to protect or overawe the civil population. It was easy to

* The force to which Lord Liverpool here referred, however, had never been a regular standing army in time of peace such as existed in the years immediately after 1815.

say that the Government was tackling a domestic problem with the mentality and the method begotten by its long experience of a foreign war. Even in the twentieth century there have been critics of the Liverpool Administration who liken the position of the Government, vis-à-vis the people, to that of a garrison quartered in the midst of a hostile population. Paradoxically enough, such historians find their predecessors in Regency England among the Whigs and Radicals who were the most inveterate opponents of any scheme to replace the regular army with an adequate civilian police-force.

The criticism of the Government's military-mindedness reached its crescendo when, in 1818, the Duke of Wellington was admitted to the Cabinet, and when, in the following year, there occurred the 'massacre' of Peterloo. The admission of Wellington took place for a variety of reasons. There was the fact that his occupation was gone with the evacuation of France after the Congress of Aix-la-Chapelle; there was the natural desire to honour a man who had served his country well; and there was the purely tactical consideration that it was more convenient to have the Duke's keen and critical intelligence inside the Cabinet than outside it. For, although he was a Tory of the Tories, the Duke was no respecter of persons. When Napoleon escaped from Elba, he described the Government as 'abject and wretched in intellect'. When he was offered Cabinet rank in 1818, he stipulated that his acceptance should not be taken as binding him to the Government's policy in any future period.[10] As for Peterloo, the presence of the Duke in the Cabinet afforded an easy alibi for Lord Liverpool and a simple argument from cause to effect, in the minds of men like Henry Brougham. Yet the order to the Hussars at Manchester came not from the central Government but from the local magistrates, and if the Government in London supported the action of the magistrates it is exceedingly difficult to imagine what else they could have done. Liverpool claimed that their action was 'substantially right', although he refused to agree that it was 'in all its parts prudent'. As he put it, 'there remained no alternative but to support them.'[11]

The truth is that the loudest and most persistent voices in demanding military measures came from other quarters than the Cabinet. They came from owners of machinery, frightened manufacturers, nervous magistrates, noble Lords in charge of County Lieutenancies, and honest alarmists like the Poet Laureate. The Home Office Papers for the period 1812–20 are full of demands from manufacturers for stronger military protection. Lord Kenyon, after Peterloo, recommended the formation of 'armed associations of the Well-disposed' in the 'disaffected' localities: a sure way of starting a civil war. The Poet Laureate, who lived at Keswick in the Lakes, was scenting sedition 'even among these mountains' and warning Lord Liverpool that if the military were withdrawn from London, 'four and twenty hours would not elapse before the tri-coloured flag would be planted upon Carlton House'.[12] The Prime Minister, however, was not impressed. He was prepared to keep the army on foot, but he was steadily opposed to any hasty recourse to abnormal methods of keeping the peace. He preferred, as ever, to place his trust in the traditional institutions of the country and the 'gradual effect of the general policy of the Government'. This was not stupid optimism, but the well-based and knowledgeable confidence of an hereditary governor. There was something shameful and humiliating, to men of Lord Liverpool's antecedents, in having to resort to anything other than the traditional laws and institutions, methods and machinery, of his country in maintaining the peace and order of England. Such recourse might be necessary in continental countries, or in Ireland. But in *England*? Perish the thought.*

Indeed, it was the native conservatism of Lord Liverpool that was to prove the best guarantee of the liberties of the country he ruled. And in this, there was, after all, something heroic. Luddites, Blanketeers, hunger-marchers and armed insurgents to the left of him; anxious noblemen, frightened manufacturers, panicky magistrates and Poet Laureate to the right of him; Lord Liverpool steadily pursued his middle course of piecemeal measures and traditional methods with the invincible resolve of the hereditary governor who never doubted the ultimate and eternal rightness of the 'traditional

---

* Apart from the resort to extraordinary measures to combat a fifth column at the crisis of the French Revolution (1796–9), 'the British Government had never employed since 1688 any methods to put down rebellion, save the ordinary process of the law': see Halévy, *History of the English People*, Vol. II, p. 20.

modes of behaviour' of his class and his country. Nor did he generally consider it incumbent upon him to apologize or explain, let alone to modify his policy in face of public clamour. 'On questions of inferior magnitude,' he once said, 'it might be very well for a minister to give up his private judgement to the opinion of the public.' On major issues, however, 'a man should stand and fall by his own judgement.' Public opinion had its uses, but there were many cases where a statesman 'by acting in conformity to public opinion might occasion the country much mischief'.[13] Thus Edmund Burke had spoken in the House of Commons, a generation earlier: 'I cannot indeed take it upon me to say that I have the honour *to follow* the sense of the people. The truth is, I *met it on the way*, while I was pursuing their interest according to my own ideas.'[14] It was the aristocratic tradition of the statesman, of the Member of Parliament in relation to his constituents, of the nature of parliamentary government itself, as it runs from Burke to Peel, and beyond.

It is this that lies behind the assertion of Lord Liverpool's biographer when he described Lord Liverpool as 'the very last who, in the strict sense of the word, can be said to have governed England.'[15] And perhaps all that it says is, that ultimately the job of a government is to govern. Certainly, Lord Liverpool and his colleagues not only believed that they were the natural and rightful possessors of authority; they believed in authority itself. To them, politics was not simply a matter of finding out what the people want and giving it to them. Such a defection from the principle of authority would turn parliament into a mere body of delegates and its leaders into a body of camp-followers. The duty of statesmen was to lead the people as they, the governors, thought best. And such a doctrine entails the sacrifice of popularity. Indeed, there must always be something inherently suspect about a popular government, or a popular statesman. Castlereagh, who was in most respects a caricature of his age and his class in all things concerning domestic government, summed it up best of all when he declared that, between popularity and unpopularity, 'unpopularity is the more convenient and gentlemanlike.'

Chapter 9

ALARM

Those who are old enough to have a distinct recollection of those times are astonished now to think how great was the panic which could exist without any evidence at all: how prodigious were the radical forces which were always heard of, but never seen ... how country gentlemen, well-armed, scoured the fields and lanes, and met on heaths to fight the enemy who never came: how, even in the midst of towns, young ladies carried heavy planks and iron-ing-boards, to barricade windows, in preparation for sieges from thousands of rebels whose footfall was long listened for in vain through the darkness of the night.

HARRIET MARTINEAU, 1849

You talked of expected horrors in London, and instead of instantly conceiving, as any rational creature would have done, that such words could relate only to a circulating library, she pictured to herself a mob of three thousand men assembling in St George's Fields; the Bank attacked, the Tower threatened, the streets of London flowing with blood.

JANE AUSTEN, 1816

POLITICS has been defined as the art of directing public force, and certainly the first duty of every government is the maintenance of public order. No English government has ever shown less prudery in the execution of this primary function than the government of Lord Liverpool. Indeed, it sometimes seemed that in matters domestic this government thought that its primary function was also its final function. 'It was of little moment to Lord Sidmouth', wrote his biographer, the Dean of Norwich, 'from what cause this treasonable spirit originated, since in every case it was equally his duty to put it down.'[1] The inscrutable workings of Divine Providence, the philosophy of Adam Smith, even the weather, might be

justly cited as alibis for governmental inquiry into the causes of
the discontents. Had not Mr Pitt himself taught his disciples the
political significance of rain? A few days of rain, Mr Pitt had said,
might produce consequences for which even he could not discover
a remedy. 'This admission of England's wisest statesman', remarks
the Hon. George Pellew, 'shows how little real control mankind
have over the sources of their prosperity, and how entirely dependent they are, even for the means of subsistence, on the mercy and
protection of Divine Providence.'[2] Henry Addington expressed
the point more tersely when he wrote in 1812 : 'Man cannot create
abundance where Providence has inflicted scarcity.' In short : 'The
alleviation of the difficulties is not to be looked for from the intervention of the Government and Parliament.'[3]

It has become a commonplace of historians that economic distress was the parent of political consciousness and activity on the
part of the working class, and that this process of cause and effect
was particularly marked in Regency England. It can be shown
quite clearly that, at least from the moment when Thomas Hardy
and his friends founded the London Corresponding Society in 1792,
working men took up the cause of parliamentary reform in the
hope of procuring a legislative body which would remedy their
material distress. The peculiar interest of reformist politics under
the Regency is to be found in the race, for it was no less, in which
the popular leaders were engaged for the harnessing of economic
discontent to the cause of political reform. Their concern was to
prevent economic distress from venting itself in such forms of direct
action as machine-breaking, strikes and demonstrations of violence,
and to turn the energies of the sufferers to political association for
the immediate political purpose of reforming the House of Commons. 'Had you possessed 70,000 votes for the election of Members
to sit in that House,' a weavers' spokesman demanded of his fellow
workers, after the rejection of a Minimum Wage Petition in 1811,
'would your application have been treated with such indifference,
not to say inattention? We believe not.'[4] William Cobbett's *Letter
to the Luddites*, in November 1816, like his *Address to the Journeymen and Labourers*, of October in the same year, was concerned to
persuade the artisan that direct action, and all forms of violence,
were the principal enemies of reform. All working-class energies,

he insisted, should be bent to the peaceable political task of securing the franchise, whereafter all else would follow. The same purpose was served by Major Cartwright's campaign in 1811, 1812 and 1813, for the founding of Hampden Clubs in the midland and northern industrial districts.

To Lord Liverpool and his colleagues all this was doubly objectionable; first, because in their view the labouring people were not susceptible of political life, except the politics of loyalty and obedience; and secondly, because it was rank heresy according to the tenets of true political economy. To suggest that the people possessed any right to representation *as the people*, or as distinct from virtual representation, was political heresy. To suggest that parliament should be reformed in order to remedy economic ills was a flagrant contradiction of the principles of *laissez-faire*. Thus, instead of regarding Cobbett, Cartwright and the rest as allies in the cause of social order, they regarded them as the promoters of mischievous confusion, crass and ill-intentioned preachers of a peculiarly dangerous kind of heresy: the heresy that confounds social distress with political agitation. It was their intention to delude the people into believing that social evils could be remedied by political change, to create a wholly artificial alliance between Politics and Economics. It is no easy matter, at this time of day, to acknowledge their sincerity in this attitude. It is very easy to regard them as merely frightened for the security of their own economic and political authority. In fact, their fears in this matter were the least part of their total apprehension. Their favourite adjective, when referring to the labouring poor, was not 'revolutionary' but 'deluded'. They were intent less upon exaggerating the disturbed and dangerous state of the country (although they rightly realized that it was dangerously disturbed), than upon correcting the false impression that there was any necessary connexion between political opinions and social distress.

In all this, the facts were for long enough on their side. There is scarcely any sign of political intention in the machine-breaking movement which raged in the midlands and the north at the time when the Liverpool Administration came into power. The disturbances of 1815 and 1816 were similarly the work of Luddites and bread-rioters. The Derbyshire Rising of 1817 was the action of deluded and desperate men whose declared intention was to 'turn out and fight for bread'. The wretched Blanketeers set out for London in the same year in order to ask the Prince Regent 'why trade was slack'. It was not until 1819 that popular agitation took on a coherent political character, and even at Peterloo there were banners denouncing the Corn Laws. Yet, throughout these years, the Radical leaders – Cartwright, Cobbett, Hunt – were struggling to canalize the energies of their followers into political channels. It was their task to change the facts, to bring about the very connexion between social distress and political opinion which the Government correctly, and with evident satisfaction, declined to acknowledge. They succeeded. Peterloo was the grim celebration of their success. Lord Liverpool, however, was still speaking in the last year of the Regency as he had spoken in the first year of that agitated epoch. In 1812 he accepted the report of the Secret Committee of the House of Lords on the nature of the Luddite disturbances: 'that the rioters were to a great extent tools in the hands of those whose turbulence and disloyalty derived no provocation from poverty ....'[5] In 1819, in the debate on the conduct of the magistrates at Peterloo, he declared that the distress of the people arose 'from the state of an internal trade which was affected by foreign commerce. . . . Whatever might be the circumstances of that distress, it was not connected with political causes.'[6] His diagnosis was the same in both cases: a basis of distress occasioned by causes beyond the Government's control, and the provocative conduct of some few ill-disposed persons who wished to make political capital out of their fellow creatures' sufferings. It had been the same in France in 1789: a few disaffected persons playing upon widespread distress. 'In every instance it was the desperate conduct of the few, and the fears of the many, that produced revolutions.' After all, his Lordship had been present at the taking of the Bastille, as he reminded the House; and surely his Lordship ought to know what he was talking about.[7]

It was under the influence of this persuasion that the Government was faced with a desperate and politically-minded minority, which must be prevented from harnessing the distresses of a non-political majority to their wicked purposes, that the Liverpool Administration evolved the technique of repression generally known as 'Alarm'. It was, like so much else in the policy of this Administration, taken over from William Pitt. It consisted of a simple and invariable sequence of events. In the first instance, the Government announces that it is in possession of certain information, derived from unspecified sources, relative to actual or threatened disturbances in the country. Secondly, this information is entrusted to Secret Committees, generally of both Houses, for examination and report. Thirdly, the Houses receive reports from the Secret Committees, and, on the strength thereof, Government moves certain legislative action: the Suspension of the Habeas Corpus Act for a specified period, and generally certain measures to strengthen the hand of the Executive in dealing with public assemblies and the press. At the end of the specified period, Government moves either the restoration of the Habeas Corpus Act or its suspension for a further period. When the emergency comes to an end, an Act of Indemnity is brought in to absolve Ministers from actions at law consequent upon their use of their temporary and exceptional powers. At this stage, a general debate takes place on Government's conduct during the period of 'Alarm'. At no stage does Government reveal the sources of its information. The personal safety of certain 'useful individuals' is said to depend upon secrecy being maintained in this matter. Everyone knows, however, that these 'useful individuals' are spies and informers, and sometimes the question of their employment is given an airing in the parliamentary debates, the Opposition producing information derived from private inquiry of its own, or from the press. 'Airing', however, is as far as the matter ever gets, and at no time is the Government ever shaken in either its majority or its self-esteem on account of the policy of 'Alarm'.

There were three periods of 'Alarm' during Lord Liverpool's Administration. The first began with the new government's arrival in power in June 1812, and lasted until the end of the year. The second began in February 1817, and lasted until January 1818: this was the most critical period, when the Habeas Corpus Act was suspended for nearly twelve months. The last period began with the Peterloo 'massacre' in August 1819, and may be said to have lasted until the execution of the Cato Street conspirators in the following March. The spring of 1820, which saw the end of the

Regency, saw the end also of 'Alarm' as a policy. Its incidence lies fairly and squarely within the eight years which preceded the 'liberalizing' of the Administration in the twenties, the period during which Lord Sidmouth occupied the office of Home Secretary, when Lord Castlereagh was Leader of the House of Commons, and when Lord Eldon exercised overbearing influence from the Woolsack. Its equivocal paraphernalia of spies, secret committees, treason trials, and soldiers serving as policemen, exposed the Government to the charge of fabricating plots in order to suppress them, of resorting to continental methods of repression, and of generally running away from its own shadow.

The question of the 'continental' taint which is supposed to have afflicted this government has already been discussed. As for the methods, they will be seen both in their operation and in their effects, in the narration that follows, and no attempt will be made in this place to prejudge the issue. Here it is intended only to give some account of the machinery at the Government's disposal at that time for the maintenance of the public peace, and to point out some of the contemporary conditions which governed its use.[8]

At the head of the system, if system it may just be called, was the Home Office. As a specialized branch of administration, it was comparatively young, and its importance only imperfectly realized. It was both understaffed and undistinguished. In the year 1812, when it was taken over by Lord Sidmouth, *The Times* described it as 'the sink of all the imbecility attached to every ministry for the last thirty years ... the most unimportant of the three offices of state'.[9] *The Times* called for its instant and radical reform, in view of 'the most delicate and difficult affairs assigned to its management', but there is no evidence that Lord Sidmouth either intended or achieved anything in this direction. The Home Office was the clearing-house for a voluminous stream of correspondence which poured in from magistrates, manufacturers, informers and police-agents in every part of the kingdom. Here was sifted and appraised the mass of information which formed the basis of Government's action, or inaction, at every crisis in the maintenance of the public peace. Here spies were employed and interviewed, state-prisoners examined, orders dispatched for the muster of yeomanry and militia or for the assistance of the regular forces of the Crown. The finances of the department were supplied from the Secret Service Fund, and the Home Secretary was in close touch with the Law Officers of the Crown, the Judges, and the heads of the armed forces. Secret agents were employed quite arbitrarily and according to the personal judgement of the Home Secretary. They were generally men who offered their services, and they were paid according to results: 'no sedition – no pay' seems to have been the rule, with the consequence that there was rarely a lack of sedition. In no sense were these agents trained or professional servants; indeed their chief defect was their amateurishness. At no time was there a 'spy system'. Granted that spies were necessary, it would have been better for all parties alike if there had been some system in the manner of their employment.

The Home Office had correspondents but no servants or agents in the provinces. The peace-keeping machinery of the country in 1812 was almost precisely what it had been in 1588. There was a small, quasi-official police-force in London. Outside London, all that existed was amateur, voluntary and unpaid. In effect, the peace and quiet of the country depended, as it had always depended, upon the public spirit and interest of the landed aristocracy, great and small, and on the capacity for self-help and voluntary service in the ordinary citizen. England was, as the late Élie Halévy showed, 'in very truth the country of self-government ....' Without the willing and able activity of the Lord Lieutenant, the Justice of the Peace, and the self-organized and self-ordered citizens of the towns, the Home Office – and the Government as a whole – would have been either paralysed or compelled to resort to military rule.

The weakness of the system, such as it was, lay in its extremities – its hands and feet, so to speak. The village constable might deal with a burglar, and a Bow Street Runner might be sent down to arrest a dangerous fugitive from justice. But to deal with the widespread organization of machine-breakers, bread-rioters, hunger-marchers, strikers and deluded yokels, the only solution was a professional police force, trained, controlled and paid by local bodies on the strength of local taxation. Not only was such an organization non-existent, but the mere suggestion of instituting such a body was regarded with horror as 'continental' and 'tyrannous'.* Moreover, outside the ancient boroughs, there existed no local bodies to supply the organ of management and control required by such a force. The great majority of industrial towns possessed no elective institutions of government until 1835, and another half-century was to pass before the English counties possessed elective councils. The remarkable fact is not that England of the Regency experienced considerable disorder, but that she did not experience a great deal more of it. An increasingly rich and industrial and populous country was attempting to subsist on the peace-keeping machinery which had scarcely proved adequate in the age of the Spanish Armada.

The Lord Lieutenant, who was normally the greatest landowner in the shire, was a Tudor creation. He represented the Crown in the county, and to him the Home Office was in the habit of first communicating its intentions: the 'Alarm' tactics of 1817, for example, opened with Sidmouth's circular letter to the Lords Lieutenant. He had full powers to call out the yeomanry and militia, and he regularly presided over the meetings of the county magistrates. In normal times he might spend much of his time in London, but in the troubled years of the Regency he did his duty regularly and energetically in his county. Particularly energetic were the Dukes of Newcastle and Rutland in the Luddite areas of Nottinghamshire and Leicestershire, and Earl Fitzwilliam in the West Riding of Yorkshire. The Lord Lieutenant had practically superseded the Sheriff as the active agent of executive power in the shires.

The real hands and feet of the administration, however, were the Justices of the Peace. There were some five thousand of them in 1812. They were chosen by the Crown on the recommendations of the Lords Lieutenant, and the traditional qualifications for the office were residence in the county and an annual income of £100 from freehold land. They were an exclusive body. The Anglican clergy had been recently admitted in large numbers. Perhaps a

---

* 'They have an admirable police at Paris, but they pay for it dear enough. I had rather half a dozen people's throats should be cut in Ratcliffe Highway every three or four years than be subject to domiciliary visits, spies, and all the rest of Fouché's contrivances.' J. W. Ward, *Letters to Ivy*, 27 December 1811, p. 146.

quarter of the entire body was constituted by the 'squarsons', or what Cobbett called 'the Black Dragoons'. Manufacturers, however, were still jealously excluded from the Bench in most districts, notably in industrial Lancashire. Their powers were parallel to those of the Lords Lieutenant, and they were frequently in direct communication with the Home Office. In their Quarter Sessions they were empowered to organize measures of defence and to call upon both the yeomanry and the militia. Individually, the Justice had the power to read the Riot Act, order the dispersal of mobs, enrol special constables and issue warrants for arrest. He could also order the assistance of regular troops within his area.

Everything depended upon the courage, integrity and vigour of the individual Justice. Among the Home Office Papers of this time, some half-dozen names constantly recur. The most ubiquitous was the Rev. Mr Hay, for nearly twenty years chairman of the Manchester and Salford Bench of Magistrates. Mr Hay corresponded prolifically with the Home Secretary, the local military and his fellow justices. He ran an elaborate local intelligence service, with a clearing-house for the reports of spies, to which all members of his Bench sent the information collected by their agents. Always ready for trouble and quick to prevent it, the Rev. Mr Hay practically constituted himself permanent police-magistrate for the West Riding of Yorkshire. In the north, also, we find the industrious Mr Prescott of Stockport, Colonel Fletcher of Bolton, and Captain Chippendale of Oldham. In the Luddite areas of Nottinghamshire we find such energetic figures as the Rev. Mr Becher and Mr Sherbrooke, Colonel Rolleston and Mr Mundy. In some districts, however, there was a shortage of the right men for the work. In others, the loneliness of the locality led to reluctance to act independently and vigorously. On the whole, far more magistrates were apathetic than over-zealous.

The efficiency of the Justices of the Peace in the urban areas was greatly affected, for good or ill, by the existence or otherwise of a corporate town. By far the greater number of disturbances in these years occurred where there was no corporate authority. Such rapidly-growing centres of population as Manchester, Bolton, Stockport, Huddersfield and Halifax, were all unincorporate, and all were at one time or another storm centres of disorder. Even

when a town had a Mayor and Corporation, the government was
frequently corrupt and inefficient, as at Leicester. But there was at
least a framework in such centres for an active policy on the part
of the Justices: a centre for regular consultation, machinery for
organizing the defence of property, a reliable source of income to
cover expenses, and a regular supply of man-power for enlistment
for special duty. The possibilities afforded by a reasonably efficient
corporate town were best illustrated by the case of Nottingham.
Lying hard by Sherwood Forest, the supposed headquarters of
'King Ludd' himself, Nottingham had every incentive to develop
an effective system of defence. During the worst Luddite period,
1811–12, the town possessed an efficient body of regular, paid
police, and, under the Nottingham Peace Bill, a well-organized
system of Watch and Ward. The citizens themselves formed a
large and useful body of special constables. The Town Clerk managed a valuable, but very expensive, system of informers. The experience gained in the machine-breaking period enabled the town
to meet the perils of the post-war years with considerable confidence. Justices, constables and yeomanry were all ready and waiting for the arrival of the Derbyshire rebels on the anxious night of
9–10 June 1817. But even Nottingham had to ask for the assistance
of regular troops, and in 1815 alone the Home Office paid £600
towards the cost of its secret intelligence service.

The forces at the disposal of the local authorities consisted of
the yeomanry and militia, a few regular police, a great many
special constables, and certain quasi-voluntary defence organizations such as the patrols for Watch and Ward. The regular police
were exiguous in the extreme. A few murders in Wapping in
1811–12 were capable of spreading a sense of perilous insecurity
throughout the whole metropolis. On such occasions people were
beginning to realize the defenceless condition of the wealthiest
capital in Europe. When the Spa Fields rioters set out to capture
the Tower of London in the winter of 1816–17, they were turned
aside by the Lord Mayor and five constables. Leicester, in the
middle of the Luddite area, had six constables in 1812. Oldham
had two. Manchester had a Borough-Reeve and constables appointed by the Lord of the Manor; but it also had Deputy Constable Joseph Nadin and a small force of paid officers who made up

in sadistic zest what they lacked in numbers. In general, England still lived in the age of Dogberry and Verges. Not that the local authorities, in many cases, were blind to the necessity for a regular and adequate system of police. 'A permanent police establishment with regular police is the only solution', wrote Mr Allsop, a Nottingham solicitor, to Lord Sidmouth in October 1816.[10] Justices of the Peace, and more especially exasperated soldiers who found themselves called upon to undertake police duties, reiterated the point again and again. But public opinion resisted the idea as savouring of 'national degeneracy'. A policeman, it was felt, would be a kind of spy. England had still to learn that she might have worse spies than policemen.

The militia and the yeomanry were, at least in idea, the 'citizen army'. By the Militia Act of 1757, militiamen were chosen by ballot in each county. The officers were chosen by the Lords Lieutenant, and must possess real estate varying in value according to their rank: £400 in the case of Colonels, £50 in the case of Ensigns. The ranks of the militia reflected fairly faithfully the social hierarchy of the county. Thus the militia was not a citizen-army in the democratic sense of the term, only in the sense that it was neither a professional nor a standing army. Apart from brief spells of annual training, its members were occupied in the normal life of the ordinary citizen. Thus it was a force which was unlikely to survive the decease of a rural civilization. Already, the prevalence of paid substitutes had robbed it of much of its intended character. It was local in composition and command, but financed by central government. It was intended for local purposes, and to resist attempted invasion, not for service overseas. A Troop of Yeomanry consisted of fifty or sixty mounted men; a Regiment of Militia consisted of six or seven hundred infantry. Together, they made up a useful force for patrol work. The entire county strength was on foot in the machine-breaking areas in 1812. Confronted by a mass demonstration of artisans at the Manchester Meeting in 1819, however, the yeomanry proved a calamitous failure. Peterloo proved the Waterloo of the yeomanry.

Such was the peace-keeping organization of Regency England. When the Liverpool Administration came into office in 1812, it had already proved itself inadaquate to cope with the widespread machine-breaking movement of the midlands and the north. Reluctantly, in the face of a threatened breakdown of all law and order in the most populous districts of England, the central government had come to the rescue with professional magistrates and police-officers, detachments of the regular army, and funds for espionage. In 1812 there were already more troops in the Luddite areas than had gone to the Peninsula with Wellesley in 1808.[11] Twelve hundred regular horse and foot were stationed in the midland and northern counties. The industrial areas had taken on a strikingly military appearance, with soldiers quartered at every inn, and great camps established in Sherwood Forest and on Kersal Moor. The clatter of hoofs and the tramp of redcoats sounded everywhere, by day and night. It was proved that unceasing patrols over the whole area, to make the military as ubiquitous as the Luddites themselves, was the only solution for the activities of the machine-wreckers. The army, indeed, had already become the police-force of industrial England.

The Government had acted with reluctance, and in response to local clamour. Although special measures were taken, and even special legislation was adopted, from time to time, Lord Liverpool clung resolutely to his opinion that the responsibility lay with 'the gentlemen of the parish'. He had been a Colonel of the Kentish Militia himself in the grim years 1795–6, and most of his colleagues had played their full part in the local activities of the country gentlemen. The fact that Nottinghamshire and Yorkshire were not the home counties, and that 1812–20 was a time of very different emergencies from those of 1795–1800, seems to have weighed with him not at all. 'The property of the country must be taught to protect itself', he wrote to a Yorkshire correspondent in 1819. 'The active disaffected in any quarter are not very numerous. The majority go with the tide, and if they see all the zeal and activity on one side, and only apathy on the other, their choice cannot be expected to be doubtful.'[12] In fact, the Government expected the gentlemen of the parish to do their duty, and it had serious doubts whether they were living up to the high standards of their forefathers. The Home Secretary rapped the Nottinghamshire magistrates over the knuckles in 1816 with something of the acerbity of squire writing to a careless gamekeeper: 'The prevailing impression certainly was that there was a want of vigilance and activity in the magistracy.'[13] The classic Tory and landed conception of government and its functions comes out in the concluding sentence: 'Government could do no more than give the impulse, and all the aid that could be afforded, to the execution of the laws.'[14] Unfortunately, a magistracy which had been pushed and prodded into activity for so long, had also to be congratulated – or at any rate supported – when their excessive activity produced the tragedy of Peterloo. Peterloo, in fact, put to the test the faith and fearlessness of Liverpool and his colleagues. They did not hesitate. Imprudent and precipitate the Manchester magistrates may have been, Lord Liverpool observed, 'but, whatever judgement might be formed in this respect, being satisfied that they were substantially right, there remained no alternative but to support them.'[15] Lord Sidmouth, in conveying the thanks of the Prince Regent to the magistrates and yeomanry for their conduct, was acting on what he believed to be an essential principle of government – to acquire the confidence of the magistracy by readiness to support them 'in all honest, reasonable and well-intended acts, without inquiring too minutely whether they might have performed their duty a little better or a little worse'.[16] George Canning, the exponent of a later and more liberal Toryism, was at one with his elders at least in this. 'To let down the magistrates', he wrote, after Peterloo, 'would be to invite their resignation, and to lose all gratuitous service in the counties liable to disturbance for ever.'[17]

Thus, while the policy of 'Alarm', with its supposedly un-English features of Secret Committees and spies and soldiers, may seem to import an alien spirit into the government of Regency England, the Administration of Lord Liverpool remained obstinately faithful to the traditional governmental concepts of the English aristocracy. A people is preserved from the worst effects of disorder in times of rapid social transition less by its laws than by its conventions, by what have been called its 'traditions of behaviour'. Perhaps it is as well, after all, that the governors of Regency England were somewhat behind the times.

Chapter 10

THE MACHINE-BREAKERS

The general persuasion of the persons engaged in those transactions appears to be that all the societies in the country are directed in their motions by a Secret Committee, and this Secret Committee is therefore the great mover of the whole machine; and it is established ... that societies are formed in different parts of the country; that these societies are governed by their respective secret committees; that delegates are continually dispatched from one place to another, for the purpose of concerting their plans ...

> *Report of the Secret Committee of the House of Lords on the Disturbed State of Certain Counties, 1812*

The guilty may fear, but no vengeance he aims
At the honest man's life or estate.
His wrath is entirely confined to wide frames
And to those that old prices abate.
These engines of mischief were sentenced to die
By unanimous vote of the Trade;
And Ludd who can all opposition defy
Was the grand Executioner made.

> *General Ludd's Triumph, 1812*

THE Regency was not the first time that England had experienced the terrifying phenomenon of machine-breaking. As early as 1779 the failure of a Bill to regulate the frame-knitting industry had resulted in three hundred frames being smashed and flung into the streets. And this resort to direct action had succeeded. The masters had agreed to a price-list which gave the trade prosperity for twenty-five years. By 1810, however, the war-time Orders in Council, and the decline of the eighteenth-century cult of the elegant leg, had led to a deterioration in the standard of craftsmanship in stocking-making, and to a general cheapening of the trade. It was in an attempt to intimidate certain masters who resorted to a type of production which lowered the standards of the craft and brought evil effects upon the hosiery market in general, that the Nottingham knitters took up the hammer. They were opposed not to the use of new machines, but to the abuse of old ones, and in particular the 'wide frames' which produced the broad pieces of fabric which were made into 'cut-ups'.

The industry was for the most part organized on a domestic basis, the stockinger hiring his frame from the master and working in his own 'shop' upon yarn handed out to him, and turning in the finished article to the master for marketing. Thus, with the frames scattered about in scores of small towns and villages around the big towns, the instruments of production were difficult to protect. The forces of 'General Ludd' could sweep through a whole village, or strings of villages, within an hour or two on a dark night, smashing frames wherever they could be found, and vanishing into the darkness beyond hope of pursuit. Between March 1811 and February 1812, they broke about a thousand machines at the cost of between £6,000 and £10,000. Such was the loyalty of the extraordinary fraternity of the machine-wreckers, so swift and sure were their attacks, and so inadequate were the traditional forces of law and order to cope with them, that central government felt obliged to institute special legislation. Machine-breaking had been made a capital offence as early as 1721. Now the law was rendered more effective, and a special Act was passed to secure the peace of the City of Nottingham. At the Nottingham Assizes of March 1812, seven Luddites were sentenced to transportation for life, and two were acquitted.

Scarcely a month later, the Luddite movement in the neighbouring county of Yorkshire reached a climax in the attack on William Cartwright's mill at Rawfolds in Liversedge, not far from Huddersfield. Cartwright and a handful of soldiers held the mill against some one hundred and fifty attackers drawn from the neighbouring towns and villages, and two of the assailants were mortally wounded. Charlotte Brontë has immortalized this midnight affray in *Shirley*. A week later, an attempt was made on Cartwright's life, and on 28 April another manufacturer, William Horsfall, was mortally wounded in an ambush as he rode home from Huddersfield market.

When Lord Sidmouth took over the Home Office in June, the crisis of 1812 had passed its peak. But at once there began, on the part of the Government, that technique of attack which was to become so familiar in subsequent periods of 'Alarm'. Early in July, both Houses of Parliament set up Secret Committees for the examination of evidence from the disturbed areas. Major Searle, who commanded the South Devon Militia at Sheffield, had sent to the Home Secretary on 30 June certain information supplied by 'a person whom I believe to be intelligent and worthy of confidence', but who 'is fearful of having his name known, for he says his life would be the penalty'. This information contained a copy of the 'secret oath' of the conspirators and avowed that the disaffected had organized themselves by a system of delegates running from London to Glasgow. The delegates, it was stated, meet in committees up and down the country in order to concert a common plan of action. The plan is to create disturbances in the provinces in order to draw away the troops from London and thus facilitate a rising in the capital. They were stated to possess large quantities of arms and a system of signalling by gun-fire which would come into operation at the outbreak of the revolution.[1] Here, then, are the classic features of 'Alarm' as we are to see them again and again in the following years: information from a hidden source, a concerted scheme covering the whole country, the running links of travelling delegates, and the ultimate objective of revolution.

The Secret Committees of both Houses reported that the fact of an extensive military organization was fully established, and on the strength of this Lord Sidmouth introduced on 23 July a Bill to preserve the public peace of the disturbed districts and to give additional powers to the magistrates. It passed through both Houses and was to remain in force until 25 March 1813. By the autumn, the Home Office had completed its arrangements for the trial of the captured Luddites. In January 1813, three men were charged at York with the murder of Mr Horsfall, and were found guilty and hanged. Fourteen others, who had been concerned with the attack on Cartwright's mill or with kindred activities, followed them to the gallows a week later. Sidmouth, and his colleague Lord Ellenborough, expected the executions to have 'the happiest effects in various parts of the kingdom', and certainly the *Annual Register* attributed the comparative calm of the year 1813 to the result of the trials at York.[2] On the day of the executions, Sidmouth broached the question of withdrawing the military from the disturbed areas.[3] In February, Lord Fitzwilliam, Lord Lieutenant of the West Riding, reported that his magistrates were optimistic about the temper of the people, and thought that the patrols of regular troops might be dispensed with, except in the big towns.[4] By the spring, many of the troops had been withdrawn, and in March Lord Sidmouth could write: 'The people are sound and firm. A most material and happy change ...'[5]

Direct action in the form of strikes or machine-breaking was to continue, on and off, for many years after the severe measures of 1813. For a time, it is true, the framework-knitters sought to secure relief by legislation. A Bill to regulate the trade, and in particular to prohibit the cheap and nasty 'cut-ups', failed in the House of Lords. Still they persevered in the ways of peace, trying the experiment of a Trade Society to promote their purposes. Carefully constructed to keep within the law against combinations, this Society consisted of a federation of local units with a central committee of delegates. Attacked as an illegal combination in 1814, it quickly collapsed. Thereupon, the Nottingham knitters resorted again to frame-breaking in desperation. This outburst culminated in the great breaking at Heathcote and Boden's mill at Loughborough on the night of 28 June 1816, at which fifty-three frames were smashed at a cost of £6,000, and for which six men were executed and three transported. After this, frame-breaking subsided in Nottinghamshire and Leicestershire, partly perhaps under the influence of Cobbett's *Letter to the Luddites* which appeared in November of that year. But there were always some who tended to put their faith in direct action. One of them, Jeremiah Brandreth, headed the Derbyshire Rising in June 1817. It is more than probable that 'the Nottingham Captain', as he called himself, had served his apprenticeship in machine-breaking, for he is known to have been a framework-knitter. Eight or nine thousand of the knitters were on strike in 1817, and some fifteen hundred in 1819, after a further attempt

to secure a Bill against 'cut-ups'. In 1819, the masters were induc.
to agree to a satisfactory 'price-list', but the agreement was not kept
and strikes occurred again in 1821 and 1824. Wearily, gallantly,
year after year, the doomed framework-knitters struggled on with
strike and petition.

What lay behind the alarmist suspicions that the Luddite movement of 1812 betokened the onset of revolution? There can be no
doubt that the spring of 1812 was a highly critical time. A large
part of the army was overseas, the country was engaged in two
foreign wars, and was experiencing the worst trade depression of
the half-century, if we except the winter of 1816–17. Little wonder
that the Rev. Patrick Brontë had taken to firing a pistol out of his
bedroom window every morning at Haworth Parsonage, and Robert
Southey at Keswick had felt obliged to 'take down a rusty gun and
manfully load it for the satisfaction of the family', not to mention
his acquisition of a watchman's rattle at the request of the children's
governess, in case 'the ugly fellows' should come.[6] General Mait-
land, however, who commanded the regular forces in the northern
area, steadfastly refused to believe in the imminence of revolution.[7]
Lord Fitzwilliam, Lord Lieutenant of the West Riding, held that
'outrage and conspiracy ... are the offspring of distress and want of
employment ... fostered and rendered formidable by nothing but
the want of trade.'[8] Ponsonby, leading the Whig Opposition in the
House of Commons, probably summed up the matter accurately
when he said that the Luddites had 'mixed themselves with those
who had political objects in view'. Among a population accustomed
to violence by night attacks on property by armed men, material
for the sponsors of political insurrection was obviously present. Yet
no attempt was made at the trial of the machine-breakers to connect
their activities with political objectives, for, as we have seen, it was
the deliberate policy of the Government to deny the necessary
nature of an alliance between economic distress and political
opinions. James Towle, awaiting execution for his part in the great
breaking at Loughborough, steadily maintained that 'he knows of
no persons in the higher ranks of life that are connected with
them.' Leaders like Cobbett and Cartwright, whom a man like
Towle would doubtless include in the category of the 'higher ranks',
never tired of dissuading the knitters from violence, and persis-

...rn them to the 'root of all evil' – the corrupt
...estminster.

...vidence goes to show that Luddism was an essentially
...nomenon, devoid of national and political ramifications;
...air of blackened faces, secret oaths, and threatening letters.
...eneral Ludd was something of an industrial Robin Hood. His
headquarters were supposed to be in Sherwood Forest. His followers
combined the morals of Robin Hood with the methods of gang-
sters. Their extraordinary loyalty to each other, their fearsome
secret oaths by which they swore to wreak 'unceasing vengeance'
upon traitors, invited the attention of spies and *agents provocateurs*,
and the Government depended upon the reports of these unscrupulous and often illiterate individuals for their perverted information
as to what was going on. Thus, it was a certain 'B' (or 'Mr Bent')
who, in a number of semi-illiterate reports which still repose among
the Home Office Papers for 1812, evoked in the imagination of his
employers the fantasy of 'a general insurrection' which was due to
occur on 1 May, or early in that month. It was 'B' who reported
the existence of Secret Committees in the northern towns. Mr 'B'
worked at Stockport. At Bolton, a certain 'S' (or 'Mr Stones') rivalled
Mr 'B' in his zeal for 'something serious in the way of destruction'.
This gentleman seems to have taken it upon himself to assure the
Secret Committee of Bolton that a number of Radical gentlemen in
London, including Lord Cochrane, Sir Francis Burdett and Mr Whit-
bread, were waiting upon their endeavours to achieve a revolution
'to put the great men down'. On 24 April 1812, he prevailed upon
them to burn down a factory at West Houghton. In such manner
were the names of the respectable London Radicals taken in vain by
agents provocateurs in provincial England as early as 1812.[9]

While Luddism as a movement lacked political affiliation, there
are signs nevertheless that certain individuals within the movement were capable of recruitment to the cause of parliamentary
reform. The Luddite committee at Manchester, for example, under
the guidance of John Buckley, a weaver and a lay-preacher, refused
to have anything to do with the proposals of Mr 'S' for the campaign which ended in the burning of the factory. Buckley turned
its activities instead in the direction of parliamentary reform. His
career is an interesting illustration of what Ponsonby meant when

he said that Luddism did not originate in political principles, but that the Luddites had 'mixed themselves with those who had political objects in view'. Buckley, as a parliamentary reformer, found it difficult to live down his Luddite connexion in the past. When he was invited to attend a meeting at the Manchester Exchange, on 8 April 1812, which had been called by 'a few gentlemen of the town' in order to protest against certain resolutions of thanks to the Prince Regent, the meeting was called off by the authorities. No doubt they foresaw the kind of opposition which would be associated with John Buckley. As it was, a large crowd arrived at the Exchange and proceeded to sack it. Buckley and his committee, however, took no part in this, or in the other serious outrages which took place in the Manchester district during the weeks that followed. Instead, they were busy preparing an Address on Parliamentary Reform to the Prince Regent, and a similar petition to the House of Commons. It appears, however, that the Committee still retained its Luddite rites of admission by secret oath, and in June thirty-eight of its members were arrested at a public house in Manchester on a charge of administering an illegal oath to one Samuel Fleming. Fleming was a spy. He had gone to the meeting for the purpose of getting himself 'twisted-in'. At the trial no evidence was forthcoming except that of the spy, and the thirty-eight were acquitted. The thirty-eight were referred to as 'the Manchester Luddites', but they were in fact parliamentary reformers. Even Mr 'B', who had got himself elected as their Treasurer, could report nothing of their activities more 'seditious' than the intention to promote peace and parliamentary reform.[10]

Finally, there is John Baines, the hatter of Halifax. John Baines was a survivor of the political movement of the nineties. He was fond of declaring that his eyes had been opened by the French Revolution. 'I have waited long for the dawn of the coming day,' said John Baines, 'and it may be, old as I am, I shall yet see the glorious triumph of democracy.'[2] Here was a politician who saw in Luddism but a passing phase in the battle for the people's cause. The young men who wielded the sledgehammers in the year 1812 had been children in the great days of Revolutionary France. John Baines, and the men of his generation, had longer memories. Sentenced with four of his fellows for tendering illegal oaths, he could declare confidently that the midnight fraternities of the machine-wreckers were but an episode in the grand movement of the people 'rising in their majesty'. It was to John Baines and men of his kind, men who could think of England as well as Yorkshire, of ballot-boxes as well as bludgeons, of the suffrage as well as sledgehammers, that the politics of Cartwright and Cobbett and Hunt were to appeal in the years that were dawning. Major John Cartwright, coming north with his petitions and his Hampden Clubs; William Cobbett's *Political Register*, the 'tuppeny trash', flung down from the London coach as it dashed through the northern towns and villages; Orator Hunt's leathern lungs roaring from the hustings in St Peter's Fields: these were to find their sounding-board in the places where once the northern air had rung with the harsh and futile clang of the hammers. London was coming to the country.

Chapter 11

THE LONDON LEADERS

No one needs to be told that the whole popular
liberties of this country, and, by connection and
consequence, of the world, depend upon the electors
of Westminster.
                              The European Magazine

The genius of England ... may therefore now be
imagined standing as a herald on the loftiest battlements of freedom's fair castle. ... May we not suppose him to cry: Lo! a mighty change is at hand;
stand to your arms! Be vigilant that ye may be
victorious ...
                              MAJOR JOHN CARTWRIGHT, 1810

THE revolution which was accomplished in England in the later
eighteenth century, and during the early years of the nineteenth,
was never dominated by London in the manner in which the French
Revolution was dominated by Paris. The absence of concentration
at the capital, and the presence of a vigorous political life in the
provinces, helped to ensure that the process of change should be
slow, persuasive, and organic. Burke had spoken of 'a constitutional policy working after the pattern of nature', and it is remarkable how often England has undergone revolution according to the
model approved by her greatest conservative statesman. 'Thus',
Burke rejoiced, 'by preserving the method of nature in the conduct
of the state, in what we improve, we are never wholly new; in what
we retain, we are never wholly obsolete.'[1] Had London dominated
the English revolution, as Paris dominated the French, the changes
that were brought about might have been achieved more quickly,
but the total achievement would certainly have disappointed more
– because more unmeditated – hopes on the part of the people as a
whole.

Men, and groups of men, were prepared to tarry for one another.
After Pitt's repressive action in the nineties, and during the war
years which followed, there was a widespread feeling among all
classes of men that the times were inopportune for agitating the

question of a reform of parliament. Nor was this feeling in most cases the timid feeling of men in search of an excuse for doing nothing. It arose from an accurate assessment of the condition of the public mind. Sir Samuel Romilly, who described himself as a 'very moderate and gradual reformer', thought the age unripe for action. The truth was, he said, that the French Revolution had been 'in every way unfavourable to reforms'.[2] As late as 1811, Sir Philip Francis considered reform a quite hopeless enterprise. 'The country has lost its passions and is not fit for action', he wrote in that year.[3] Lord Grey, despairing of effective action after the loss of his reform motion in 1797, had retired to his estate in Northumberland, thus initiating a Whig secession from the House of Commons which lasted for three years. In moving a motion 'On the state of the country', in June 1810, he made it clear that he thought there was little prospect of the people showing themselves to be disposed to take up the question seriously and sincerely. For his part, he would wait 'until the country should have expressed its opinion'.[4] Earl Stanhope – 'Citizen Stanhope', as he had delighted to be called in the nineties, and one of the earliest champions of the cause – wrote to Major Cartwright in 1810: 'The people are yet, as it were, asleep. Nor do I know that you or your friends will wake them until events shall ....'[5] In case these despondent views should appear to be based on a merely distant prospect of the country as seen from the capital, we have the report of an agent of the Society for Constitutional Information who made a tour of the provinces in 1803. 'The country patriots are lukewarm and frightened', he wrote, 'and we have been much deceived in point of their numbers.' After travelling many hundreds of miles, he had been able to profit the Society by the sum of £8 13s. 6d. 'So much for Country Civism', he reflected.

There was, however, one old heart that never lost hope and never beat the slower for the prevailing mood of depression. This was Major John Cartwright, the veteran Radical of the nineties who was to fight the good fight until his dying breath in the year 1824. When Horne Tooke, another veteran, wrote to him in 1797: 'I think the cause of reform is dead and buried', the Major endorsed the communication: 'But J. C. is a believer in the Resurrection.'[6] Cartwright could always see the herald of change 'standing on the

battlements of freedom's fair castle'.* When it seemed that everyone else had decided for hibernation, the Major was still to be observed going forward at the charge. 'Of course', he wrote cheerfully,
in 1796, 'I get heartily cursed for disturbing the quiet of the country.' Indeed, it was his intention to sound Reveille as long as he
had breath in his body. 'Citizen' Stanhope might doubt whether
'you or your friends will wake them ....' But the Major was determined never to stop trying. It was in the year 1811, when he was
more than seventy years of age, that he undertook the first of his
great missionary tours for the purpose of planting a crop of Hampden Clubs for parliamentary reform among the working men of the
industrial north and midlands. Thereby he initiated the somewhat
equivocal and sometimes dangerous alliance between London radicalism and provincial discontent: the alliance in which Lord
Liverpool for so long refused to believe and was never to cease to
deplore.

The heart of London radicalism was the Borough of Westminster.[7] The scene of the memorable triumphs of Charles James Fox,
it had one of the largest electoral rolls in England – some 10,000
voters, mostly shopkeepers and artisans. It was the home of parliament itself and of its greatest intellectual critic Jeremy Bentham.
The election of Sir Francis Burdett as Radical member for the Borough in 1807 signalized the opening of the great epoch of London
reform politics. It set the stage for the most stirring political drama
of Regency England; a raffish, rowdy, rhetorical scene, set in the
midst of Hogarthian squalor and Brummellian refinement. At Number 16 Stratton Street, Sir Francis Burdett teaches his eldest son to
read Magna Carta. At Charing Cross, Francis Place reads political
economy behind his breeches-maker's shop, and coaches working
men in the rights and duties of true democrats. In a high room
overlooking St James's Park, Jeremy Bentham is reducing law to a
system and the mind of man to a machine, while William Hazlitt,
his next-door neighbour, makes a peep-show of the sage of radicalism for his friends, saying: 'That is the great law-giver, Bentham;
a remarkable man: he would make laws for the whole universe,

* Epigraph to this chapter: see Cartwright's *Mock Reform, Half Reform
and Constitutional Reform* (1810).

but as the sailors say, "he doesn't allow for the wind." ' Here Burdett goes in triumph beneath the banner bearing the legend: WESTMINSTER'S PRIDE AND ENGLAND'S GLORY. Here Henry Hunt goes forth to monster meetings in Spa Fields, replete with white topper and a tricolour flag. Here Arthur Thistlewood and Dr Watson and the crack-brained 'Spenceans' are to be seen dashing off to the Tower of London, under the impression that it is the Bastille. Here Cobbett sits with Cartwright and Hunt at the *Crown and Anchor* Tavern in the Strand, and longs to be off on his horse into the shires. Here Samuel Bamford and the country cousins from the north, bearing reform petitions from the Hampden Clubs, gape at the great world of London politics of which they have heard so much and in which they have placed such great and unrewarded faith. They find Sir Francis Burdett frigidly polite. He receives them in his dressing-gown, 'seeming rather to submit to association with persons of our kind', Bamford noticed, 'than to seek it'. They find Hunt vain, boastful and fickle. Cobbett and Cartwright, while friendly and staunch enough, seem disappointingly ready to content themselves with rate-payer suffrage in town, while they wrote and spoke for plain manhood suffrage in the country. As for Bentham, they have never heard of him.[8]*

Yet, in all Westminster, and perhaps in all England, the most influential Radicals were the Benthamites. True, their influence was greatest 'in the long run', and hungry working men at all times are liable to remember that in the long run we are all dead. The Benthamite Radicals paid the price of their intellectual superiority in terms of a low metabolism and a paucity of appeal to the generality of men in their own time. They occupied a very similar place in the Radical movement of Regency England to the place occupied by the Fabian Socialists in the Socialist movement nearly a century later. They were indeed the intellectual ancestors of the Fabians. They put their faith in intellectual persuasion, 'the march of Mind', judicious pressure brought to bear through the agency of men of money and influence. They detested equally the 'apostate Whigs' like Grey and Henry Brougham, and the demagogic methods of popular figures like William Cobbett and Henry Hunt. Even old Major Cartwright, with all his sobriety and respect for law,

* For Bamford at Wesminster, see also ch. 12.

found himself distrusted for his habit of direct appeal to the people. Place described Cobbett as 'too ignorant to see that the common people must ever be imbecile when not encouraged and supported by others who have money and influence.'[9] He considered 'Orator' Hunt 'a pretty sample of an ignorant, turbulent, mischief-making fellow, and a highly dangerous one, too, in turbulent times'.[10] Bentham himself, who refrained from the fraternal back-biting which afflicted Radical leadership, still expressed his contempt for Cobbett as 'a microbe struggling with a swarm of his elemental kind in a drop of water . . . .'[11] Cobbett returned the compliment by alluding to the Philosophical Radicals as 'Understrappers of the Whig oligarchy'.

It was 'a few men of business and spirit' who came together in Francis Place's house and decided to run Sir Francis Burdett as Radical candidate for Westminster in April 1807. The committee remained in being after its victory, and for the next ten years and more 'the Westminster Committee' was the focal point of Radical politics in London. Its historic link with the London Corresponding Society is to be discovered in Francis Place, 'the Radical breeches-maker of Charing Cross', who had been Chairman of the Corresponding Society in 1795, but had withdrawn in 1797. Place was a rather thin-blooded, priggish person, with all the solemnity and vanity of the self-educated. As manager of 'the Westminster Committee' he evinced none of the 'common touch' which might be expected of a working man who had served his Radical apprenticeship in the circle of Thomas Hardy. Indeed, he was for several years suspected by the more popular leaders as a spy. The suspicion was wholly unfounded, but there was something secretive and mole-like about this thin, grey-faced man with the hard pale eyes and the thin bushy hair, threading his way in and out of the full-blooded drama of Westminster politics, always shunning the lime-light, infinitely patient of converting the world by Benthamic common sense.

Behind the Westminster Committee, remote and unseen, was Jeremy Bentham, the hermit of Queen Square Place. This prosy, prolix, carpet-slippered figure of a music-hall philosopher was never in prison, never faced the hustings, never knew either the applause or the abuse of the mob. Sixty-eight years old in 1815, he was to die on the day when the Great Reform Bill of 1832 received the Royal Assent. His life-time covers appropriately the revolution in English public life whose presiding spirit he represented better than any other figure of his age. In Jeremy Bentham is embodied the challenge to aristocratic monopoly, to the spirit of 'Burkism' in politics, to guess-work and amateur trifling in administration. Under the influence of his greatest disciple, James Mill, and as a consequence of his own experience of the Tory governments of his day, he had come to see that his doctrine of 'the greatest happiness of the greatest number' could only be implemented by a government democratically elected and controlled, and by administration at the hands of a professional civil service selected not by aristocratic patronage but by public examination. The work of Bentham, it has been said, was to carry the world of government and administration out of the age of humbug into the age of humdrum.

In the political arena, Bentham was represented by his numerous disciples, men like Place, Burdett, Romilly, and – somewhat equivocally – Brougham. The Westminster Committee was the caucus of the Philosophic Radicals, and Sir Francis Burdett was its spokesman in the House of Commons. True, Burdett was a country gentleman of ancient family and enormous wealth, an unlikely convert, it might have been thought, to the urban, utilitarian, middle-class politics of the Benthamite Radicals.[12] He had learnt the alphabet of reform in Horne Tooke's garden at Wimbledon in the nineties. Sickened of the Whig Party by their record in the Ministry of All the Talents, he might have retired, like Grey, to his country estates after the death of Fox. But Burdett was fond of the limelight, and he genuinely believed that it was the duty of men of rank and property to follow their conscience wherever it might lead them. If it led them to the leadership of a Radical movement for parliamentary reform, they must follow it there, too. The Westminster Radicals were fully aware of Burdett's social value to their cause. He amply fulfilled Place's criterion of 'money and influence' without whose patronage the common people must ever be imbecile, although there came a time when Place was to describe Burdett as 'too rich, too lazy, and too high'. Sir Francis had a habit of retiring to the comparative safety of the hunting-field when things grew too fierce and vulgar at Westminster, as in the crisis of

the winter of 1816–17. He would not, he said, be made a catspaw
by hooligans like 'Orator' Hunt. In this, the Philosophic Radicals,
who equally detested Hunt, could scarcely blame him.

Cobbett, who hated what he called 'feelosofers' ('My God, how
I hate them!'), Radical or otherwise, with the unreasoning hatred
with which he hated tea, could both understand and approve of
Sir Francis Burdett, whom he described as the most influential and
popular man in England with 'the really efficient part of the
people'. He quarrelled with the baronet, early and late, but he
recognized in him the aristocratic counterpart of himself: a Tory
who was wiser than the Tories of his time. Like Cobbett, Burdett
was genuinely attached to the kingly government and the whole
constitution of England. Neither man was a Radical or a Democrat
in the proletarian sense of the term. They both stood for parliamentary reform not because it looked forward to the proletarian
state, but because they believed it looked back to an ideal society
which was being destroyed by stock-jobbers and the riff-raff of the
cities. They wanted to unearth the true, ancient constitution from
beneath the parasitic growth of fund-lords and financiers. Their
cry was never forward to mathematical democracy, but back to the
ancient right of the commoners of England before the days when
Whigs and money-grubbers robbed them of their inheritance. They
were predecessors of Disraeli and Young England, not of John
Bright and the Great Exhibition. Theirs was the politics of the old,
landed England. They were countrymen, the one the squire, the
other the yeoman. Burdett was trying to do his hereditary duty as
a landed gentleman every bit as sincerely as was Lord Liverpool:
to maintain the traditional leadership of the country gentleman in
an age that had turned to the town. Cobbett was trying to vindicate the yeoman outlook under the same conditions. After 1832,
Burdett voted with the Tories, and Cobbett found himself voting
against such 'progressive' measures of the reformed Parliament as
the new Poor Law with a conservative animosity that would have
astonished Lord Liverpool.

With Cobbett[13] we arrive at the first of the London leaders of
Regency England who were responsible for the education of the
provincial working class in the politics of reform. He was qualified
for this work by three characteristics: his social origins, his preju-

dices and his prose. Bentham, Burdett, Place, all belonged essentially to London, and to Westminster. Cobbett, like the great majority of his countrymen, was the child and the champion of rural England. 'Born in a farm house, bred up at the plough tail, with a smock-frock on my back, taking great delight in all the pursuits of farmers, liking their society', was it not natural that he should champion the basic humanity of his countrymen rather than any ideological palaver about rights, classes, and such-like fictitious entities? To him, London and its ways were a dark and evil mystery. Like the Tory Robert Southey, he considered it to be an excrescence on the body politic. He called it, more simply, 'the Wen'. Riding out to see the people in the shires, Cobbett went not as a tourist but as a home-comer. He knew the people of England as few men have known them, before or since, because he was one of them. His prejudices were their prejudices, and Cobbett lived on his prejudices as other men live on ideas. He shared especially their prejudice in favour of wholesome living: white bread, red meat and beer. He summed up both his politics and his religion when he said: 'A full belly to the labourer is the foundation of public morals and the only real source of public peace.'[14] While the intolerable 'feel-osofers' talked their nonsense, he was away on his horse,

hearing what gentlemen, farmers, tradesmen, journeymen, labourers, women, girls, boys, and all have to say; reasoning with some, laughing with others, and observing all that passes .... At the end of a tramp like this you get impressed upon your mind a true picture, not only of the state of the country, but of the state of people's minds throughout the country.[15]

Cobbett almost elevated his prejudices to the status of ideas, and he did this in some of the most lucid, direct and unaffected prose that is to be found in the whole of the rich field of English political journalism. He accepted the institutions of his country as the *sine qua non*. It would have given him as much pain, he said, to see a change in the 'form of the government' as it would have given to any man in England. King, Lords and Commons were right and proper; but 'when I say Commons, I *mean* Commons, and by Commons I mean men elected by the free voice of the untitled and unprivileged part of the people'.[16] For thus, he believed, the Commons had once been, in the good old days before 'the light of Protestantism and the march of mind ... turned beer into water.' At heart, Cobbett believed in Merry England, a golden age when Englishmen had white bread, red meat and malt beer; when the classes understood one another, when the country had been unsundered and unsullied by the irresponsibility of manufacturers, stock-jobbers and Jews. To restore his country to her condition in that golden time was the governing passion of his life, and the first thing necessary was to make the Commons once more the Commons, by a wholesome measure of parliamentary reform. This, and the means he employed for this purpose, is what puts Cobbett in the 'popular' or non-philosophic group of Radical leaders, along with Cartwright and Hunt. The *Political Register* was never ambiguous and never dull. It was read by the village schoolmaster or the parish clerk to the local politicians in a thousand alehouses over the length and breadth of England. When landlords objected, fearing for their licences, Cobbett reduced the price to twopence, and thereafter the 'tuppenny trash' could be read by the individual on his own hearth. From the winter of 1816 onwards, Bamford tells us, Cobbett's writings were read on nearly every cottage hearth in the manufacturing districts. Their effect was to direct the workman to the true cause of his distress and the true method of redress: peaceful petitioning for a reform of the suffrage. Riots, Bamford adds, never regained their ancient vogue after Cobbett's influence gained ascendancy. This was probably an exaggeration, but at least the petitioning movement went ahead with redoubled energy.[17]

It was here that Major John Cartwright took up the tale. While Cobbett advocated petitioning, the Major organized it. The popular reform movement of Regency England may truly be said to have been launched in the year of the Prince Regent's arrival at the head of the State, and it was launched by Major Cartwright's personal tour of the midland counties in 1811. On his return, he joined forces with Burdett to found the 'Hampden Club' in London, and in 1813 he was off again, touring the midlands and the north in order to sow a crop of Hampden Clubs in the industrial districts. It was through the agency of these Clubs that the great petitioning movement of 1816–17 got under way.

Major John Cartwright[18] was one of those rare bores who are the salt of the earth. Older even than Jeremy Bentham (he was born in 1740), he came of the same fertile tradition of eighteenth-century English eccentrics. He belonged to an old Nottinghamshire family which had owed an increase in its fortunes to the despoliation of the monasteries and a kinship with Archbishop Cranmer. A reformer almost from childhood, one of his earliest memories was of his uncle, Viscount Tyrconnel, stirring the fire violently during family prayers when the Prayer for the Parliament was read, and muttering to himself 'Nothing but a miracle can mend them.' After eighteen years in the Navy, the young John Cartwright plunged into the movement to mend them – the Lords and Commons of England: and from the publication of his first reform pamphlet, *Take your Choice*, in 1776, to his death in 1824, he worked for the cause with unflagging energy. He wrote scores of tracts, pamphlets and books, answered hundreds of letters every week, took the chair at innumerable meetings, made long and earnest speeches, financed Radical journals, and even designed a Temple of Naval Celebration, or 'Hieronauticon', in his spare time. At the age of seventy-two, he thought nothing of touring nine hundred miles in twenty-nine days in post-chaises in January weather on the rudimentary roads of old England, in order to carry the gospel of reform to working men of the north and midlands. He was a man of limited intelligence, extreme obstinacy and very little sense of humour. He desired his nephew to hang up the Declaration of Rights in his rooms at Oxford, and objected to giving presents to children on the score that 'it was a species of immorality to employ *bribery* and *corruption* even to a child.' Kind-hearted, pompous, courageous, possessed of the simple faith and enthusiasm of a child, he was more truly loved than any other leader of his time. His frame was tall and spare, his face long and wizened, his eyes whimsical, his upper lip rather too long, his mouth a long thin line. His usual dress was a loose jacket and knee-breeches, and his grey hair hung in thick, untidy locks under his battered cocked hat. With his box of petition-forms under his arm and an endless stock of hope in his heart, the Major crosses the scene in these years at the charge.

When the revival of reform politics began in 1807, Cartwright was already known as 'the Father of Reform'. He had been a founder of the Society for the Promotion of Constitutional Information as long ago as 1780, and he had given evidence in the Treason Trials of 1794. All through the years of eclipse, the Major kept the torch of reform secretly burning, ready to greet the herald of change when he should appear on the battlements of freedom's fair castle. His rhetoric, his unconquerable hope, and his reputation as a veteran of the pre-Revolutionary movement of the days of Wilkes, Horne Tooke and Priestley, have led to the tendency to dismiss John Cartwright as a doctrinaire gas-bag of the eighteenth-century type. Any undue attention to his innumerable and prosy writings might well support that impression, for they are replete with the arid philosophy of the Age of Reason – Laws of Nature, the Return to Simplicity, Human Perfectibility – all the bag of tricks with capital letters and long quotations. Teach the People the First Principles of the Law of Nature, and they will see that all existing Governments are based on Force and Fraud; that Nobles, Priests, Soldiers and Taxes are props of Despotism and enemies of Liberty; and that Knowledge is Power. History, for Cartwright, was a story of decline and fall from the virtuous democracy of the Saxons, assisted by the wickedness of 'the crafty illegitimate of Normandy', or William the Conqueror and his robber barons. The democratic constitution of the Saxons was destroyed, submerged, overlaid, distorted, by continental cunning and chicanery, and the purpose of patriotic reformers was to recover it in all its pristine purity.

This, however, is not the Major Cartwright who matters in the story of Regency England. Had he never written a pamphlet his influence would have remained unimpaired. Cartwright's impact on his age was in the field of action. Even in the early days he had tried to counteract the utopian plans of Tom Paine and the pure republicans. He was one of the first to point out the lack of con-nexion between the Friends of the People and the people itself. And now, in 1811, he went into provincial England to find out what the people were like. What he discovered deeply wounded his warm and compassionate heart. The spectacle of poverty and disease which confronted him on that first tour in 1811, however, did not deter him from going again, and yet again. When his friends expostulated with him, he defended himself thus: 'English gentlemen are perpetually travelling. . . . Some go to see lakes and mountains. Were it not allowable to travel for seeing the actual conditions of a starving people?'[19] He was no stranger among 'the dregs of society'. In the militia, he had 'associated with even the worst of men to be found in the night-cellars of London and with felons from Newgate'. He was, his niece and biographer tells us, 'not a mere student ... but a man who had lived and acted in the world, and had mixed with persons of various professions and in all ranks of life.'[20] Nevertheless, or perhaps just because he knew 'the people' of whom he spoke and wrote, Cartwright never lost a certain distrust of them. 'His experience of the lower orders', writes his niece, 'led him to remark that they preferred confiding their interests to persons of more consideration than themselves, and that they generally evinced a jealous dislike to raise those of their own standing to stations of importance.'[21] As for the tactics of reform, 'the worthy old Major', as Samuel Bamford tells us, taught his disciples to take as their watchword: 'Hold fast by the laws.' He had nothing but contempt for those who preached the 'ignis fatuus' of expediency, but he had no desire to overthrow established authority. Like most English reformers, he had learnt a lesson from the French Revolution, a noble cause which had become the sport of 'the mean, revengeful, murderous spirit of a small faction'.

Cartwright's clubs were intended to be local or provincial versions of the Hampden Club in London, which he had joined with Burdett in founding in 1812. This they were not, and could never be, for the Hampden Club in London was essentially a gathering of 'men of wealth and influence', open to all owners of, or heirs to, a £300 rental from landed property – the qualification for candidature for the House of Commons. Its subscription was two guineas. Among the members were the Duke of Norfolk, the Earl of Oxford, Lord Cochrane, Lord Byron and other large landed proprietors. Cartwright realized well enough that the high qualification for membership would prevent it from becoming the real nucleus of a national union. 'It of a certainty is, and must continue to be', he wrote, 'an exceptional institution in the eyes of a great part of the community.' He felt obliged to resign his own membership for one year because it was hinted that many persons of rank and influence were kept away by his presence. Just so had he frightened Grey

and co. out of the Friends of the People in 1794. In any case, however, the decline of the club was rapid enough. In 1814 only three
members attended, and on 15 March 1815, the Major attended
alone. In the same year, one of the members wrote to Cartwright
that he had long given up hope of the club ever being instrumental
in procuring parliamentary reform; that it was paralysed by eva-
sion, apathy and neglect; and that it had become purposeless. In
1819 it died a natural death.[22]

The Hampden Club has been described as the focus of reform
politics in London. This it never was. The Government chose to
look upon it as a hot-bed of sedition. This was even more fantastic.
Its significance lies elsewhere. It may be said to have served as
Major Cartwright's platonic 'idea', the vision which he hugged to
his brave and expansive bosom as he went about his missionary
activities in the industrial areas of midland and northern England
in these years. It was the model laid up in heaven, to which he
would point as he walked and talked among the provincial working men in the course of their political education. It was his
counterpart of Cobbett's journalism and Henry Hunt's oratory.
George Canning once described the Major as 'the old heart in London from which the veins of sedition in the country are supplied.'
The Major was more modest. He thought of himself rather as a
missionary. Like a Wesleyan preacher, he toured provincial England with his gospel: the gospel of parliamentary reform, the first
condition of bringing the Kingdom of Heaven down to earth. 'One
step more', he wrote to his wife, in 1815, 'and your prophecy will
be completed, that I shall become a field preacher.'[23] And like John
Wesley, he left a crop of local associations in his wake, little groups
of workmen who were prepared to organize themselves–sometimes,
significantly, as in the case of Samuel Bamford's village of Middleton, in Lancashire, in the very building which had once been used
as a Wesleyan chapel.[24] It was the purpose of these local organizations to spread the gospel, to exchange ideas by travelling delegates
– who might be compared to the circuit-preachers of the Methodists – and to secure signatures for petitions to parliament, begging
it to reform itself. It is not difficult to understand how readily all
this fitted into the framework provided earlier by the Corresponding Society, as well as its affinity with the organization of the

Methodist movement. All three, Methodism, Corresponding Society and Hampden Clubs possessed the same general structure: the central inspiration, the local group, and the travelling preachers or delegates.

The local Hampden Clubs wished to imitate their London exemplar. In 1812, Cartwright was informed by persons connected with the disturbed Luddite areas, that they wished to have the advice and countenance of the London Club 'for turning the discontents into a legal channel favourable to parliamentary reform', and that they saw in the London Club a standard beneath which all friends of reform might rally.[25] Thus Major Cartwright went on tour in response to demand – the demand of those working men in the provinces who were turning from direct action to the parliamentary reform movement. Yet, when he wrote in 1814 that the club should be the heart, and its committee the brain, of the movement, the London Club consisted of no more than three active members. No doubt Major Cartwright omitted to mention this depressing fact when he spoke to the workmen of Sheffield or Manchester, and no doubt those hopeful hearts liked to imagine that the London Club was a large, active, influential body of reformers. Certainly they regarded it as an oracle. This reverential attitude towards a mythically powerful headquarters in London was to prove one of the greatest dangers which arose out of the attempt of the London Radicals to proselytize and organize the provinces. Any gentleman of ostensible respectability with a plausible story, coming among the provincial workmen in the name of 'the Hampden Club in London', was assured of credence. He came in 1817, and he was Oliver the Spy.

Cobbett, with his shrewd sense of political possibilities, had uttered his warning against the dangers of the club movement from the beginning. 'I advise my countrymen to have nothing to do with any *Political Club*, any secret *Cabals*, any *Correspondencies*', he wrote in the *Political Register*; 'but to trust to *individual exertions* and *open meetings*.' He admitted that such clubs contained many worthy and zealous men, 'but', he added, 'I shall be very difficult to be made believe that they are thus employing themselves in the best and most effectual way.' While he always spoke with respect, and sometimes with affection, of Cartwright – to whom, indeed, he owed his own conversion to the cause of genuine parliamentary reform – he still could not see that anything good would ever be done by such an organ as the Hampden Club, 'or meeting and *talking* about what they are to *talk* about next time'.[26] Besides, he was fairly sure that William Cobbett and the *Political Register* alone were quite equal to directing the reform movement. There was an element of jealousy in his attitude. Yet, as events were to prove, his apprehensions about the dangers of the Hampden Club movement were justified, although he could scarcely have been expected to anticipate the precise form that these dangers were to take. There is no reason to assume that Cartwright himself ever realized how his work was to make straight the path for the *agent provocateur*. He was content to believe, with pardonable pride, that the Hampden Club, for all that it was 'lamentably defective, cold, and inefficient', had nevertheless 'by its name, and the use that has been made of that name, been instrumental in generating the petitions for reform of more than a million of men'.[27] What other uses had been made of that name he, mercifully, never knew.

To Cobbett's journalism and Cartwright's clubs there were added Hunt's lungs. 'Orator' Hunt[28] was a clear case of the natural demagogue. He came of a prosperous farming family of Wiltshire, representing indeed that very class of enclosing landlords which Cobbett so detested. A man of fine physique and graceful proportions – the novelist's dream of a Regency 'Corinthian' as portrayed by the late Jeffrey Farnol – he was a boxer, a good shot, and a furious rider to hounds. Adopting the cause of Radical Reform, he took it as he took his fences – with a sort of brutal energy and terrifying bravado. To Henry Hunt, the objective of the chase was 'universal suffrage – or nothing'. His part in its promotion was dictated by his physical energy. He was born to cut a figure before a mob. His lungs were of enormous power and endurance. He could make himself heard at great distances in the open air. No Hampden Clubs for him: only the hustings, the waggon, the concourse of Spa Fields, London, or St Peter's Fields, Manchester. He gained an immense reputation as a mob-orator, and immense notoriety as a firebrand. There is no doubt that he did much to bring the cause of reform home to the working class, but there is no less doubt that he did more by his vanity, boastfulness and posturing to bring it into disrepute with peaceable men. He was an embarrassing ally at the best of times. At the worst he was a liar and a bully.

Finally, like a disreputable tail on the body of London Radical leadership, there were the Spenceans, a small group of physical force fanatics who shared no more profound a principle than an uncritical admiration for the aims and methods of the Jacobins of the Terror. Insignificant in numbers and defective in leadership, they yet contrived from time to time to give the impression of the tail wagging the dog. The peculiar circumstances which made this possible will be examined later, but here it is necessary to examine briefly their always dubious claim to figure in the leadership of London radicalism.

The 'Spenceans' were, indeed, a small inner circle of a more extensive and quite harmless party known as 'The Society of Spencean Philanthropists', founded by one Thomas Evans, in 1814, to promote the views of the late Thomas Spence, a Yorkshire schoolmaster, whom we have already seen contributing his mite to the melting-pot of ideas which bubbled so furiously in the opening years of the Regency.[29] Spence had lectured on his famous 'Plan' before the Newcastle Philosophical Society as long ago as 1775 : a plan for remedying all the ills of mankind by a system of parochial communism in land. In the nineties he kept a bookstall in Chancery Lane and hawked his periodical, *Pigs' Meat: or Lessons for the Swinish Multitude*, in a baker's barrow. The Society founded in his name, and after his death, was concerned to promote knowledge of his Plan, and held meetings in a variety of public houses in the East End of London. It was here, within the philanthropic confines of a society designed for the discussion of 'subjects calculated to enlighten the human understanding', that there nested the queer characters, half crazy and half criminal, who envisaged a repeat performance of the Terror in Regency London.

Chief among them was the celebrated Dr Watson, an obscure medical practitioner, a man of about fifty, of whom Samuel Bamford reports 'there was something of polish in his gait and manners, and a degree of neatness and respectability in his dress.' He had, Bamford thought, 'probably a better heart than head'.[30] With him went his son, known as 'the younger Watson', a young lunatic who laboured under the impression that the Tower of London was the Bastille. Then there was Preston, a lame man, who nevertheless managed to scramble on to a wall of the Tower and call upon the Guard to surrender. And there was a gloomy ruffian who cast himself for the role of Marcus Brutus, although his name was Arthur Thistlewood. In all London, and perhaps in all England, this futile little gang were the only advocates of physical force as a consistent policy. It was supposed that they had plans for a murderous 'anticavalry machine', known as 'the night-cat'; a device for smothering the soldiers in barracks; a scheme for capturing the Tower of London and setting up a Committee of Public Safety at the Mansion House. All this would have been merely silly, had they not advertised their supposititious alliance with Burdett, Cartwright and Admiral Cochrane. Thus they contrived to create wholly false impressions in the minds not only of the Government (who saw them through the eyes of one Castle, an informer), but also in the imaginations of provincial working men of the simpler sort. For, if the name of Major Cartwright were on the lips of men like these, what might not be the real purpose of the Hampden Clubs which he had founded in the industrial areas during his tours of 1811 and 1813? And again, the provincial delegates of the Hampden Clubs, visiting London with their petitions in the winter of 1816–17, what impression of Burdett and Cartwright might they not carry home with them after associating – as some of them did associate – with the queer company at the *Cock*, the *Mulberry Tree* or the *Nag's Head*? Moreover, if a government spy were to go down to the industrial areas with talk of Burdett and Cartwright as leaders of 'the Revolution' – the general rising which would begin in London whenever the men of Sheffield, Leeds, Nottingham – or even Pentrich – should give the signal ...? It was thus, by the magnification of small ambiguities, that 'Alarm' was born. It was thus, by the wild and futile fancies of a handful of fanatics in the taverns of East London, that the advocates of physical force were enabled to create confusion and tragedy out of all proportion to their numbers or importance.

Chapter 12

THE COUNTRY COUSINS

On the 1st of January, 1817, a meeting of delegates
from twenty-one petitioning bodies was held in our
chapel, when resolutions were passed declaratory of
the right of every male to vote, who paid taxes. . . .
The Hampden Club of London ... having issued
circulars for a meeting of delegates at the *Crown
and Anchor*, for the purpose of discussing a Bill to
be presented to the House of Commons, embracing
the reform we sought, I was chosen to represent the
Middleton Club on that occasion.

SAMUEL BAMFORD:
Passages in the Life of a Radical

EARLY in the month of January 1817, a large number of earnest,
peaceable and neatly-dressed artisans might have been seen making
their way from north, east and west towards the capital city of
England. They travelled singly or in pairs, some trudging on foot
through the wintry countryside, some begging lifts from wag-
goners, a few perched like half-frozen birds on the tops of mail-
coaches. They were converging on the *Crown and Anchor* tavern
in the Strand, that famous meeting-house of Radical politicians.
Now, the first-fruits of the labours of Thomas Hardy, John Cartwright and William Cobbett were to be gathered into the old
threshing-floor of reformism. A new generation, a new class of the
people, almost a new world, was arriving on the scene: shoemakers
like William Benbow, from Birch, weavers like Samuel Bamford of
Middleton, nondescript artisans like Joseph Mitchell, cutlers and
bleachers, coopers and porters, smiths and puddlers. At last, the
country cousins were coming to town.

They travelled through towns and villages, beside fens and fields,
which had lately seen distress flare into public commotion. The
previous summer had seen bread-rioting in the East Anglican towns
of Ely, Littleport and Downham Market, disturbances which had
necessitated the summons of the yeomanry and which had led to
the execution of five ring-leaders. A little later, the unemployed

colliers and iron-workers of South Wales – deeply depressed by the falling-off of the iron trade with the coming of peace – had staged an orderly demonstration in the form of a hunger-march with waggons of coal as far as St Albans. The same summer saw a revival of machine-wrecking at Nottingham. As the wet summer wore on into a wet autumn, the corn was still green in the fields at harvest-time, and by October the price was a guinea a bushel in Yorkshire. There was serious rioting at Birmingham by the end of that month. Mr Nadin, Deputy Constable of Manchester, informed the Home Secretary that 'the lower orders are everywhere meeting in large bodies and are very clamorous' and that 'the delegates' were afoot again. He reported talk of 'a general union of the lower orders throughout the kingdom'. In one sense, Mr Nadin was right. The delegates were certainly afoot again, and the lower orders certainly had visions of a general union. But the delegates were afoot on the business of securing petitions from Cartwright's clubs, and their ultimate objective was not the Tower of London, but the *Crown and Anchor* tavern. The union they sought was a union behind Burdett, Cartwright and Cobbett for a reform of the House of Commons; not behind Dr Watson and Arthur Thistlewood for the establishment of a Committee of Public Safety.

The summons had come from London at the end of August 1816, when Burdett and Cochrane, Francis Place and James Mill – in fact, the Benthamite Radicals of the Borough – held a public meeting at Westminster, calling for an organized campaign of petitions throughout the country, each district to send up two delegates as petition-bearers to London in time for the opening of the next session of parliament. At once, the Hampden Clubs got busy, and all through the autumn and early winter there was great coming and going in the provinces. Lancashire, with its cotton-spinning multitudes, was naturally very much to the fore. Oldham had its Union Society under the chairmanship of a Methodist Unitarian preacher; its members were, in the main, skilled workers. The Middleton Society, of which Samuel Bamford was Secretary, also had a Methodist connexion. The Manchester Society was the nucleus of Lancashire reform politics; the others looked to it as a centre, and on the eve of the departure of the delegates for London, it convened a meeting of them all at Middleton. Similarly, the clubs were busy in Yorkshire, especially at Sheffield, Leeds and Barnsley. There were a number of Hampden Clubs, each with sixty members, at Norwich, and Leicestershire possessed not only a very active Club in the county town, but a large number scattered about in the villages. Leicester served to coordinate the activities of the Clubs in Leicestershire, as Manchester served in Lancashire, and both were in touch with London. John Knight, Chairman of the Manchester organization, was a friend of Cartwright. Burdett himself sent down advice on the number of delegates who should travel to London.

It is not difficult to imagine how all this preparation should have appeared from the desk of the Home Secretary. Studying his reports from what he chose to call 'the disaffected areas', Lord Sidmouth is scarcely to be blamed for adopting an attitude of watchful apprehension; indeed, he would be very much to blame had he adopted any other. He had before him not only the rather lurid reports of Deputy Constable Nadin, but a whole budget of information submitted by the agents employed by local magistrates. The Town Clerk of Leicester, for example, reported that his agent had discovered that the Hampden Clubs in the villages there were 'solely impressed with the belief that Revolution was the object, and were no further interested than to hold themselves in readiness to fight when necessary'. Again, Colonel Chippendale of Manchester reported that his agent believed that the people there had been expecting a revolutionary move in London, and that crowds awaited the arrival of the London Mail and the news that the Tower had fallen. Sir John Byng reported much the same hopeful excitement in Yorkshire.

The fact was, that certain events in London during November and early December had aroused a faint revolutionary echo in the distant districts of the north and midlands, and indeed had served to prejudice the wholly peaceful hopes of the Hampden Club delegates as they prepared for their southward journey. On 15 November, Henry Hunt held an open-air meeting in Spa Fields for the purpose of securing a show of hands for the election of himself and Sir Francis Burdett to carry a petition to the Prince Regent from the people of London itself. It is said that some 10,000 people were present. The 'Orator' addressed them from the window of a public house, accompanied with a tricolour flag and a Cap of Liberty. He enlarged upon the evils of high prices and over-taxation, the greed of the borough-mongers and sinecurists, the necessity for parliamentary reform. No doubt he was typically 'Orator Hunt', with his wild gestures and his passionate vituperation. He made no appeal to force, although he did advise his hearers to sign the petition 'before physical force' was 'applied'. The meeting passed off peaceably enough, with Hunt and Burdett elected as petition-bearers. Four days later, however, Burdett wrote to Hunt to decline the honour of assisting him in carrying the petition to the Regent. 'I am determined not to be made a cat's-paw of', he said, 'and not to insult the Prince Regent.' The petition embodied the full Radical programme: universal male suffrage, annual parliaments, vote by ballot. Burdett's affinities, as we have seen, were rather with the Benthamite or Philosophic Radicals, who generally confined themselves to a demand for the franchise 'co-incident with direct taxation'. In any case, Burdett disliked Hunt as a rival demagogue, and a vulgar, mob-stealing one at that. Hunt at once accused Burdett of running away. He announced his abandonment of the idea of the Baronet's ever doing 'anything effectually to relieve the people'. Cartwright and Cobbett did their best to persuade Hunt to 'give up for the present the principle of universal suffrage in order to shape our course to his [Burdett's] views'. Hunt refused. He would not, he said, 'accommodate the whim and fickle and faithless leader'. The rift in the London leadership had shown itself, in both personalities and programmes, more than two months before the country cousins reached London.[1]

Hunt held to his course. He bore the petition single-handed, and was twice refused admission to the Regent's presence. On 2 December, a second meeting was held in Spa Fields, this time to protest against the contemptuous treatment of the petitioners. An even larger crowd assembled to await the arrival of the frustrated hero. Hunt was driving down Cheapside when he was met by one Castle, an informer, who told him that he was too late: 'the people' had taken the Tower of London. Disregarding this clumsy attempt to implicate him, Hunt drove on to Spa Fields. There a strange spectacle confronted him. In the midst of the crowd – *his* crowd – stood a waggon decorated with banners, one of which announced the wishful thought: THE BRAVE SOLDIERS ARE OUR FRIENDS, and in the waggon stood the celebrated Dr Watson, his no less celebrated son, Arthur Thistlewood, and a number of other habitués of the *Cock* and the *Mulberry Tree*, those East End resorts of the Society of Spencean Philanthropists. Dr Watson was mopping his brow after concluding a heated oration, and his son was at present rendering a spirited performance of Camille Desmoulin's café-table exhortation to the patriots of Paris before the taking of the Bastille. 'If they will not give us what we want,' he screamed, 'shall we not take it? Are you willing to take it? Will you go and take it? If I jump down amongst you, will you come and take it?' At every question, the cry of 'Yes!' grew louder from the crowd, and the next thing that the displaced 'Orator' Hunt saw was young Watson leaping into the crowd with a tricolour flag, *en route* for the Tower of London.

A leaven of sailors in the crowd supplied a useful impetus, and a gunsmith's shop on Snow Hill supplied a number of firearms. Having killed a pedestrian, the mob made for the Royal Exchange, and there were confronted by Alderman Shaw and half a dozen constables. 'I did not perceive any arms,' Shaw said later. 'We got five constables in all; the whole party consisted of eight.' They arrested three of the leaders, and by nightfall the troops had restored order in the City.[2] 'Five fanatics hounded on by a spy' is not an inaccurate description of the affair. But the Government decided to flatter the leaders with a charge of High Treason, and, on the production of Castle, the informer, as a witness, they were acquitted. If anything further had been required to alienate Burdett and the Philosophic Radicals from the Hunt–Cartwright–Cobbett leadership at this time, it was certainly supplied by this tragicomic interlude on the part of the physical force fanatics. Similarly, if Lord Sidmouth required further confirmation of his suspicions as to what was going on in the country districts, with their network of clubs, their travelling delegates, and their concentration upon the capital, he may well have felt that he now possessed it.

It is against this disturbed and ambiguous background that we must view the arrival of Samuel Bamford and the concourse of country cousins for the great conference at the *Crown and Anchor* on 22 January 1817. It is safe to say that few of them can have been aware of the change which had overtaken the situation since the issue of the summons to London in the late summer; the widening breach between their leaders; the gravity of the concern felt by Lord Sidmouth and his colleagues of the Cabinet. There is something pitifully ironic about the spectacle of these hopeful, earnest artisans, the first of their kind to enter upon the stage of metropolitan politics, arriving upon a scene already darkened by the fears, the follies and the rivalries of contending factions. They came in faith and hope; they were to depart in despair or in desperation.

For most, if not for quite all, of them, this must have been their first encounter with the capital; and, from the account left to us by Bamford, we may see something of what they saw, and feel something of what they felt. Although he wrote many years after the event, and in the chastened mood of the veteran, the pages in which he records his first sojourn in Regency London are still among the freshest that he ever wrote.[3] They are, indeed, unique. English autobiography is rich enough in memoirs of young men who 'came to town to seek their fortunes' or to sow their wild oats. Boswell, Bewick, Haydon and many more have shown us the London of George III from the angle of the youthful adventurer. Bamford gives us something quite different from these: the wondering, critical, inquisitive mind of a young working-class politician, the first of his kind. He has come, this pioneer invader of the preserves of the monopolists, to sit in council with his chosen leaders in a great cause, to say his say in the midst of the gentlemen who have been merely great names to him and his kind until now. He is to see Henry Hunt and Major Cartwright, William Cobbett and Sir Francis Burdett, in the flesh, and face to face. He, one of the great unenfranchised, is to walk and talk in Westminster. He is to feel himself to be some kind of member of parliament, the member for Middleton, seated in the conclave at the *Crown and Anchor*.

Descending from the coach at the *Elephant and Castle*, Bamford was met by William Benbow, a shoemaker from Birch, near Middleton, a fellow delegate who had been in town for some time, and who took him to lodge with him at Buckingham Gate. That very night, they went together to the *Crown and Anchor*, and Bamford was astonished to find himself in a large hall, 'wonderfully grand

and silent for a tavern'. Within a few minutes he found himself gazing with 'curiosity and awe' upon the celebrated Henry Hunt. That gentleman fully came up to Bamford's expectations, with his fashionable blue coat and topped boots, his mobile features and magnificent legs. In the course of the next few days, Bamford went with some of his fellow delegates to wait upon both William Cobbett and Sir Francis Burdett. They met Cobbett at his office in Newcastle Street, Strand, unmistakably the gentleman-farmer in town; six feet high, portly, with fresh round cheeks and twinkling small grey eyes; dressed in a blue coat, with a swansdown waist-coat, and topped boots; wonderfully clean and fresh in his linen; the perfect example of what he always professed to be – the well-lined, stout-hearted, bantering countryman. Sir Francis Burdett received the visitors at his fine house in Park Place, a cold, gloomy, sparsely furnished mansion. The Baronet appeared in his dressing-gown and slippers, his white cotton stockings hanging loose about his long spare legs, and his neck devoid of a cravat. No refreshment was offered, and the great man seemed to submit to rather than to seek conversation with his humble visitors. He spoke guardedly of the prospects of universal suffrage. It is clear that Bamford was unaware of recent events which had chilled Burdett's enthusiasm for the petitioning movement. On the other hand, Lord Cochrane was 'cordial and unaffected'. He and Lady Cochrane provided 'a brief refection'. The delegates were captivated, and 'no health was ever drunk with more sincere goodwill than was Lord Cochrane's.' In the event, it was Lord Cochrane who was to carry the petitions to the House of Commons.

When the great day of the *Crown and Anchor* meeting arrived, the strains and stresses within the Radical leadership became dramatically apparent. In the first place, Sir Francis Burdett stayed away, and Bamford tells us that 'the absence of the Baronet was the subject of much observation by the delegates.' For, after all, Burdett was not only the Radical member for Westminster, the great hope of the cause in the House of Commons, but Chairman of the Hampden Club. In his absence, the chair was taken by Major Cartwright, and it was explained to the meeting that a resolution for household suffrage was proposed 'in deference to his [Burdett's] wishes', and that Mr Cobbett would second it. It must have come as a consider-

able shock to the country delegates, few of whom were householders, and who had been collecting petitions for universal suffrage,
to hear their old mentor, Major Cartwright, and the editor of the
Political Register, advocating a measure which would have left the
greater part of the working class of England where they had always
been – outside the electoral pale of the Constitution. They must
have asked themselves, were Cartwright and Cobbett democrats in
the country and oligarchs in the town? And anyway, was it democratic to concede so much to the absent aristocrat who had left his
humble visitors to stand up in his drawing-room without so much
as a glass of gin and water? The delegates at once showed their
disapproval. The motion for household suffrage was opposed by
many, Bamford tells us, 'and especially by the delegates from the
manufacturing districts'. Needless to say, they found a prompt ally
in Mr Hunt, who proposed an amendment in favour of universal
suffrage in a speech which contained 'a sarcastic fling or two at the
baronet'. Cobbett maintained his support for the more limited suffrage unconvincingly, and without conviction. His attitude was
the more baffling because he had declared himself a convert to
universal suffrage at the hands of Major Cartwright in one of the
first cheap issues of the *Political Register*, exactly a month before.[4]
Now, it seemed, the great tribune had changed his mind again, and
all because the Baronet fought shy of the popular programme. In
a warm altercation with Hunt, it seemed that he could produce no
better argument than the vague assertion that universal suffrage
was 'impractical'.

It was at this point that the member for Middleton stepped into
the arena. No one seemed to have grappled with the charge that
universal suffrage was 'impractical', until Bamford arose and
pointed out that 'universal suffrage might be carried into effect by
taking the voters from the Militia list.' Hunt at once adopted this
suggestion, and Cobbett declared himself convinced. Without more
ado, resolutions in favour of universal suffrage and annual parliaments were carried. The man from Middleton had spoken, the
mighty ones had fallen into line, and the cause of the Hampden
Clubs had triumphed. London had called, London had wavered, and
the north had imposed its programme. Let it be admitted at once
that the north could not hope to hold its ground. Parliamentary

reform was not to be won by weavers passing resolutions at the *Crown and Anchor* over the heads of Sir Francis Burdett, Major Cartwright and William Cobbett. The delegates might crowd into Old Palace Yard, shouting 'Hunt! Hunt! Huzza!' as the great demagogue bore their petition for universal suffrage to the waiting Lord Cochrane, who would ride on their shoulders to the doors of St Stephen's. It was not at the hands of the Hunts and Cochranes that the first great legislative measure of reform would be won, but by the grace of the great Whig oligarchs when they should condescend to return to the leadership of the reformist cause. All the same, the little victory of the country cousins at the *Crown and Anchor* has its place in the greater story. It was just this extra-parliamentary pressure by the great excluded element of the people which provided the wind for the sails of the homing ship. It was, moreover, itself a straw in the wind of its own making. It blew from the north, and when next Henry Hunt should find himself at the head of the northern Radicals, it would not be on the occasion of a few score of delegates coming to him in London, but on the occasion of his going to some sixty thousand of their 'constituents' in St Peter's Fields, Manchester. It would be Peterloo.

Even as the shouting and the tumult died in Old Palace Yard, with the disappearance of Lord Cochrane and the petition of half a million signatures into the House of Commons, the shades were falling fast upon the efforts of the assembled delegates and their leaders. That same morning, when the Prince Regent drove to Westminster to open the new session of Parliament, a stone or a bullet – no one ever discovered precisely what it was – had penetrated the glass of his coach-window. The debate in the lower House was interrupted by a message from the House of Lords announcing this, the latest outrage of the 'disaffected', and both Houses adjourned after sending loyal and congratulatory messages to the Prince. The Cabinet had already held a hurried meeting and resolved to take steps to strengthen the arm of the executive. A few days later, certain documents purporting to contain secret information relative to the disordered state of the country were presented to both Houses, and a joint Secret Committee was appointed to examine and report on them. 'The Pop-Gun Plot', as it was called, had set off the second period of 'Alarm'.

Some of the *Crown and Anchor* delegates were still in London, and Bamford himself listened to the debate on the report of the Secret Committee which took place towards the end of February. He had singularly little to say on the content of the debate. One would scarcely imagine that he was witnessing the first stages of a procedure which was to drive the reform clubs underground, darken his northern hills with a sullen cloud of hate and suspicion, send half a hundred of his fellows to Botany Bay or the gallows, and land himself in custody as a state-prisoner. For, on the strength of the Secret Committee reports, the Habeas Corpus Act was to be suspended, and the executive was to be strengthened by measures to restrain seditious meetings, detain political writers under the warrant of a Secretary of State (which, in effect, meant Lord Sidmouth), and prevent and punish attempts to tamper with the loyalty of the armed forces of the Crown. The Government secured the passage of the legislation enacting these precautions without difficulty, so alarming were the reports.[5] That of the House of Lords contrived to magnify the Spa Fields Riot into a narrowly averted revolution, and went on to attribute schemes of nation-wide subversion to 'societies or clubs, established ... in all parts of Great Britain, under pretence of Parliamentary Reform ....' The House of Commons' Committee openly denounced the Hampden Clubs as aiming at 'nothing short of a Revolution'. Meanwhile, the Secretary of the Hampden Club of Middleton, Lancashire, sat in the public gallery of the House of Commons making mental notes on the contemptible conduct of 'the most illustrious assembly of freemen in the world', and wishing that he might hear the tramp of 'stern old Oliver' and his troopers on the floor.

Did the illustrious assembly obscurely feel an alien presence that day? Was nobody impelled to declare that he 'spied strangers'? Is it possible that the weaver's boy from Lancashire himself may have been aware for a fleeting moment that something more pregnant with the future of that august assembly than all Cromwell's troopers was present that day? He gives us no hint of it, although we may judge by implication that he thought the House of Commons compared unfavourably with the assembled company at the *Crown and Anchor*. Even the wickedness of the 'borough-monger crew' was unimpressive. 'Some three or four hundreds of the most ordinary-looking men I had ever beheld at one view' sums up his impression. There were a few striking exceptions : Canning, with his smooth, bare, capacious forehead, 'a spirit beaming in his looks like that of a leopard waiting to spring upon its prey'; Castlereagh with his 'handsome but immoveable features'; Burdett with his head held high in defiance; Brougham with 'his Arab soul ready to rush forth and challenge all comers ....' But the rest of 'the collective wisdom ...' – they propped up the pillars, their hats cocked awry, their arms akimbo, their quizzing-glasses much in evidence; they lolled and whispered and waved their arms; they howled 'like a kennel of hounds at feeding time'; they whinnied their mocking laughter like the damned in their bitterness; they beat the floor with their boots, snorted into their cravats, or coughed until they were black in the face. Most of all Bamford was concerned by the conduct of Henry Brougham, the stormy champion of every cause involving the emancipation of the human race, from the abolition of negro slavery to the institution of popular education. And what a fall was here ! For Brougham, after castigating the alarmist policy of the Government, proceeded to make 'a dead set at the reformers' ! The House had howled him down before. Now they listened in grateful silence. And when he sat down, they 'applauded to the very welkin'. He had subdued, but spared, his enemies; he had derided and disclaimed his friends; he had sacrificed his liberal principles to his ambition and his vanity. So thought Samuel Bamford. 'I turned from the spectacle with disgust, and sought my lodgings in a kind of stupor, almost believing that I had escaped from a monstrous dream.'

Bamford and his friends were to witness one other, and very different, conclave of Regency politicians before they left London. They were to visit the haunts of the Spenceans in the pothouse of the East End. Making their way through a low doorway, they found themselves in a dense cloud of tobacco-smoke. There they sat, the British Jacobins, each man with his long clay pipe and his pint of porter, everyone talking at once and scarcely anyone listening, save perhaps the foxy-faced Mr Castle, who was on equally familiar terms with the Home Secretary. There was the celebrated Dr Watson, out on bail and at present bearing up remarkably cheerfully under a charge of High Treason for his share in the proceedings at Spa Fields. His son, Camille Desmoulins-Watson, was in hiding somewhere in the eastern stews, with a price on his head. There was Preston, the lame man, who had managed to climb on to a wall of the Tower of London and summon the Guard to surrender the British Bastille. Arthur Thistlewood, the Brutus-to-be of the Cato Street Plot, seems to have been absent. It seems that Bamford and his fellow delegate, Joseph Mitchell, invited Dr Watson and Mr Preston to breakfast with them, and were regaled with some account of their exploits. Bamford was very soon to regret these contacts, for these new friends were already under the influence of *agents provocateurs*.

'Soon afterwards', Bamford concluded his London story, 'I left the great Babylon, heartily tired of it, and returned to Middleton ....' Not for nearly another two months did Joseph Mitchell leave the great Babylon. What he was doing during that time we do not know, but it seems probable that he took some interest in the whereabouts of the younger Watson. We know that he somehow got into touch with one Pendrill, a violent reformer who had been one of the speakers at the Spa Fields Meeting, and who had concealed the younger Watson in his house thereafter. Pendrill had in his employment a person called Richards, and, when Joseph Mitchell decided that he would return to Lancashire, Pendrill proposed that Richards should travel with him. They set off together on 23 April.

The person called Richards was 'Oliver the Spy'.

Chapter 13

SPIES AND INFORMERS

A cloud of gloom and mistrust hung over the whole
country. . . . It seemed as if the sun of freedom were
gone down, and a rayless expanse of oppression had
finally closed over us. . . . Our society, thus hopeless,
became divided and dismayed; hundreds slunk home
to their looms, nor dared to come out, save like
owls at nightfall . . .

SAMUEL BAMFORD:
Passages in the Life of a Radical

WHEN Lord Liverpool's government put the 'Alarm' mechanism
into operation in the early spring of 1817, the Radical cause was
already in ruins. Discredited by the Spa Fields episode in the previous December, London radicalism plainly revealed the divisions
in its leadership and the confused nature of its aims at the *Crown
and Anchor* meeting in January. Burdett had withdrawn to the
comparative quiet and respectability of the hunting-field. Cobbett
fled to America in March. The Spencean leaders were in hiding or
on bail for High Treason. Only 'Orator Hunt' remained to enjoy
an equivocal and blustering triumph. Major Cartwright could do
little more than contemplate ruefully the ruins of the Hampden
Clubs. The poor delegates, returning to their homes, knew themselves to be pursued by the shadow of the law. The Habeas Corpus
Suspension Act was passed on 3 March, and the Seditious Meetings
Act on the 29th. Together they had the effect of making it possible
for any magistrate to order the arrest and detention without trial
of anyone attending any meeting for reformist purposes. If the reformist cause were to go on, it must now go on in secret, with all
the attendant dangers of conspiratorial atmosphere, and all the
obvious opportunities for the worst devices of spies and informers.
Indeed, it seemed at that moment that Regency England was about
to conform to the political pattern of the continental powers, with
the grim alternatives of revolution and reaction.

Of course, it was not so. There were powerful forces of compromise and concession in all parties; modifying forces of moral suasion in the fortunately numerous and diverse religious bodies; immensely powerful traditions of behaviour in governors and governed alike. Least of all was Lord Liverpool anxious to 'come to extreme measures'. There was, as we have seen, something infinitely repellent to the English gentlemen who governed England at this time in the prospect of being obliged to resort to any other than the normal and traditional methods of preserving law and order. The remarkable thing about the measures adopted in the supposed crisis of 1817 was their lateness and their inefficiency. The information on which the Secret Committees of both Houses reported in the middle of February 1817 had been in the hands of the Home Secretary for months. The Spa Fields affair took place in early December 1816, but neither the suspension of the Habeas Corpus Act nor the additional powers for dealing with seditious meetings and the press came into operation until the following March. As for the notorious Mr Oliver, whose activities have sometimes been taken to sum up the character of government in this period, Sidmouth picked him up, like a stick out of a hedge, in April – some six weeks after the miserable 'March of the Blanketeers' was over, and only six weeks before the single armed rising of Regency England – the Derbyshire Rising of 9 June.

The truth is, that if there was a crisis in 1817, it was over before Government took anything like concerted action. The events of the early summer of that year were nothing more, and nothing less, than the tragic aftermath of the great Hampden Club movement of the winter. Disappointed and embittered men, driven to underground activity by 'Alarm' measures, found themselves under arrest. Some, like Samuel Bamford himself, were brought before the Privy Council, solemnly warned, and sent home again. Others, like Jeremiah Brandreth and the Derbyshire men, marched into High Treason, lost their lives, or were sent to Botany Bay. In July, Sidmouth reviewed all cases of detention under the Suspension Act, a number of persons were released, and by the end of the year only three were still in custody. The activities of Oliver the Spy in the industrial districts during the early summer, which culminated in the Derbyshire Rising and the subsequent spy-hunt in parliament and the press, might be likened to the action of a bread-poultice applied to certain portions of the body politic which had shown signs of serious inflammation. No doubt the similitude would have appealed to Lord Sidmouth, son of Dr Addington, and known to the Radical press as 'the Doctor'. He worked overtime during this summer and autumn, even returning to town from his summer holiday at Malvern before the rest of his family with the weary remark: 'Back to sedition and treason again ...' Indeed, one might imagine from a reading of his correspondence, the Home Office Papers marked 'Disturbances', and the lucubrations of Whig historians from Martineau to the Hammonds, that England had no other history than the history of reactionaries, Radicals and spies at this time.

Precisely what was happening in the midland and northern districts during the early summer of 1817 cannot be ascertained with any certainty. Still less certainly could it be ascertained at the time, which is why Lord Sidmouth readily accepted the proposal of Oliver the Spy to go and find out. The one safe generalization that can be made is, that the collapse of the Hampden Club movement, and the recourse of the Government to 'Alarm' tactics, had produced a highly dangerous and potentially explosive situation throughout the industrial districts. The most dangerous point in any widespread reformist movement is always the point when the movement meets its first shock of disillusion. When high hopes and enthusiasm are dashed by the spectacle of divided or pusillanimous leadership, and when the force of established authority appears invulnerable to persuasion. This point had been reached in March 1817. The delegates had seen their London leaders divided and hesitant. They had seen their positions derided or ignored. Now they were at home again, in the midst of wretchedness and want, while the shadow of the law – reinforced by measures which vastly strengthened and lengthened its arm – loomed over them like a black shadow darkening the land. They were at a loss what to do next, whether to lie low, whether to strike in blind desperation at the enemy. Worst of all, they knew not whom to trust, for even their own comrades seemed infected by the taint of treachery which breathed upon the frightened air. Some, like Samuel Bamford, decided to lie low. Others, like William Benbow, went about secretly mouthing threats of fire and slaughter to come. Still others, like Joseph Mitchell, put their faith in the desperadoes of East London, the Watsons and the Thistlewoods, who were doubtless only awaiting 'a sign from the north' – if only the north would arise in its wrath. In the poorest pot-houses of Nottingham, notably the *Three Salmons* and the *Punchbowle*, there were unemployed stockingers like Jeremiah Brandreth, working themselves up into the requisite state to 'strike a blow' – for something, preferably 'Liberty'; while John Cope, a puddler at the Butterley Ironworks, a few miles over the Derbyshire border, who had been dismissed his employment for joining a Hampden Club, was going about threatening the whole universe of kings and ministers. 'Damn the Prince Regent,' said John Cope. 'Damn the Government. I'll kill Lord Castlereagh, before I settle, and roast his heart.' There was, indeed, a plenitude of suggestions as to 'what to do next . . .'

The first thing that was done, early in March, was to organize a 'hunger-march' of weavers from Manchester to London. It was promoted principally by two headstrong working-class reformers, Bagguley and Drummond, neither of whom had any intention of taking part in the march personally. The idea was that the weavers should march in groups of ten, each man with a blanket on his back and a petition to the Prince Regent fastened to his arm. The petitions bore no political demands, only a request to His Royal Highness to take measures to remedy the wretched plight of the cotton-trade. The march began with an open-air meeting in St Peter's Fields, Manchester, where the magistrates read the Riot Act and took Messrs Bagguley and Drummond into custody. Some six or seven hundred men set out in drizzling rain. Dragoons, Yeomanry and special constables arrested many of them before they could reach Stockport; some four or five hundred got as far as Macclesfield and Leek; most of them were turned back at the Hanging Bridge over the Dove as they were about to enter Derbyshire; only one man reached London. 'Our first great absurdity', Bamford called it.[1] He had been opposed to the idea from the beginning, scenting from afar off the machinations of the Spenceans at work in Lancashire through the agency of some of his fellow delegates who had 'cultivated a rather close acquaintance with these men' during their stay in London in the previous winter. 'One of the bad schemes which accompanied us from London', he suspected.

Bad, dangerous, playing with fire, it may have been; but an 'absurdity' it was not. Indeed, in some respects 'the March of the Blanketeers' was the cleverest scheme of all, for it combined all the advantages of legality with all the opportunities of development into something else. There was no law to prevent unarmed men from making their way, in small parties, to London. Providing that they kept on the move, committed no trespass, and did not unreasonably obstruct the public highway, there was no charge that could be brought against them with any chance of securing a conviction. The Blanketeers were not riotous. When the magistrates ordered them to disperse at the beginning of the march, they did so at once: it was, in a sense, exactly what they wanted to do. When the Yeomanry took up nearly two hundred of them outside Stockport, they could not think what to do with them. The jails were full. And anyway, with what could they be charged? Vagrancy? They had their provisions in the keeping of duly appointed 'provisioners', and even a 'common purse' – albeit the keeper made off with it fairly early in the proceedings. Riotous behaviour, with intent to cause a breach of the peace? Of course, any magistrate could charge them with that: but would he have secured a conviction – against one hundred and sixty-seven of them, and with more to come? On the whole, the authorities thought it better to send them home. Yet there had always been the chance that a peaceable hunger-march would grow into an army as it moved south. . . . Lord Sidmouth was sure that this was the intention, and he was supported by the Duke of Northumberland who likened the March of the Blanketeers to the march of the Marseillois to Paris in 1792. 'I am sure, my Lord, the intended march of the delegates from Manchester to London must too forcibly have reminded your Lordship . . . .'[2] Delegates – petitioners – marching to London, inspired by some of the delegates who had, on Bamford's showing, 'cultivated a rather close acquaintance with . . .' the Watsons, Prestons and Hoopers. . . . It may well have appeared that Messrs Bagguley and Drummond had hit upon a masterstroke of tactics.

It is very easy to enlist the sympathy of posterity for the poor, innocent Blanketeers, as writers like the Hammonds have done. It is not so easy, but it is no less important, to see such phenomena against the whole troubled and ambiguous background of the year

1817. Just how considerable were the elements of delusion and ambiguity in that background may be best appreciated from the pages of Bamford's autobiography. The situation was pregnant with danger, desperately inflammable, and bedevilled by the activities of spies and informers. No one knew whom he might trust. Any wandering artisan, going from door to door, or from tavern to tavern, in the little towns of the north and midlands, might turn out to have been in the pay of a magistrate or a constable. Nor was every whisperer of sedition necessarily a spy. Embittered and desperate men, weary of the endless futility of petitioning, angry at the arrest and imprisonment of their mates, were prepared to say and do things that they would have refrained from six months before. How great was the falling away from earlier standards of behaviour among the working-class reformers is suggested by Bamford's observations.

Steadiness of conduct and consistency of principle were soon placed as it were at a distance from us. Our unity of action was relaxed ... plans were broached, quite different from any that had been recognized by the Hampden Clubs; and the people, at a loss to distinguish friends from enemies, were soon prepared for the operation of informers, who, in the natural course of their business, became also promoters of secret plots and criminal measures of various descriptions. The good and fatherly maxim of the worthy old major, 'Hold fast by the laws', was by many lost sight of.[3]

Bamford's innate good sense saved him more than once from the machinations of spies and informers. On the night after the Blanket Meeting, for instance, he received a visit from a mysterious stranger – 'a man dressed much like a dyer' – who tried to involve him in a crazy scheme to 'make a Moscow of Manchester' that very night: that is, to set fire to the town and make it a beacon for a general conflagration and insurrection.[4] Bamford never succeeded in identifying this incendiary stranger, who professed to be an emissary of a committee in Manchester which had things well in hand. It is plain, from the investigations carried out by J. L. and Barbara Hammond into the activities of the swarm of spies and secret agents at work in the industrial districts at this time, that this man was a spy.[5] Moreover, when the Secret Committee of the House of Lords later reported upon the situation between the Blanket Meeting and the Derbyshire Rising in June, it described the plans of 'the disaffected' for turning Manchester into a blazing Moscow, and for a general insurrection, in almost precisely the same terms that were employed by Bamford's unknown visitor.[6]

Samuel Bamford owed his preservation not only to his own good sense but to Lord Sidmouth. On 28 March, the 'Ardwick Bridge Conspirators' were arrested, four simple-minded individuals who had suffered themselves to be led on by a local informer to the furtherance of the design for making a Moscow of the neighbouring town of Manchester – the avenging of the captured Blanketeers incarcerated there. It was the nipping in the bud of the spy-fomented plot with which Bamford had refused to have anything to do. Nevertheless, on the day after the arrests, Bamford was whisked away to London for examination by the Privy Council. His account of this, his second visit to London, reads like a premature instalment of the adventures of the Pickwick Club, which were to begin some ten years later.[7] Young Bamford and his mates had the time of their lives as state-prisoners. They were fed like fighting-cocks, and everything was done to make their experience as guests of His Majesty's Government as jolly as possible. They found the Lords of the Privy Council civil, frank and good-humoured – about as unlike the monsters of Shelley's *Masque of Anarchy* as a row of church-wardens. Bamford was never again to be impressed by the blood-and-bones talk of men like John Cope of Butterley or William Benbow of Birch. He is, indeed, one of our earliest examples of the blessings of State education, compulsory and free of charge.

When he returned to Middleton, towards the end of April, he learnt that his old friend and co-delegate, Joseph Mitchell, was 'moving about with a well-dressed and apparently affluent stranger'. Bamford professes also to have become immediately aware of a further deterioration in the atmosphere of reformist politics in the neighbourhood. 'A secret influence had been at work during my absence, exciting to and carrying on private meetings and suspicious intrigues ....' It seems that Joseph Mitchell's well-dressed and affluent friend had been making enquiries after Samuel Bamford. Bamford went on with his work like the industrious artisan which it suited him to be when politics held out less attraction for him, but no doubt he pondered over these things in his heart. Then, one day while he was at work, a message summoned him to step over to the *Dog and Partridge*, just across the street. He went, and there he found two men from Pentrich, in Derbyshire. The elder of the two was a venerable figure, much like an Old Testament prophet, with white locks hanging upon his shoulders and a staff clasped in his ancient hand. He carried a basket which contained rolls of worsted and small articles of hosiery, which gave him the air of an old pedlar. Bamford recognized him at once as Thomas Bacon, one of the Derbyshire delegates to the *Crown and Anchor* meeting, and he scarcely needed the old man's sly reference to the contents of his basket in order to understand that Thomas Bacon was engaged in peddling something quite other than hosiery. The second man was 'a tall, decent-looking young man, much like a town's weaver, wearing a blue coat, and with a clean white apron wrapped about his waist'. His name was William Turner, and he came of a very large clan of Turners who populated Pentrich and South Wingfield, and still do to this day. His trade was actually that of a stone-mason, and he had been a soldier, and he was – as Bamford at once detected – a very decent young man.

Thomas Bacon, the Nestor of the Derbyshire reformers, was the bringer of glad tidings. He was, he said, on his way to a delegate meeting in Yorkshire, 'which would cause a finishing blow to be levelled at the borough-mongers', and he was looking for a Middleton man who 'was particularly wanted on the present occasion'. Bamford affected not to know this wanted man, and proceeded to warn the ancient Bacon of the perils besetting his present course. He assured him that 'no force would avail in overturning the present state of things' and that the Ministers of the Crown 'had eyes to see and ears to hear and tongues to whisper whatever occurred'. In fact, Bamford talked to old Bacon very much as Lord Sidmouth had talked to Samuel Bamford across the Privy Council board a few weeks earlier. Old Bacon, however, declared that he cared little for 'a traitor or two' and that young Bamford would 'soon learn something which he at present little understood'. Anyway, he was 'too old a politician to be counselled by one so young'. So saying, he finished his beer rather hastily, picked up his innocuous-looking basket, and took the road towards Manchester with his youthful disciple: 'This pertinacious old man', as Bamford calls him, was to end his days in Botany Bay, and his young friend was to die on the scaffold in Derby, after the ill-fated 'Pentrich Revolution' a few weeks later. Both, Bamford maintained, were victims of Joseph Mitchell's 'well-dressed and affluent friend', who was none other than Oliver the Spy.[8]

The plot which was now working itself out with such diabolical ingenuity was not, however, hatched at the hands of Oliver, nor of Lord Sidmouth, nor of any single person or group of persons. It represented the tragic *dénouement* of a highly intricate complex of forces and personalities. Indeed, if names are to be named, the mischief might as well be imputed to feather-headed Radicals like Joseph Mitchell, half-criminal eccentrics like the Watsons, or worthy but unimaginative old souls like Major Cartwright, as to Sidmouth and Oliver. The whole Hampden Club movement, with its travelling delegates and its London leadership, laid itself wide open – as Cobbett had predicted – to the tortuous play of ambiguity and abuse. There were the clubs, little conclaves of disappointed men congregating secretly all over the north and midlands, under the shadow of the 'Alarm' measures adopted by the Government. There was Joseph Mitchell, the Lancashire delegate, cultivating 'a rather close acquaintance' with the physical force fanatics of East London, and ferreting out the younger Watson where he lay in hiding in the house of Pendrill, whose clerk – Mr Richards – proposed to go down to Lancashire with Mitchell in order to find out just how much truth there was in that young man's talk about thousands of north-country Radicals awaiting a signal from London to rise in revolt against the borough-mongers. Mr Richards informs the Home Secretary of his projected journey with Mitchell and receives – not unnaturally – a commission from the harassed Minister to report to the Home Office on what he finds. At a delegate meeting at Wakefield, Mr Richards – now known as Mr Oliver – makes it plain that London is only waiting for Yorkshire, and old Thomas Bacon goes away from the Wakefield meeting to make it plain to the men of Pentrich that all England is only waiting for them. On 6 June, the Pentrich men march out under the leadership of Jeremiah Brandreth, the self-styled 'Nottingham Captain', and the road to Nottingham takes them to the scaffold or the hulks. Mr

Richards, alias Oliver the Spy, was a very wicked man, and Joseph Mitchell was a very foolish one; old Thomas Bacon was a pertinacious old fool, and Lord Sidmouth was a blunderer to make use of an unknown and irresponsible builder's clerk in a situation fraught with mischief. They were one and all victims of a situation whose complexity not one of them could have been expected to understand. They made history, in the sense that they were the stuff of which the history of their time was made, and history handed out to them their haloes and halters with grim partiality. It is hardly the task of the historian to attempt a retrospective redistribution.

Chapter 14

THE PENTRICH REVOLUTION

> The jurors of our Lord the King upon their oath
> present that Thomas Bacon, late of the parish of
> Pentrich, in the County of Derby, labourer; Jere-
> miah Brandreth ... otherwise called the Notting-
> ham Captain ...; William Turner ... [etc. etc.] ...
> not having the fear of God in their hearts, not
> weighing the duty of their allegiance, but being
> moved and seduced by the instigation of the Devil
> ... together with a great multitude of false traitors
> ... to the number of five hundred and more, arrayed
> and armed in a war-like manner, that is to say with
> swords, pistols, clubs, bludgeons, and other weap-
> ons ... did then with great force and violence parade
> and march in a hostile manner in and through divers
> villages, places, and public highways ... and did
> then and there maliciously and traitorously attempt
> and endeavour by force of arms to subvert and de-
> stroy the Government and Constitution of this realm
> as by law established. ...
>
> *First Count of the Indictment of Thomas Bacon,*
> *Jeremiah Brandreth, and others for High Treason*
> *before the King's Justices at Derby, 1817*

THE Regency was to have its Revolution. History has forgotten it,
partly because it took place in a remote countryside equidistant
from the populous haunts of the cotton trade and the central stage
of London, and partly because an affair of plots, pikes, night-
marching and dragoons was something of an anachronism in a
society which was undergoing an altogether more relevant revolution at the hands of manufacturers, journalists and Radical clubs.
The revolution which bears the name of Pentrich as distinct from
the revolution which bears the name of (say) Bentham, has a singularly old-fashioned air. Its style and manner belong almost, although not quite, exclusively to the old England that was passing
away. The Pentrich Revolution is revolution as Lords Liverpool and
Sidmouth understood it, indeed, as they had for long anticipated it.

It might have been arranged, if not by, at least for, the special benefit of the Home Secretary.

Lord Sidmouth had been looking forward to this event for many months, indeed ever since the Spa Fields riots in the previous winter. Secret Committees of both Houses of Parliament, reporting upon information supplied by the Home Office, rather naturally had employed similarly premonitary language. The Reports presented to both Houses on 18 and 19 February,[1] immediately after the breaking of the windows of the Prince Regent's coach at the opening of Parliament, testified to the existence of a widespread conspiracy of the labouring classes for the total overthrow of existing establishments; the employment of the Hampden Clubs as a network of revolutionary preparations; the expectation of the provinces of a *coup d'état* in the capital. Spa Fields, it was averred, was no chance-struck blow. Its failure had scotched the snake, but had not killed it. The attempt would be renewed. Indeed, all through the spring, with the March of the Blanketeers, the proposals to make a Moscow of Manchester, the Ardwick Bridge Conspiracy, Sidmouth had been receiving information from the agents of the north-country magistrates that 'the revolution' was coming. The precise date was continually being postponed. First, it was to have been 'on the first Monday after Sir Francis Burdett's motion for parliamentary reform, whenever that might be'. The date worked out to 27 May. Then it was postponed to 4 June. Finally, it was fixed for 9 June, which turned out to be the date of the Pentrich rising. When, on 12 and 20 June, the Secret Committees of both Houses reported[2] upon the latest developments in the situation, they averred that the late insurrection in Derbyshire had been the climax of a carefully concerted conspiracy which had been going on for several months and had only been frustrated from time to time by the vigilance of the authorities. The pitiful march of Jeremiah Brandreth and his Derbyshire yokels through the pouring rain of the night of 9 June had been intended as only one element in a general march of all northern England upon the capital. Elsewhere, it was intimated, the timely action of the authorities had been effective in suppressing the activities of the disaffected in their 'general plan of simultaneous or connected insurrection'.

The gratifying isolation of the Derbyshire rebels was achieved not only by the vigilance of the established authorities, but by the 'professional tour' (the phrase is Samuel Bamford's) of Oliver the Spy.[3] Oddly enough, Oliver achieved this by his extraordinary ineptitude. He seems never to have been capable of making up his mind whether he was an atomizing agent or a bread-poultice. Travelling about the north and midlands in April and May 1817 – at first with Joseph Mitchell as an innocent cicerone – he seems to have spent most of his time talking to groups of 'delegates' in low public-houses in such vague and general terms, that his hearers went away with the impression that 'the London delegate' thought the prospects of revolutionary action a good deal brighter almost everywhere than in the place where he happened to be speaking. This line of talk represents Oliver the 'Atomizer' – the informant who gave it as his opinion, on returning to London, that the revolutionary design which he had discovered during his first tour was 'a weak and impracticable scheme, and that if it could be delayed it would blow up of itself'. By the term 'blow up', it seems, Oliver meant 'blow over'. And this is, in fact, what happened. The postponement of zero-hour, which Oliver did his best to effect, gave time for the elements of active sedition to disperse under the influence of a growing sense of discouragement and frustration. His second tour was designed to discover whether anything was really to be apprehended in June. He helped to secure postponement until 4 June, 'pretending that the London people would not be ready before ....' Then, on 6 June, he lost his head and made a dash for London. For, on that day, he was arrested with a group of obscure individuals at the *Sportsman's Arms*, Thornhill Lees, and after his release became known (which happened immediately) his character as 'the London delegate' would be in ruins. Indeed, on his arrival in Nottingham on that same night of 6 June, he knew that his life was in danger. Even so, he consented to attend a meeting of delegates at the *Punchbowle*, at the urgent request of the city magistrates. He 'only consented to stay for the meeting at the solicitation of Mr Hooley and myself', wrote Mr Allsop, one of the Nottingham magistrates to Sidmouth, 'in order to furnish us with the necessary information ... his life was in the greatest danger.'[4] The Nottingham delegates had heard of his release after the arrests at Thornhill

Lees. He was put through a gruelling cross-examination at the *Punchbowle* on the evening of 7 June, and must have been glad to get away with his life.

The game was up, and the spy-hunt was on. But there was still time for the 'revolution' to break out at Pentrich on the night of 9 June, for Jeremiah Brandreth had already left Nottingham for his command in Derbyshire, and no one seems to have troubled to send after him. The notion that Brandreth went down to Pentrich to lead out the Derbyshire men on instructions from Oliver will not bear examination. There is no evidence that Brandreth ever met Oliver. The most likely link between them is supplied by that 'pertinacious old man', Thomas Bacon of Pentrich, who had heard Oliver talking of the 'coming blow' at Wakefield, several weeks earlier. But the 'pertinacious old man' stayed at home on the night of 9 June. Indeed, it seems that everyone who had ever actually heard Oliver 'holding out encouragement' or playing his alternative role of the bread-poultice, decided that discretion was the better part of valour. When he was not tacitly advocating delay, his very ineptitude as an *agent provocateur* served to promote procrastination. 'A feather-headed fellow' was the verdict of Thomas Bradley, secret agent to Mr Parker, a Sheffield magistrate, after trailing 'the London delegate' for some time without knowledge of his true identity.

When the Pentrich Revolution was over, the game of 'hunt-the-spy' became fast and furious. The parliamentary opposition and the Whig and Radical press set to work to prove that there would have been no sedition had not Oliver and Lord Sidmouth manufactured it. Historians of the same complexion, from Harriet Martineau to the Hammonds, have maintained that the outcry against 'Oliver the Spy' was an expression of national indignation against a 'system' – a certain continentally-tainted mode of government by a reactionary gang of Tories. But 'system' was there none. Instead, a broken-down master-builder of dubious morals and low-grade intelligence, who offered his services as an informer, was casually employed on terms of 'payment-by-results'. Sidmouth's offence was that he employed Oliver as indiscrimately as a man might tip a total stranger who offers to steer him through a fog. He even omitted the elementary precaution of informing local magistrates, in any systematic fashion, that this casual 'tourist' was coming into their midst. Thus we get the ludicrous spectacle of locally-employed informers spying on the spy from London, and locally-zealous magistrates arresting him – thereby depriving him of whatever value he might have had. Worst of all, Oliver went blundering into a situation which he did not understand; and the grotesque and tragic truth is, that if he had understood it, he could scarcely have played his part with more success for bringing the story to a diabolically-conceived conclusion.

So Lord Sidmouth had his 'Revolution', and it turned out to be very much the kind of revolution which one might expect to have haunted his Lordship's essentially romantic and old-fashioned mind – an affair of pistols, pikes, bill-hooks and bludgeons, parading and marching with great force and violence in and through divers villages and highways .... For its leader, also, possessed an old-fashioned and romantic mind. Jeremiah Brandreth was as little like the true revolutionary of the Regency – the politically-conscious, petition-making parliamentary reformer in fustian – as John Ball or Jack Cade or Robert Kett. The adventure which he led through the wet summer night from the sunken lanes and cornfields of south-east Derbyshire to storm the battlements of Nottingham was about as relevant to the purposes which were served by Samuel Bamford and the working-class politicians of the Hampden Clubs as a blunderbuss is relevant to a ballot-box. Not once, throughout these colourful proceedings, did Jeremiah Brandreth utter the words 'franchise' or 'manhood suffrage' or 'annual parliaments'. His whole talk was of bread, rum, a hundred guineas for every man who reached Nottingham, a 'band of music', even a pleasure-trip up the Trent. When he was asked, by a practically-minded female, what kind of government was to supersede the borough-mongers, he replied – 'a provisional government', and it is plain that he and his followers thought that a provisional government had something to do with provisions.[5]

Jeremiah Brandreth may have been a Luddite. At the time of his entering upon his command as 'the Nottingham Captain', he was described as an unemployed stockinger living on parish relief at Wilford, a parish adjoining the city from which he took his grandiloquent title. Where he originally came from, and what had been the manner of his life before his brief and disastrous appearance upon the stage of national affairs, are necessarily wrapped in that profound obscurity which once enveloped the short and simple annals of the poor. It was said that he had been at various times a drover, a whitesmith and a sailor; and, possibly, because he was thick-set, swarthy and excitable, it was suspected that he had gipsy blood. Rather inconsistently, it was also maintained that he came from Ireland or Exeter. Everyone seems to have been intent on proving that he could not have come from the solid, sober stock of the English midlands. Even his Counsel at his trial for High Treason thought it necessary to liken him to a corsair.

> Sun-burnt his cheek, his forehead high and pale
> The sable curls in wild profusion veil;
> There breathe but few whose aspect might defy
> The full encounter of his searching eye;
> There was a laughing devil in his sneer,
> That raised emotions both of rage and fear ...

Thus Mr Denman, who had been to Eton and Cambridge, and who was later to be Lord Chief Justice of England, chose to regale the Court with a quotation from Lord Byron's *The Corsair*. Mr Denman, however, reserved this quotation until his principal client had been found guilty, employing it rather in order to extenuate the offences of Brandreth's lieutenants, who, it was asserted, found it impossible to resist the commanding personality of their leader.

Those who gave evidence of Jeremiah Brandreth's demeanour and appearance during the march upon Nottingham were much struck by the difference in his appearance as he stood in the dock at Derby. 'His dress and general appearance had been very much altered,' one witness declared. Previously he had on a pair of grey trousers, a brownish great-coat, was shaved, and looked decent. Another described him as a stocky young man with a leather apron twisted about his waist to serve as a pistol-belt. He had 'large whiskers coming round his face, but no beard'. The truth would seem to be that Brandreth's terrifying aspect in Court was simply the result of his obdurate refusal to be shaved while awaiting his trial. The father of Herbert Spencer, a precise and respectable citizen of Derby at this time, has left us a sketch of the man as he appeared at the bar of judgement, and it depicts a gloomy ruffian, low-browed, unshaven, with his shabby coat-collar drawn up to his shaggy hair and beard. This was, no doubt, the portrait that respectable citizens of Derby wished to see, just as Mr Denman's word-picture in terms of Byron's Corsair was the portrait most likely to influence a jury of Derbyshire farmers in acquitting the man's duped and deluded followers. It is probable, however, that Brandreth looked very much like any other resolute young Luddite of the stocking-weaving villages of the Nottingham-Derbyshire border country. After his conviction, he wrote to his wife like a repentant Methodist; and he died bravely, forgiving his enemies.

Jeremiah Brandreth was indeed the traditional rebel: the stalwart, desperate fellow who burns with desire to strike a blow for – something, although he may not know precisely what. He was the kind of man that Samuel Bamford might have been, had that rather self-righteous weaver's boy lacked the literacy and the political education which he gained from Sunday School and Hampden Club. He was old-fashioned almost to the point of reaction. He possessed one fixed idea: that the Government must be overthrown and the poor men of England vindicated in the form of better victuals and brighter living. He talked not of ballot-boxes, but of rum, guineas, bands of music and pleasure parties on the Trent. But first, always first, came the desperate and dangerous task of overthrowing the Government. It was his fierce obsession with this immediate task that gave him his hold over his associates, the children – like himself – of the old, rough, often brutal, always passionate world of the poor. That world, with its recent memories of the Jacobite armies, the gallows, the press-gang and the prize-ring, was passing away. Brandreth had known no other, and he carried its traditions of violence, in word and deed, into the political arena of the Regency. The tradition died with Arthur Thistlewood, a very few years later, and George Borrow was to compose its swan-song. It was because he spoke and acted in those terms that he was able to lead out the last rebel host that ever marched through England.

Action was the passion of a man of his sort and his breeding.

There is no need to take seriously the 'monumental inscription'
proposed for him by the egregious *Black Dwarf* :

FORMED BY NATURE FOR DEEDS OF DARING,
HIS SOUL POSSESSED A DEGREE OF
PERSONAL COURAGE
AND AN EXTENT OF SELF-COMMAND
WHICH
UNDER THE SMILES OF FORTUNE MIGHT
HAVE ENABLED HIM
TO ECLIPSE THE FAME OF MARLBOROUGH
AND RIVAL THE GLORY OF NAPOLEON.

But the marching-song which he taught his followers breathes
action in every line :

Every man his skill must try,
He must turn out and not deny.
No bloody soldier must he dread.
He must turn out and fight for bread.
The time has come, you plainly see,
The Government opposed must be.

These are not the accents of Mr Richards, alias Oliver the Spy. No
word here of the impatience of the London leaders, the readiness of
Sir Francis Burdett and Major Cartwright to set up a Committee of
Public Safety at the Mansion House, if only the men of Pentrich
will raise the standard of revolution in the north. As one witness
said : 'It was a provision government they talked about,' for they
thought that 'a provisional government' had something to do with
provisions. Moreover, the good times coming included something
more attractive than bread. 'You will be kept on roast beef and ale
while you are along with us,' the Nottingham Captain promised
reluctant recruits on the march.

It was to set in motion this peculiarly enjoyable kind of revolution that Jeremiah Brandreth went down from Nottingham to Pentrich, a remote village in the foothills of the Peak of Derbyshire, on
Saturday, 7 June 1817. He set out, in fact, on the very day when
Oliver the Spy reached Nottingham on his retreat from the embarrassing misadventure at Thornhill Lees, to undergo his alarming

cross-examination at the hands of the city Patriots who had good reason to suspect that he was a spy. There is no evidence that Brandreth met Oliver on that Saturday, or indeed at any other time. But the Nestor of the Pentrich Patriots was the aged Thomas Bacon, who had certainly heard Oliver holding forth at the Wakefield meeting on the prospective 'simultaneous operation all over the country' which was to put down the borough-mongers. One might have expected old Thomas Bacon to have welcomed 'the Nottingham Captain' when he arrived at Pentrich in order to take charge of the Derbyshire branch of this 'simultaneous operation'. In fact, however, old Bacon seems to have held aloof. He certainly took no part in the rising on the following Monday night. There seems no doubt that he, like the Nottingham Patriots, had good reason to suspect the identity of Oliver. Did he attempt to warn or to dissuade Brandreth when he arrived at Pentrich? It is impossible to tell. All that we can be sure about is this: Brandreth was determined to lead out the Pentrich men, spy or no spy. There was ample opportunity for both Bacon and the Nottingham Patriots to warn him. Possibly either, or both, did so. But Brandreth went ahead. Nor did he ever utter one word of recrimination afterwards. Only William Turner, one of his lieutenants, was to cry out on the scaffold: 'This is all Oliver and the Government ....' And Turner was that 'decent-looking young man' who had drunk ale at the *Dog and Partridge* with Samuel Bamford on his way northward, to the Wakefield meeting with old Bacon.

No, Jeremiah Brandreth, like Lord Sidmouth, was determined to have his revolution. He was perfectly open about his mission when he set up his headquarters at the *White Horse* in Pentrich on the Sunday morning after his arrival. There he sat in the bar-parlour, with a map spread before him, explaining his plan of campaign to all comers, including a couple of special constables from the Butterley Ironworks. These latter seem to have been bemused by the open conspiracy, with its details for disposing of the local magistrate,* manufacturing bullets from the lead stripped from church roofs on the road to Nottingham, and procuring 'a man and

---

* This operation was described as 'drawing the badger'. It involved lighting a fire outside the magistrate's front door and then shooting him when he came out.

a gun' from every farmhouse along the line of march. One of them even contributed sixpence to a silver collection which was taken up for the expenses of a scout who was to go to Nottingham 'to see how they were getting on'. And neither of them appears to have reported what he saw and heard at the *White Horse* on that Sunday morning. They 'thought this was all foolish talk'.

'Seven drunken paupers in an ale-house on a Sunday, and without arms.' Thus Counsel for the Defence was to describe Jeremiah Brandreth's council of war. A tactical understatement, perhaps, on the part of a barrister with a hopeless case to defend. Similarly, Counsel for the Defence was to protest that the events of the night of Monday, 9 June, amounted only to 'aggravated riot'. These, however, were hardly the views of the farmers and labourers who were hounded from their beds and over the commons and field-tracks of the Pentrich district at the points of pikes and the muzzles of pistols during that long-remembered night. Even today the people of Pentrich talk of 'the Pentrich Revolution'. Oral tradition has handed down much that finds no place in the cold, close-printed columns of *State Trials*, 1817. There are beds of docks and nettles where great-grandfathers of men still alive hid themselves until the tramp of marching feet had died away down the lane; there are holes in plaster ceilings where pikes were pushed through bedroom floors to stir the revolutionary fervour of heavy sleepers; plantations where ash-poles were cut down to serve as pikestaffs; quarries where bundles of pikes were stored against the fateful night; cow-horns that were kept for sounding signals from one party to another as they diverged and converged in their great sweep on the scattered farms for men and guns. There was a good deal of eating and drinking; bread and cheese at midnight in an orchard, and unpaid bills at the Ripley taverns. And there was the rain.

The rain began after the frustrated Battle of Butterley. It came at the worst possible psychological moment. The Nottingham Captain had spoken confidently of the outcome of the 'Battle of Butterley'. For one thing, some of his followers bore a grudge against the management of the Butterley Ironworks for their dismissal on account of their membership of a local Hampden Club. For another thing, it was said that John Cope (the braggart who rejoiced in the prospect of roasting Lord Castlereagh's heart) had been secretly manufacturing munitions there for some weeks past. At the very least, it was hoped that the captured ironworks would afford a potential arsenal for the revolution. Yet, when Brandreth had drawn up his motley army before the foundry-gates in the early morning light, he had been worsted by the courageous demeanour of Mr Goodwin, the manager, who had advised the rebels to go home and avoid a hanging. Some, it seems, had gone. Others felt that the Captain's command had been badly shaken at the first brush with established authority. It was then, as they tramped away towards Ripley and the Nottingham border, that it began to rain. All along the last ten miles of the march into Nottingham-shire, single figures and small groups of men were to be seen steal-ing away across the fields. The Captain threatened to shoot the deserters, and was only prevented by the threat of retaliation by knives and pikes. When Launcelot Rolleston, a magistrate, ap-peared at the head of a party of hussars on Giltbrook Hill, the rem-nant of the revolutionary army threw down its arms and fled. Casualties throughout the affair amounted to one farm-servant, shot through a kitchen window by the Nottingham Captain while the unfortunate fellow was putting on his boots.

Apart from some mild agitation on the part of expectant crowds at Huddersfield and Nottingham, the rest of England remained per-fectly peaceful on the night of 9 June. Only Brandreth and Lord Sidmouth, it seems, had expected anything else. Brandreth had talked throughout the night about 'clouds from the north' which would sweep down and carry all before them. At the crossing of the Erewash into Nottinghamshire, he had tried to hearten his dis-pirited supporters with news that Nottingham had fallen; although it was noticed that it was Brandreth himself and not the scout who had returned from that city, who conveyed this information to the marchers. No doubt all this was the remote echo of what Oliver had said might be expected to happen. No doubt, also, Brandeth was inspired with the will to believe. As for the Home Secretary, before the month of June was out, he was able to rejoice in the publica-tion of Reports by Secret Committees of both Houses of Parliament, in which the Pentrich Revolution was put in its proper setting as part of 'some general plan of simultaneous or connected insurrec-tion; the object of which was, after consolidating a sufficient force, to march upon London, and there to overturn the existing Government and to establish a republic'. In the autumn, Lord Sidmouth fell ill, but towards the end of October he was reported to have 'derived more benefit from the termination of the Derby trials than from all that the medical men could give him'.

The outcome of the Derby trials was a foregone conclusion. The Government took care of that. There was to be no risk of an acquittal this time, as after Spa Fields, because of public revelation of the activities of a spy. The case of Mr Oliver had been a *cause célèbre*, both in the press and parliament, for many weeks since the exposure of his activities at Thornhill Lees by the *Leeds Mercury* : the exposure which had endangered his life and limbs on his southward retreat through Nottingham on the eve of the Pentrich rising. Every care was taken by the Crown Solicitors to arrange the proceedings at Derby in such a way that the Defence should have no chance to plead provocation. Those historians, however, who have chosen to see in this a diabolical machination on the part of the Government,* have neglected to observe one important fact which was perfectly obvious to the lawyers engaged in the case for the defence of the Pentrich men. It is expressed thus, in an endorsement on the reverse of the brief[6] for the prisoners :

In regard to the Proof that this Crime was committed by the Excitement of Oliver the Spy, it is to be apprehended that *such proof is inadmissable*, and if admissable, it does not lessen the Malignity of the Offence whether committed at the Instigation of a Government Spy, or at the Instance of any other Person ...

Quite apart from the admissibility or otherwise of such proof, the Defence was well enough aware that it was also impossible. The Defence was unable to produce a single witness who could swear that he had heard Oliver inciting people to insurrection, or that any of the Pentrich prisoners had been present on any of the occasions when he had done this. There remained only the forlorn hope that Oliver's name might be dragged in, in order (as the Brief puts it) 'to raise an Impression in the Minds of the Jury favourable to the

* Taking their cue, no doubt, from misinformed or uninformed contemporaries like Sir Samuel Romilly, who stated in the House of Commons, on 27 January 1818 that 'in his conscience, he believed that the whole of that insurrection was the work of the persons sent by Government'.

Prisoners'. The Defence did, indeed, strive to raise such an impression by veiled references to 'something here behind the curtains which ought to be brought forward to public view', and to 'the real author of these riots [who] was entirely kept out of sight, while it was sought to make victims of the villagers who were dupes of his artifices.' Oliver was never mentioned by name. Doubtless the Defence was well aware that the Prosecution had that gentleman safely stowed away at the *George Inn* nearby, and were prepared to produce him in court for the purpose of confronting the prisoners with him, if need be. It proved more profitable, indeed, to put the blame on Cobbett and 'incendiary' journalists.

The trial lasted for ten days. Forty-seven false traitors were named in the Indictment. Two hundred and sixty-eight witnesses were called. The report of the proceedings occupies more than six hundred columns of the *State Trials*. And at the end, Brandreth and three other ring-leaders were sentenced to death, twenty-three were sentenced to transportation on various terms of imprisonment, and the rest were acquitted. It was a pitiful harvest. Many of the accused appeared in court in smock-frocks or the fustian dress of quarrymen and iron-founders. The Chief Baron of His Majesty's Exchequer, however, who presided over a Bench crowded with legal luminaries, maintained the orthodox attitude of the Prime Minister, and all good sons of Adam Smith, that economic distress was not to be corrected by political activity. Indeed, the Chief Baron denied that the accused had been turned to political agitation by economic motives, and added – perfectly correctly – that in any case such motivation would be quite irrelevant to their guilt or innocence. 'The question was, was this insurrection calculated to accomplish ... a reform in the Government, to bring about a revolution, or for any other public purpose? It was no excuse to say that these persons were poor. The distress they might labour under was no excuse, if they intended to overturn the Government ....' The Attorney-General, Sir Samuel Shepherd, in his turn, demanded to know: 'What did they commit this act for? Did they ask for bread? No! ... Some attempt had been made to induce the jury to believe that the object these men had in view was bread, but he would submit to them whether men who were wanting bread, whose only object was to procure food, would talk about overturning the Government, the pulling down of the Parliament Houses, and obtaining the keys of the Tower?'

On Monday, 7 November 1817, Jeremiah Brandreth, William Turner and Isaac Ludham* were hanged on Nun's Green, in front of Derby Gaol, and their heads afterwards severed from their bodies, in the presence of a vast crowd of spectators. The Prince Regent had graciously remitted the quartering which was customary in the case of High Treason. Nevertheless, Lord Colchester expressed his gratification that the event had served to remove the mischievous delusion that 'High Treason was an offence for which low persons were not punishable'. Another privilige of the aristocracy had been extended to the oncoming democracy. Another challenge had been successfully delivered to 'the monopolists of varied experience'.

* The fourth man sentenced to death, George Weightman, was respited on account of his youth and good character.

Chapter 15

PETERLOO

They determined to put down the multitude. They
thought they were imitating Mr Pitt because they
mistook disorganization for sedition.

DISRAELI: *Coningsby*

It was deemed expedient that this meeting should
be as morally effective as possible, and that it should
exhibit a spectacle such as had never before been
witnessed in England. . . . There was no hyperbole in
the statement which a magistrate afterwards made
on oath, that 'the party with the blue and green
banners came upon the field in beautiful order!'
adding, I think, that 'not until then did he become
alarmed.'

BAMFORD: *Passages in the Life of a Radical*

THE execution of the Derbyshire rebels coincided with the death
of the Princess Charlotte, the Heir Presumptive, in child-bed, and
the Hermit of Marlow took it upon himself to improve the occasion
in a pamphlet entitled *We Pity the Plumage, but Forget the Dying
Bird*. Some have liked to imagine that Shelley made one of the
crowd of spectators at Nun's Green on that November morning,
and that he was inspired by the horrid spectacle to compose this
splendid lament for the death of liberty. In truth, however, the poet
spoke no more than was felt by the generality of his countrymen.
The fate of these men, and the circumstances of which it was the
characteristic and the consequence, constituted a calamity no less
to be mourned than the death of the heir to the throne. The feeling
was widespread that these men were state victims; that they died
in consequence of the diseased condition of the body politic.

To diagnose this disease in terms of a monstrous accession of
wickedness on the part of the King's Ministers, however, was over-
simple. The disease from which England was suffering was rather
one of disorganization than of diabolical possession. A new kind of
society was coming painfully to birth within the old, and both the

minds of men and their political institutions were undergoing a difficult process of adaptation. In the unfolding of this larger story, the Pentrich rising was all but irrelevant. It contributed nothing to the growth of political self-consciousness on the part of the people, although it doubtless contributed something to the growth of the social conscience which was to hasten the process of social and administrative reform in Victorian England. If it served to reveal and discredit the use of spies and informers, it was still many years before the English people learnt to regard a properly trained and regulated police force as a normal and essential condition of a well-governed community. If it served to brand Lord Sidmouth as a scaremonger and a hypocrite, it certainly did nothing to shake either the self-esteem or the parliamentary majority of the Liverpool Administration. It required a far more startling example of the tragic possibilities of social disorganization before the mood of either the nation or its governors should change with that finality which marks the arrival of a new era. It required Peterloo.

The two years which prepared that melancholy event were a time of rapid vicissitudes in the prosperity of the people and in vitality of Radical politics. The two things were, *pace* Lord Liverpool, closely connected as ever. Lord Sidmouth himself admitted as much. There was a good harvest in 1817; between June and September, the price of wheat fell from 111s. 6d. to 75s. a quarter. Consols rose from 63 to 83. Foreign markets were recovering, and there was an increased demand for our manufactures. 'Our situation and prospects at home are improving', the Home Secretary wrote to Lord Exmouth. 'The materials for disaffection to work upon are less abundant and less susceptible than at the corresponding period last year.'[1] On 10 September, Lord Exmouth could reply: 'Every article of life is falling, the panic amongst farmers is wearing off, and above all, that hitherto marketable article, discontent, is everywhere disappearing.' Even so, his Lordship saw fit to offer thanks for these blessings to the appropriate quarter. 'We owe our present peaceful and happy prospects to your firmness and prompt exertions in keeping down the democrats.'[2]

However, while the commercial prosperity of the country was increasing, wages still remained low, and the workers in the textile trades continued to attempt to secure their share in the increased prosperity of their employers by direct action. The year 1818 was, indeed, notable for its strikes. Both the jenny-spinners and the power-loom weavers struck at Stockport, and the spinners were joined shortly by the bricksetters, joiners, carpenters and dyers. By July, some twenty thousand were on strike in Manchester. They spent their time in parading the streets with banners, a form of demonstration which greatly disturbed the minds of the authorities and greatly disappointed their own more politically-minded leaders. Men of the old guard, Drummond, Bagguley, Ogden, Knight and Benbow – many of them newly released from custody under the Suspension Act – turned again to their old task of attempting to direct the attention of the strikers to the root cause of their distress and the indispensable condition of its remedy: the unreformed House of Commons and the winning of the franchise. It was uphill work. Parliamentary reform, or the politics of 'the long run', seemed to be as difficult a cause as ever to promote among men who were striking for the means to buy bread. 'I do not by any means think that the system of turning out in the different trades is connected with this idea', wrote Mr Norris, stipendiary magistrate at Manchester, to Lord Sidmouth in July, 'or that the sentiment itself has taken root in the minds of the mass of the population, yet I am disposed to think that this idea gains ground ....'[3] The old group-and-delegate system, for so long the favourite device of the political agitators of the Hampden Club movement, was being employed in Lancashire this summer for purely and immediately economic purposes. When the magistrates seized the papers of the Spinners' Committee on 29 August, they reported that the object of the organizers was 'of the most serious nature in a commercial point of view, though nothing of a *political* nature *seems* mixed with it.'[4] Messrs Bagguley and Drummond tried hard to mix something political with it, even to the point of martyrdom. John Bagguley was set upon and beaten by a mob of strikers at Manchester on 24 August. He was howled down when he tried to address a meeting of weavers at Stockport. His 'Mule-spinners' Address to the Public',[5] with its bitter onslaught upon the upstart cotton lords, was repudiated by the Spinners' Committee.

If the spinners and weavers had persuaded themselves that direct action would serve their purposes more effectively than political organization, they were quickly disillusioned. The weavers gained some slight and temporary success, but the spinners found themselves compelled to return to work on their masters' terms in September. Then, with the autumn, general conditions deteriorated again. The harvest of 1818 was poor. Excessive importation of raw cotton, silk and wool led to feverish production and a glutted market. The winter, and the early months of 1819, saw political methods and motives gaining ground again. Bamford records two interesting meetings for political reform late in 1818. At the first, near Middleton, it was resolved to present reform petitions to both Houses, and William Benbow gained some applause for the proposal that the people should march to London and present their petitions at the point of the sword. At the second, at Lydgate, Bamford himself proposed that the women should join in the show of hands on reform resolutions – a proposal which led, he tells us, to the formation of female reform unions.[6] It is clear that during the early months of 1819, the political movement which was to culminate in Peterloo was getting under way. On 18 January, Henry Hunt held what might be described as a bloodless rehearsal of the Manchester Meeting on the actual terrain of the calamitous encounter of the following August.

As the summer of 1819 advanced, the political reform movement not only increased in *tempo*; it reverted to the temper, the tactics, and even the *personnel* of the vigorous and confident days before the fiasco of the winter of 1816–17. With the removal of the ban on public meetings, which had had the disastrous effect of driving agitation into the dark ways of underground conspiracy, meetings were held once more in the open air : sometimes monster meetings which, it was suspected, were intended to teach the people 'to estimate their own numerical force . . . .'[7] Meetings which had been intended for no political purpose might be invaded and turned to political ends by the parliamentary reformers. For example, when forty thousand poor weavers met at Glasgow on 16 June in order to petition the Prince Regent for passage money to Canada for the hopelessly unemployed, an amendment was moved that no good was to be expected from anything but annual parliaments, universal suffrage and a reduction of taxation. It was carried, after speeches denouncing emigration and petitioning – although it was said that its supporters knocked down the hands of those who opposed it. At these meetings, the old 'politicals' who had regarded Luddism, hunger-marching and the adventures of Jeremiah Brandreth as futile irrelevancies, were now to be observed in their element. Some of them, like Joseph Harrison and Sir Charles Wolseley, were veterans of the nineties. Others, like Samuel Bamford and his friend 'Doctor' Healey, the Falstaff of the movement, were the children of Cartwright's Clubs. The Major himself was out and about again, snuffing the fresh breeze from the north with the zest of the old war-horse. And, of course, Orator Hunt, the idol of the open-air meeting, was furbishing up the famous white topper to serve once more as the beacon of reform, from Westminster to Manchester. Other signs and symbols, too, were showing themselves again, after the long winter of Radical discomfiture, notably the tricolour banner and the Cap of Liberty. The very name 'Radical' came into common use in this year.

More important than the revival of the old paraphernalia was the recourse to the old tactics. Conventions, anti-parliaments, mock elections, these devices for the discomfiture of the corrupt institution at Westminster had a history that went back to the days of Wilkes and Middlesex, and to the great campaign for Economical Reform in 1780.* Nothing, indeed, short of statutory treason itself, was so calculated to affront the susceptibilities of England's governors as the implied challenge to the sovereignty of Parliament which lay in a mock election. It had been bad enough when, in the winter of 1816–17, the delegates of the Hampden Clubs had assembled at the *Crown and Anchor* tavern. Now, in 1819, the old game began again, with renewed insolence and even greater menace, at the hands of gentlemen like Sir Charles Wolseley. On 28 June, this gentleman–Radical, of the Burdett tradition, presided at a meeting at Stockport, where, beneath a Cap of Liberty, he swore eternal faith in annual parliaments and universal suffrage. Sir Charles, like Lord Liverpool, had been present at the taking of the Bastille. Unlike Lord Liverpool, he was fond of declaring that this qualified him to take part in the attack on the Bastilles of his native land. When, a fortnight later, this aristocratic firebrand was elected 'Legislative Attorney and Representative of the People of Birmingham',

* See pp. 82–6.

188

the Government thought the joke – never in good taste – had gone
far enough. Sir Charles was sent to prison for eighteen months for
seditious words uttered at Stockport. Some ten days later, the *Manchester Observer* printed an advertisement for a meeting to be held
in St Peter's Fields in that town on 9 August, for the purpose of
adopting Major Cartwright's plan of parliamentary reform and to
elect a 'representative' for Manchester. Henry Hunt was billed to
play Sir Charles's role at Manchester.

Such was the inception of the Manchester meeting, known to
history as 'Peterloo'. Legend has diminished its singularity at the
behest of outraged feelings, thereby obscuring its significance in
the larger story to which it belongs. Peterloo was no ordinary
meeting of 'distressed persons' hounded down by a heartless magistracy. It was no culmination of a ruthless government's rough-
handling of a long-standing menace from the 'mobility'. On the
part of the people, it was the culmination of many years of political
education at the hands of the Cartwright–Cobbett–Hunt group of
Radicals: the point at which Parliamentary Reform came of age
as a popular programme. On the part of the governors, it was the
death-bed of an outmoded conception of 'the people' – that multitude which, according to Burke, remained when the politically
effective half-million ('the public') had been abstracted: 'the rest
who, when feeble, are the objects of protection, when strong, the
means of force.'* At Peterloo, 'the rest' were obviously – frighten-
ingly – 'strong', and therefore the object of force. They were the
more strong, and the more alarming, because they were organized.
Not until the watching magistrates observed 'the beautiful order'
of the contingents arriving at St Peter's Fields, did they feel alarm.
They mistook not disorganization, but its opposite, for sedition.

For, after all, the thing was unbelievable. Here were fifty, perhaps sixty thousand men and women who belonged, by every
tradition of the older English society, to the vast, politically excluded world of the workshop and the loom, the coal-seam and
the shovel. They had come dressed in their Sunday clothes,
wives and children included, trooping into Manchester in orderly array, unarmed and cheerful, at the command of Mr Hunt,
who had required them to bring 'no other weapon than that

* See p. 48.

of an approving conscience'. They were peaceable, they were orderly, and they knew what they wanted. Their banners bore such devices as: UNITY AND STRENGTH, LIBERTY AND FRATERNITY, PARLIAMENTS ANNUAL, SUFFRAGE UNIVERSAL. True, there were Caps of Liberty, in crimson velvet, and 'Doctor' Healey's contingent, the Lees and Saddleworth Union, bore a pitch-black banner with staring white words EQUAL REPRESENTATION OR DEATH; but even this was accompanied by a heart and two clasped hands adorned with the word LOVE. No pains had been spared to show the world that working-class reformers knew how to conduct themselves with order and sobriety. Many of them had spent the summer evenings, for weeks past, out on the moors, learning how to march in rank and wheel in column, at the instruction of old soldiers; a species of rehearsal which had greatly alarmed the authorities. It was intended, as Bamford[8] put it, to disarm criticism 'by a display of cleanliness, sobriety and decorum such as we had never before exhibited'. To the gentlemen who watched the fruit of all this painstaking preparation, as it showed itself at eleven o'clock on the morning of 16 August, from the high windows of a house overlooking St Peter's Fields, such 'beautiful order' was in itself a symptom of untold menace. They could not know that they were watching the arrival of a new era no less certainly than their breathren of Paris, who, exactly thirty years earlier, had watched the Third Estate walking to Versailles. For them, these marching feet held only the echo of the mob; and the gaily decorated hustings in the middle of St Peter's Fields gave up the thin, ghostly shadow of a guillotine.

For the greatest demagogue in England was on his way to the heart of this vast assembly. Cheering swelled up from the far side of the Fields, as a barouche appeared, covered with blue and white flags, drawn along by the people. It came through a lane in the crowd, and presently Henry Hunt stepped forth and ascended the hustings, the famous white top hat gleaming in the sunshine, the focal point of fifty thousand pairs of eyes. Then the band played 'God save the King', and many of the people took off their hats, in imitation – it is to be hoped – of the white topper. Then Mr Hunt began to speak.

The lane down which Henry Hunt had come now disappeared.

But another lane, long prepared, and leading from the hustings to the house at the corner of Mount Street, remained open. It was lined by special constables, and it was to be used for the purpose of arresting Mr Hunt, if and when such a proceeding seemed necessary to the watching magistrates. The fact that this decision had been left in abeyance has sometimes been supposed to indicate a certain irresolution on the part of the authorities. Why, if Mr Hunt's presence was calculated to produce a breach of the peace – and it was upon that ground that his arrest was finally based – did not the magistrates arrest him at once, or – better still – before he could arrive at St Peter's Fields? These questions were asked at the time, and they have often been asked since, notably by those who contrive to combine criticism of the authorities for their 'continental' habits of preventive action with condemnation of those same authorities for not acting upon them. The fact is, however, that the Manchester meeting was perfectly legal and was concerned with a perfectly respectable purpose. Its sponsors had taken legal advice, after issuing their original advertisement announcing that it would proceed to elect a 'representative' for Manchester. They were informed that 'the intention of choosing representatives, contrary to existing law, tends greatly to render the proposed meeting seditious.' In consequence, the date was postponed to 16 August, and the purpose was declared to be that of considering 'the propriety of adopting the most *legal* and *effectual* means of obtaining Reform of the Commons House of Parliament'. It would be difficult to imagine a milder or less tendentious expression of a political purpose. As for Mr Hunt, he could, of course, have been arrested on his way to the meeting if anyone had been prepared to swear an affidavit that his presence there was likely to cause a breach of the peace. Plenty of people could have been found prepared to do this. The Rev. Edward Stanley, a sympathetic observer who watched the whole of the proceedings from a window immediately above the room where the magistrates were stationed, afterwards stated upon his oath that any crowd under the control of Henry Hunt must have been a dangerous crowd.[9] The necessary affidavit was sworn, indeed, and the warrant for Hunt's arrest was ready long before he arrived on the scene. The fact that no attempt was made to arrest him until the proceedings had already begun can only be attributed to the desire of Mr Hulton and his fellow magistrates to wait and see – as Hulton put it – what the complexion of the meeting might be: a peculiarly English attitude on the part of the representatives of a peculiarly English government, who fully shared the dislike of the Prime Minister himself for 'coming to extremes'.

The fact is that the magistrates at Peterloo were precisely those 'gentlemen of the parish' in whom Lord Liverpool – even against the advice of less complacent friends, like Lord Grenville – delighted to put his trust. Three months after Peterloo, the Prime Minister was still content to limit public meetings to 'parochial meetings' which, he predicted, 'would generally be flat', and where 'the gentlemen who live in the parish would have influence enough to check those with whom they are so intimately connected and whose actions in this respect could not be concealed from them.' Lord Grenville was willing to agree that this might do for the country, but he inquired rather pertinently: 'How will it apply to the metropolis and the great towns which are at present the chief seat of this evil? The real inhabitants of a single parish may amount to many thousands or tens of thousands, and are so little known to each other that no person could discriminate ....' In fact, Grenville pointed out, the existing system of peace-keeping was 'originally adapted to a state of our society to which the present bears no resemblance.'[10] It would be rash, indeed, to assume that Mr Hulton and his colleagues at Peterloo had ever seen one man in a thousand of those who assembled in St Peter's Fields. As for the peace-keeping machinery of the town of Manchester, it was a feudal relic: it consisted of a Court Leet, a Deputy Constable, and reeves. It possessed no regular police-force. The forces available on this occasion, for dealing with a crowd of some fifty or sixty thousand people, were the special constables who now formed a ring round the hustings and a lane from the hustings to the house where the magistrates sat, and a body of local civilians dressed in regimentals and known as 'the Manchester and Salford Yeomanry'. In reserve and out of sight, like a secret confession of the absurdity of the situation, there were standing by six troops of the 15th Hussars, nearly the whole of the 31st Regiment, several companies of the 88th, and a troop of Horse Artillery: the whole under the command of Colonel Guy L'Estrange. As usual, in Regency England, the regular forces of the

Crown were likely to be called upon to perform the duties of a police-force.

It would have been better for everyone concerned if the magistrates had placed the duty of arresting Mr Hunt and dispersing the crowd, once these measures had been decided upon, in the hands of the regular troops. Correct formation and skilful handling of horses will suffice to break up any unarmed assembly without the use of sabres and with the minimum of bodily injury. It may be assumed that the 15th Hussars, who were wearing their Waterloo medals, were not thirsting for the blood of the unarmed weavers of Lancashire, their wives and their children. The straightforward, humane and manly account of their behaviour which has been handed down to us by one of their officers, Lieutenant Jolliffe,[11] would alone serve as good evidence for that. But the 15th Hussars were not called upon until a tragic overture had been performed by the Manchester and Salford Yeomanry. 'The stupid boobies of yeomanry cavalry', the *Manchester Observer* called them, 'fawning dependents of the great, with a few fools and a greater proportion of coxcombs, who imagine they acquire considerable importance by wearing regimentals'. Perhaps there was always something a trifle ridiculous about the Yeomanry. It really depended upon who composed it. On the one hand, there were the gentlemen and farmers of the Home Counties, where Lords Sidmouth and Liverpool had led respectable levies in the nineties, and where Edward Gibbon claimed to have learnt something of the discipline of the Legions. On the other hand, there were the small masters, inn-keepers and tradesmen of Manchester: the butcher, the baker and the candlestick-maker on horseback. The Manchester and Salford Yeomanry consisted almost exclusively of cheesemongers, ironmongers and newly enriched manufacturers, and the people of Manchester and district thought them a joke, and a not very good joke. It was to their very great disadvantage that they were on their native heath, the only people in all that populous scene who really belonged to the place* and to whom the place belonged. They were defending their own property. Unfortunately, they had not properly learnt how to control their horses.

* The magistrates, like most of the crowd, came from the neighbouring districts.

It was upon these gentlemen that the magistrates called for assistance when Deputy Constable Nadin protested that he was unable to execute the warrants for the arrest of Mr Hunt without military assistance. They came charging into the Field, knocking down a woman and killing her child on the way, and when they appeared Mr Hunt pointed at them and said something which 'excited a shout from those immediately about him, which was re-echoed with fearful animation by the rest of the multitude.'[12] Halting in disorder, they then proceeded to advance into the crowd, converging upon the hustings. The crowd stood fast. There was little opportunity for flight in that densely packed multitude. For a moment it looked as if the people were to triumph by their very physical inability to retreat. However, some of the Yeomanry reached the hustings, and Mr Hunt was hustled along the lane of special constables to the magistrates' house. Then it became apparent to the watching magistrates that the Yeomanry were stuck. There they sat, stranded on their horses, all over the Field, hemmed in by the jeering, pressing crowd, unable either to advance or to retire, and no doubt looking extremely foolish.

It was at this point that the 15th Hussars were summoned to the scene. Here is Lieutenant Jolliffe's description of what he saw:

It was then for the first time that I saw the Manchester troop of Yeomanry; they were scattered singly or in small groups over the greater part of the Field, literally hemmed up and hedged into the mob so that they were powerless either to make an impression or to escape; in fact, they were in the power of those whom they were designed to overawe, and it required only a glance to discover their helpless position, and the necessity of our being brought to their rescue.

Jolliffe thought the Manchester Yeomanry, 'and the manner in which they were made use of (to say the least) greatly aggravated the disasters of the day.' They lacked the knowledge of a trained military body, and 'they were placed, most unwisely, as it appeared, under the immediate command and order of the civil authority.'[13]

Colonel Guy L'Estrange, halting the Hussars on the edge of this ludicrous scene, looked up to the magistrates' window for his orders.

'Good God, sir,' Mr Hulton called down to the Colonel, 'do you not see how they are attacking the Yeomanry? Disperse the crowd.'

The Hussars advanced with drawn swords, and Mr Hulton turned away from the window because he 'would rather not see any advance of the military'.

The Hussars, Lieutenant Jolliffe records, drove the people forward with the flat of their swords: 'but sometimes, as is almost inevitably the case when men are placed in such situations, the edge was used.' He also asserts that

although nine out of ten of the sabre wounds were caused by the Hussars, it redounds to the humane forebearance of the men of the 15th that more wounds were not received, when the vast numbers are taken into consideration with whom they were brought into hostile collision; beyond all doubt, however, the far greater amount of injuries were from the pressure of the routed multitude.[14]

It was all over in a very few minutes. The crowd was fleeing along the streets towards the open country, and St Peter's Fields was littered with hats, bonnets, shawls, shoes, musical instruments, and the bodies of the dead and injured. In the midst stood the hustings with its broken flag-staffs and tattered banners. A group of Yeomanry loosened their horses' girths, adjusted their accoutrements, and wiped their sabres. Over all, the hot August sunshine filtered down through a cloud of dust. It was a battle-field. It was Peterloo.

Many years were to pass before it became possible for the public mind to form anything like a dispassionate picture of what happened at Peterloo. Even before the horrid sound of that fatal collision had died away, the air was clamorous with futile questions. Had the crowd thrown brickbats? Had anyone fired a pistol? Had anyone read the Riot Act? Whether anyone had done, or left undone, any of these things, the stark fact remained that a peaceable crowd, engaged in a legitimate form of demonstration, had been ridden down by armed men, and one way or another eleven people had been killed and many hundreds injured. The event was at once christened 'the Massacre of Peterloo' in sardonic reference to the glorious victory of four years earlier; and, for many years to come, the Radical cause was to make grateful use of cheap engravings which depicted ferociously-whiskered cavalrymen prancing with flashing swords above heaps of prostrate men and women. The Whigs, too, after their long and sulky hibernation, were stirred to assume once more their role of traditional leaders of the people. Peterloo afforded them an irresistible opportunity to resurrect the bogy of military rule. Earl Fitzwilliam immediately associated himself with a requisition to the High Sheriff of Yorkshire to summon a County Meeting, and was dismissed from his Lieutenancy of the West Riding for his pains. Earl Grey thought it necessary to explain to the Duke of Devonshire, the head of the Whig Party, that in associating himself with Earl Fitzwilliam in this, he repudiated 'any disposition to give countenance to the opinions and the practices of Mr Hunt and his associates ....' His Lordship was simply concerned that 'the people' should not 'find themselves abandoned by their natural protectors ....'[15] The Radical leaders, however, who had borne the heat and the burden of the day for so long, were not disposed to stand aside in favour of those who – in their view – had shirked the task of leadership in the dark and dangerous years. Henry Hunt, released on bail, entered London in triumph; and although he was to go to prison for two and a half years, the Radicals won both the seats for the Borough of Westminster in the spring of 1820 and retained them until 1832. Sir Francis Burdett, not to be outdone in the race for martyrdom by Earl Fitzwilliam, got himself fined £2,000 and imprisoned for three months for a libellous letter of protest to his constituents.

Burdett wrote in righteous indignation on the strength of newspaper reports of Peterloo. The reply of the Prince Regent to an Address of Protest from the Common Council of the City of London, at the beginning of September – that they appeared to know little or nothing either of the circumstances which preceded the late meeting at Manchester, or of those who attended it – probably applied equally to Burdett and a good many other persons and groups of persons who rushed into print at this time. Certainly, the Government showed no immediate disposition either to apologize or to explain. The magistrates and the military were thanked, on behalf of the Prince Regent, for their 'prompt, decisive and efficient measures for the preservation of public tranquillity'. The

Home Secretary and his colleagues acted throughout upon what Lord Sidmouth privately expressed as

an essential principle of government – namely, to acquire the confidence of the magistracy, especially in critical times, by showing a readiness to support them in all honest, reasonable, and well-intended acts, without inquiring too minutely whether they might have performed their duty a little better or a little worse.[16]

It was a principle in which not only diehards like Lord Eldon, but liberal Tories like George Canning, equally concurred.* Nor should it be forgotten that, while many supporters of the Administration deeply regretted the sufferings incurred at Manchester, and were prepared to criticize the way in which the situation had been handled, the Government lost little or none of its hold upon the opinion and the suffrages of the country as a whole. The Address was received with the customary large majorities at the opening of Parliament in November, and the six Acts† which came before Parliament before the adjournment at the end of December met with general approval, even if they gave rise to strenuous debate in many of their details.

Then, as if specially designed to vindicate this, the last phase of the policy of 'Alarm', Arthur Thistlewood and the remnants of the physical-force party played straight into the Government's hands with the 'Cato Street Plot'. Thistlewood was a bankrupt and broken-down officer of the militia who had been acquitted, amidst general laughter, with the rest of the Spa Fields rioters in the winter of 1816–17, after the Government had committed the egregious error of charging them with High Treason. The laughter rankled, and Thistlewood's malignant disposition was not improved by twelve months' imprisonment in Horsham Gaol for attempting a breach of the peace by challenging Lord Sidmouth to a duel with sword or pistol. He came out of prison in time to hear the cries and clamour over Peterloo, and made up his mind on the spot that the Ministers of the Crown should die, each and every

* See p. 122.

† 60 George III, cap. 1 (to prohibit drilling); 60 Geo. III, cap. 2 (to restrict the right to bear arms); 60 Geo. III, cap. 6 (to regulate the right of public meeting); 60 Geo. III, caps. 4 and 8 (to check and punish libels); 60 Geo. III, cap. 9 (for taxing newspapers).

one of them, by a single and supreme act of vengeance. 'High Treason was committed against the people at Manchester,' he declared, at his trial. 'I resolved that the lives of the instigators of massacre should atone for the souls of murdered innocents.' Like an atom-bomb traitor, Thistlewood cast himself for the role of an outraged Providence. With a handful of devoted followers, he would make his way into the dining-room of Lord Harrowby, where the members of the Cabinet sat at table. He would announce the arrival of the moment of truth by the simple words: 'My Lords, I have as good men here as your Manchester Yeomanry. Enter Citizens, and do your duty.' The heads of the Ministers were to be carried through the streets on pikes, and Arthur Thistlewood was to sit at the Mansion House along with Sir Francis Burdett, Major Cartwright, and other worthies, as the first President of the Britannic Republic. With the assistance of a spy and an informer, however, the emissaries of divine justice were surprised in their stable-loft at Cato Street while still in the act of buckling on their swords and butcher's-knives.[17]

The Cato Street Plot was discovered too late to feature as an episode of the Regency. George III had died nearly a month earlier, and the Prince Regent was now George IV. This is a pity, for Thistlewood's design, in the stark simplicity of its style and the wretched inadequacy of its detail, bears the hall-mark of the Regency, with its unique blend of squalor and bravura. On the other hand, there is Arthur Thistlewood's assumption of the gestures and the eloquence of the classical tyrannicide; he justified himself at his trial by references to Brutus and Cassius. On the other hand, there is the drunken horror of the ruffianly guttersnipes with whose assistance he proposed to carry through his *coup*. One perceives the unlighted courtyards, the thieves' kitchens and the cesspools which infected the Age of Elegance east of Regent Street; the gimcrack plaster behind the Nash façade; the inglorious aspect of Prinny when he took off his stays. The whole thing rings hollow like one of Lord Sidmouth's plots. 'An expectation prevailed', his Lordship declared, when it was all over, 'amongst the disaffected in the northern parts of the kingdom that an important blow would be struck in London prior to the expiration of the month of February.'[18] Yet no scrap of evidence has ever been produced to show that the Cato Street Plot had any affiliation with anything beyond the tiny circle of its pitiful protagonists. With its frustration, the unclean birds who had nested within the Society of Spencean Philanthropists, and who had bedevilled the cause of Radical reform politics for so long, disappeared for ever.

It was too late. The triumph of the parliamentary reform programme of Cartwright, Cobbett and Hunt, signalized by the great and tragic rally at Peterloo, had put midland and northern England beyond the range of influence of men like Arthur Thistlewood. No Joseph Mitchells or William Benbows went down to Lancashire from the *Cock* and the *Mulberry Tree* in 1820, and no Olivers either. There was no Thomas Bacon to carry the glad tidings of Thistlewood's coming *coup* to the rustics of South Derbyshire. Thomas Bacon was in Botany Bay. Had some new emissary of the physical-force faction arrived in his stead, he would have gone away with a flea in his ear. It was not simply a case of 'once bitten, twice shy'. It was a case of conversion to Cartwright and Cobbett.

That is the true significance of Peterloo. It marked the point of final conversion of provincial England to the doctrine of 'first things first'. The ship which had tacked and lain becalmed for so long among the shoals and shallows of Luddism, hunger-marching, strikes and sabotage, was coming to port. Of course, there were still shoals and shallows ahead. Even at the time of Peterloo, agitation for a Minimum Wage Bill was being carried on at Bolton and Stockport; and much of the driving force behind the parliamentary reform agitation of 1819 and subsequent years was derived from hatred of the Combination Laws. In 1821, Cobbett was still trying to convince the framework-knitters that a political programme was the only way out of their distress, and that all else must serve as a mischievous red herring across the track of real and permanent amelioration. Powerful contemporary thinkers like Thomas Carlyle long preferred to think that Peterloo itself was concerned with the right to work rather than with the right to vote; and it is true that there were Anti-Corn-Law banners as well as Suffrage Banners at the Manchester meeting. All this is true, and yet the greater truth remains. Henceforth, the people were to stand with ever greater fortitude behind that great movement, which, stage by stage throughout the nineteenth century, was to impose a new political order upon a new society. It was to be a political order consciously, even mechanically, contrived – consonant with a society which had decided, for better or for worse, to live by machines.

With Peterloo, and the departure of Regency England, parliamentary reform had come of age.

BIBLIOGRAPHY

I. MANUSCRIPT AND PUBLIC RECORDS

Home Office Papers. Disturbances, 1812–20
Additional Manuscripts in the British Museum
Hansard, Parliamentary Debates, Old Series to 1820, New Series after
    1820
State Trials, vols. XXV, XXXII and XXXIII
Annual Register, 1812–20
Reports of Committees, 1817, vol. IV

II. PRESS AND PAMPHLETS

The Times
Cobbett's Political Register. Rural Rides (Everyman edition, 2 vols.)
The Black Dwarf

Address to the Friends of Free Inquiry and the Common Good, by the
    Derby Society for Political Information, 1792
Encomiastic Advice, by Philo-Filmer, Derby 1793
Reason urged against Precedent, by Henry Yorke, 1793
We Pity the Plumage, but Forget the Dying Bird, by The Hermit of
    Marlow (P. B. Shelley), 1817
The Green Bag Plot, by Henry Hunt, 1819

III. BIOGRAPHIES AND MEMOIRS

Assheton-Smith, Thomas: *Reminiscences of,* by Sir John E. Eardley-
    Wilmot, 1869
Bamford, Samuel, *Passages in the Life of a Radical,* ed. Henry Dunckley,
    2 vols., 1893
Bewick, Thomas: *Life and Letters of,* ed. Thomas Landseer, 2 vols., 1871
Brougham, Lord: *and the Whig Party,* by Arthur Aspinall, 1927
Burdett, Sir Francis, *and his Times,* by M. W. Patterson, 2 vols., 1931
Cartwright, Major John: *Life and Correspondence of,* by F. D. Cart-
    wright, 2 vols., 1826
Castlereagh: *The Rise of,* by H. M. Hyde, 1933
Cobbett, William, *Progress of a Ploughboy to a Seat in Parliament,* ed.
    W. Reitzel, 1933
Crabb, Robinson, Henry: *The Diary, Reminiscences and Correspondence
    of,* ed. Thomas Sadler, 1892

Eldon: *Life of*, by Horace Twiss, 3 vols., 1844

Eldon, John, Earl of: The Life, Political and Official of, Anon., 1827

Haydon, Benjamin Robert, *Autobiography and Journals*, published as *The Life of Haydon* in 3 vols. by Tom Taylor, 1853 (World's Classics edition, ed. Edmund Blunden, 1927)

Heron, Sir Robert, *Notes*, n.d.

Holcroft, Thomas: Life of, by William Hazlitt, 1816 (World's Classics edition, 1926)

Jay, William: Recollections of, by his son Cyrus Jay, 1859

Liverpool, Robert Banks Jenkinson, Earl of: Life and Administration of, by C. D. Yonge, 3 vols., 1868

Lovett, William: Life and Struggles of, 1876 (republished in Bohn's Popular Library, 2 vols., 1920)

Mill, James, by Alexander Bain, 1862

Owen, Robert: Life of, 2 vols., 1858

Place, Francis: Life of, by Graham Wallas, 1908

Romilly, Sir Samuel, Memoirs, 1840

Scott, Sir Walter: Life of, by J. G. Lockhart, 7 vols., 1837–8 (abridged by Lockhart in one volume, 1848)

Sidmouth, Henry Addington, First Viscount: Life and Correspondence of, by Hon. George Pellew, 3 vols., 1847

Southey, Robert: Life and Correspondence of, ed. Cuthbert Southey, 6 vols., 1848–50

Tierney, George, by H. K. Olphin, 1934

Tytler, Patrick Fraser: Memoir of, 1859

IV. POLITICAL WRITINGS (MAINLY CONTEMPORARY)

Edmund Burke, *Works*, World's Classics or Bohn's Standard Library

Thomas Carlyle, *Chartism*, 1839

Major John Cartwright, *Take Your Choice*, 1776
  Mock Reform, Half Reform and Constitutional Reform, 1810

S. T. Coleridge, *A Lay Sermon*, 1816
  Second Lay Sermon, 1817
  Biographia Literaria, 1817

James Mill, *On Government* (1819–20), ed. Ernest Barker, 1937

John Stuart Mill, essays on Coleridge (1840) and Bentham (1839), in *Dissertations and Discussions*, 1859

P. B. Shelley, *A Philosophical View of Reform*, 1819–20

Robert Southey, *Colloquies on Society*, 1830

Thomas Spence, *A Lecture read at the Newcastle Philosophical Society*,

BIBLIOGRAPHY

1775 (republished in *Pioneers of Land Reform*, ed. M. Beer, Bohn's Popular Library 1920)

Sir John Walsh, *Popular Opinions on Reform considered*, 1831

V. GENERAL WORKS OF REFERENCE

H. W. C. Davis, *The Age of Grey and Peel*, 1929

Sir Ernest Barker, *Traditions of Civility*, 1948, ch. VII

P. A. Brown, *The French Revolution in English History*, 1918

F. A. Bruton, *Three Accounts of Peterloo*, 1921

H. Butterfield, *George III, Lord North and the People*, 1949

Sir John Clapham, *An Economic History of Modern Britain*, vol. I, 1926

F. O. Darvall, *Public Order and Popular Disturbance in Regency England*, 1934

Keith Feiling, essay on Liverpool in *Sketches in Nineteenth Century Biography*, 1930

Dorothy George, *England in Transition*, 1931 (reprinted with additions, Penguin, 1953)

Élie Halévy, *History of the English People in the Nineteenth Century*, vol. I (*England in 1815*) and vol. II (*The Liberal Awakening*), English trans., 1924–6

J. L. and B. Hammond, *The Town Labourer*, 1917
  The Skilled Labourer, 1919

Harriet Martineau, *History of the Thirty Years' Peace*, 1849

John Summerson, *Georgian London*, 1945

W. R. Brock, *Lord Liverpool and Liberal Toryism*, 1939

VI. SOME RELEVANT NOVELS

George Borrow, *Lavengro*, 1851
  The Romany Rye, 1857

Disraeli, *Coningsby*, 1844

Charlotte Brontë, *Shirley*, 1849

Mark Rutherford, *The Revolution in Tanner's Lane*, 1887

VII. MISCELLANEOUS

Matthew Arnold, essay on Democracy (1861) in *Mixed Essays*, 1879 (popular edition issued by John Murray, 1903)

Sir Charles Oman, essay on the Cato Street Plot in *The Unfortunate Colonel Despard*, 1922

Disraeli, *Vindication of the English Constitution*, 1835

John Neal, *The Pentrich Revolution*, Ripley, Derbyshire, 1895

George Theodore Wilkinson, *The Cato Street Conspiracy*, 1820

NOTES

CHAPTER 1 WATERLOO

1 See Robert Gittings, *Famous Meeting* (1956).
2 P. B. Shelley, *A Defence of Poetry* (1821) and *A Philosophical View of Reform* (1819–20), reprinted in *Political Tracts of Wordsworth, Coleridge and Shelley*, ed. R. J. White (C.U.P. 1953) – see especially pp. 204 and 228–9.
3 Sir Robert Heron, *Notes* (n.d.), p. 64
4 *Black Dwarf*, no. 10, 2 April 1817, and no. 46, 10 December 1817
5 ibid., no 46, 10 December 1817
6 Major John Cartwright, *Mock Reform, Half Reform, and Constitutional Reform* (1810)
7 Letter quoted in Arthur Aspinall, *Lord Brougham and the Whig Party* (1927), p. 97
8 Élie Halévy, *History of the English People in the Nineteenth Century* (English trans. 1924–6), vol. II, Introduction, p. ix.
9 J. L. and B. Hammond, *The Skilled Labourer* (1919), p. 371
10 S. T. Coleridge, *Biographia Literaria* (1817), ch. X
11 Harriet Martineau, *History of the Thirty Years' Peace* (1849), vol. I, p. 56
12 Sir J. H. Clapham, *An Economic History of Modern Britain*, vol. I (1926), p. 184
13 Samuel Bamford, *Passages in the Life of a Radical*, ed. H. Dunckley (1893), vol. II, p. 31.
14 John Summerson, *Georgian London* (1945), p. 165
15 ibid.

CHAPTER 2 OLD ENGLAND: SOCIAL LANDSCAPE

1 William Cobbett, *A Tour in Scotland* (1832), pp. 208–11
2 ibid.
3 Thomas Carlyle, *Chartism* (1839), ch. II 'Statistics'
4 See especially Dorothy George, *England in Transition* (1931: reprinted with additions in Penguin Books, 1953).
5 *Life and Correspondence of Robert Southey*, ed. C. Southey (1848–50), vol. I, p. 64
6 D. H. Lawrence, *Phoenix* (1936), pp. 133–40

7 Macaulay, 'Southey's *Colloquies on Society*' (January 1830) in *Critical and Historical Essays*

8 Cobbett's *Political Register*, XXX, 23 March 1816, pp. 362–3

9 Adam Smith, *The Wealth of Nations* (1776), book V, ch. I, part III, art. 11

10 *Political Register*, LXXXI, 21 September 1833

11 Cobbett, *Advice to Young Men* (1829), pp. 256–7

12 *Political Register*, XXXVIII, 17 March 1821

13 Élie Halévy, *History of the English People in the Nineteenth Century* (English trans. 1924–6), vol. I, p. 36

14 ibid., vol. II, Introduction, p. vi

15 J. G. Lockhart, *Life of Scott* (1837–8); version abridged by Lockhart (1848), pp. 99–101

16 *Memoir of Patrick Fraser Tytler* (1859), p. 68

17 *Life and Correspondence of Robert Southey* (as above) vol. III, p. 71

18 Lockhart, op. cit. (1848 version), p. 56

19 Benjamin Robert Haydon, *Autobiography and Journals*, published as *The Life of Haydon* by Tom Taylor (1853), vol. I, p. 5

20 George Borrow, *Lavengro* (1851), ch. I; *The Romany Rye* (1857), Appendix, ch. VII

21 *Recollections of William Jay* by his son Cyrus Jay (1859), p. 37

22 *Life and Struggles of William Lovett* (1876); Bohn's Popular Library (1920), p. 1

23 Samuel Bamford, *Passages in the Life of a Radical*, ed. H. Dunckley (1893), vol. I, *Early Days*, pp. 33 and 158–9

24 James Hill, *On Government* (1819–20); ed. E. Barker (C.U.P. 1937), pp. 71–3

25 Bamford, op. cit., vol. I, p. 38

26 Cobbett, *Rural Ride* dated 21 November 1821; see Everyman edition of *Rural Rides*, vol. I, p. 38

27 Cobbett, *Rural Rides*, Everyman edition, vol. I, p. 249

CHAPTER 3   OLD ENGLAND: THE PEOPLE

1 George Borrow, *The Romany Rye* (1857), Appendix, ch. X

2 Samuel Bamford, *Passages in the Life of a Radical*, ed. H. Dunckley (1893), vol. I, *Early Days*, p. 101

3 *Life and Struggles of William Lovett* (1876); Bohn's Popular Library (1920), vol. I, p. 21

4 Bamford, op. cit., vol. I, pp. 46–7

5 Lovett, op. cit., vol. I, pp. 2–3

6 Bamford, op. cit., vol. I, pp. 206–7

7   ibid., vol. II, ch XXVI

8   S. T. Coleridge, *The Statesman's Manual* (1816); reprinted in *Political Tracts of Wordsworth, Coleridge and Shelley*, ed. R. J. White (C.U.P. 1953), p. 11

9   Edmund Burke, *Letters on a Regicide Peace* (1795–7), Letter I; Bohn's Standard Library, *Works of Burke*, vol. V, pp. 189–99

10 Matthew Arnold, *Mixed Essays* (1879); popular edition issued by John Murray (1903), pp. 17–18

11 A. Aspinall, *Lord Brougham and the Whig Party* (1927), p. 91

12 See Shelley's pamphlet, *We Pity the Plumage but Forget the Dying Bird* (1817), under pseudonym 'The Hermit of Marlow'.

13 Benjamin Robert Haydon, *Autobiography and Journals*, published as *The Life of Haydon* by Tom Taylor (1853), vol II, pp. 139–41

14 Sir J. E. Eardley-Wilmot, *Reminiscences of Thomas Assheton-Smith* (second ed. 1860), pp. 2 and 238

15 Bamford, op. cit., vol. II, p. 211

16 Eardley-Wilmot, op. cit., pp. 9–10 and 12

17 Sir Robert Heron, *Notes* (n.d.)

18 ibid., p. 104

19 Hon. G. Pellew, *Life and Correspondence of Henry Addington, First Viscount Sidmouth* (1847), vol. III, p. 162.

20 Burke, *Reflections on the French Revolution* (1790); World's Classics, *Works of Burke*, vol. IV, p. 36

21 H. Butterfield, *George III, Lord North and the People* (1949), p. 183

CHAPTER 4   THE MELTING-POT

1   S. T. Coleridge, *Biographia Literaria* (1817), ch. X

2   C. D. Yonge, *Life and Administration of Robert Banks Jenkinson, Second Earl of Liverpool* (1868), vol. II, pp. 300–307; latter reprinted in *Political Thought of S. T. Coleridge*, ed. R. J. White (1938)

3   Hon. G. Pellew, *Life and Correspondence of Henry Addington, First Viscount Sidmouth* (1847), vol. III, pp. 85, 90, and 145

4   Hansard, *Parliamentary Debates*, XXX, 177

5   ibid, XLI, 497

6   Thomas Carlyle, *Chartism* (1839), ch. VI

7   John Stuart Mill, essay on Coleridge (1840) in *Dissertations and Discussions* (1859)

8   See *Observations on the Political Tendency of the late Public Meeting for returning thanks to G. L. Wardle, Esq.* by A. South Briton (London 1809).

9   *Life and Correspondence of Robert Southey*, ed. C. Southey (1848–

50), vol. IV, letters of November 1816 and February 1817; see also Southey's *Essays, Moral and Political* (1832).

10 *Life and Correspondence of Robert Southey* (as above), vol. III, p. 226

11 P. B. Shelley, *A Philosophical View of Reform* (1819–20); reprinted in *Political Tracts of Wordsworth, Coleridge and Shelley*, ed. R. J. White (C.U.P. 1953), pp. 239–40

12 ibid., pp. 7–53

13 *Life of Robert Owen* (1858), vol. IA, pp. 115–16

14 Spence's Plan may be found in *Pioneers of Land Reform*, ed. M. Beer, Bohn's Popular Library (1920).

15 *Black Dwarf*, no. 6, 5 March 1817

16 ibid., no. 3, 12 February 1817

CHAPTER 5 CHALLENGE TO MONOPOLISTS

1 Hon. G. Pellew, *Life and Correspondence of Henry Addington, First Viscount Sidmouth* (1847), vol. III, p. 162

2 *Life and Correspondence of Robert Southey*, ed. C. Southey (1848–50), vol. III, p. 169

3 J. G. Lockhart, *Life of Scott* (1837–8), vol. II, p. 260

4 Shelley, *We Pity the Plumage, but Forget the Dying Bird* (1817)

5 *Life and Letters of Thomas Bewick*, ed. Thomas Landseer (London 1871), vol. I, pp. 24–5

6 William Cobbett, *Rural Rides*, Everyman edition, vol. I, pp. 5–6

7 S. T. Coleridge, *Biographia Literaria* (1817), ch. III, first footnote. See also *The Statesman's Manual* (p. 1 in reprinted text, *Political Tracts of Wordsworth, Coleridge and Shelley*, ed. R. J. White, C.U.P. 1953). There are also interesting references to the same problem in Coleridge's *Unpublished Letters*, ed. E. Leslie Griggs (1932), vol. II, pp. 193–5.

8 James Gillman, *Life of Coleridge* (1838), pp. 329–32. See also Kathleen Colburn, *Coleridge's Philosophical Lectures* (1949), *passim*.

9 *The Diary, Reminiscences and Correspondence of Henry Crabb Robinson*, ed. Thomas Sadler (1892), vol. II, p. 86

10 A. Aspinall, *Lord Brougham and the Whig Party* (1927), pp. 232–5

11 *Life and Struggles of William Lovett* (1876); Bohn's Popular Library (1920), vol. I, pp. 36–7

12 ibid., p. 35

13 H. Crabb Robinson, op. cit., vol. II, p. 228

14 *Life and Correspondence of Robert Southey* (as above), vol. III, p. 342n

15 *Black Dwarf*, no. 19, 4 June 1817
16 Samuel Bamford, *Passages in the Life of a Radical*, ed. H. Dunckley (1893), vol. II, pp. 11–12
17 See *Autobiography of William Jay* (1854) and *Recollections of William Jay* my his son Cyrus Jay (1859).
18 See Major John Cartwright, *Mock Reform, Half Reform, and Constitutional Reform* (1810)
19 Philo-Filmer, *Encomiastic Advice* (1793)
20 Sir Francis Burdett, Speech of 15 June 1908, *Edinburgh Annual Register*, I, 271

CHAPTER 6 POLITICAL TRANSLATION

1 *Hansard, Parliamentary Debates*, XVII, 581.
2 Sir John Walsh, *Popular Opinions on Parliamentary Reform Considered* (1831), p. 38
3 Benjamin Disraeli, *Vindication of the English Constitution* (1835), XII and XXI
4 Edmund Burke, *Thoughts on the Causes of the Present Discontents* (1770); World's Classics, Works of Burke, vol. II, p. 50
5 *Letters of S. T. Coleridge*, ed. E. H. Coleridge (1895), p. 635
6 William Paley, *Principles of Morals and Legislation* (1785); 1814 edition, vol. I, pp. 217–18 (book 6, ch. 7)
7 P. B. Shelley, *A Philosophical View of Reform* (1819–20); reprinted in *Political Tracts of Wordsworth, Coleridge and Shelley*, ed. R. J. White (C.U.P. 1953), pp. 229–30
8 See Herbert Butterfield, *George III, Lord North and the People* (1949), p. 183
9 See Sir Ernest Baker, *Traditions of Civility* (1948), pp. 294–5.
10 *Parliamentary History*, xviii, 1288–98
11 *State Trials*, vol. XXV, pp. 590–92
12 Butterfield, op. cit., pp. 242–8
13 P. A. Brown, *The French Revolution in English History* (1918), pp. 134–5
14 C. D. Yonge, *Life and Administration of Robert Banks Jenkinson, Second Earl of Liverpool* (1868), vol. II, pp. 431–4

CHAPTER 7 THE GOVERNORS

1 *The Life, Political and Official, of John, Earl of Eldon* (1827). This anonymous study is to be preferred in all respects to the official piety of the standard life by Twiss.
2 See H. M. Hyde's invaluable study, *The Rise of Castlereagh* (1933) –

indispensable for correcting the fantasies of contemporary and most later writers on the career of Castlereagh.

3 *Hansard, Parliamentary Debates, 1815, 177*

4 *Diary and Correspondence of Lord Colchester*, by the second Lord Colchester (1861), vol. II, p. 584

5 Hon. G. Pellew, *Life and Correspondence of Henry Addington, First Viscount Sidmouth* (1847), vol. III, p. 162

6 For the early life of Castlereagh, see H. M. Hyde, op. cit.

7 For details of the career of Robert Banks Jenkinson, second Earl of Liverpool, see the standard life by C. D. Yonge (1868). There is also an anonymous sketch by a contemporary, *Memoirs of the Earl of Liverpool* (1827). The best recent study is W. R. Brock's *Lord Liverpool and Liberal Toryism* (1941), which does more than any other work to increase our understanding of this government.

8 See Pellew, op. cit.

9 C. D. Yonge, *Life and Administration of Robert Banks Jenkinson, Second Earl of Liverpool* (1868), vol. I, pp. 9–12

10 ibid., pp. 14–15

11 ibid., p. 16

12 ibid., pp. 25–6

13 See Hyde, op. cit., *passim.*

14 Benjamin Disraeli, *Coningsby* (1844), book I, ch. 1

15 K. Feiling, *Sketches of Nineteenth Century Biography* (1930), p. 29

16 See Coleridge's letter to the Prime Minister (outlined pp. 57–8 of this book), C. D. Yonge, op. cit., vol. II, pp. 300–307; reprinted with abbreviations in *Political Thought of S. T. Coleridge*, ed. R. J. White (1938).

17 Matthew Arnold, 'Democracy' in *Mixed Essays* (1879); popular edition issued by John Murray (1903)

CHAPTER 8 THE MIND OF THE GOVERNORS

1 C. D. Yonge, *Life and Administration of Robert Banks Jenkinson, Second Earl of Liverpool* (1868), vol. I, pp. 399–400

2 ibid., vol. I I, pp. 270–71

3 J. L. and B. Hammond, *The Skilled Labourer* (1919), p. 371

4 See H. K. Olphin, *George Tierney* (1934), ch. II.

5 C. D. Yonge, op. cit., vol. II, p. 132

6 *Life and Correspondence of Robert Southey*, ed. C. Southey (1848–50), vol. IV, pp. 60–61

7 Yonge, op. cit., vol. II, pp. 235–43

8 Benjamin Robert Haydon, *Autobiography and Journals*, published as *The Life of Haydon* by Tom Taylor (1853), vol. II, pp. 265–6

9 Yonge, op. cit., vol. I, p. 36

10 ibid., vol. II, p. 378

11 ibid., p. 410

12 ibid., pp. 298–300

13 ibid., vol. I, p. 36

14 Edmund Burke, *Speech on Economical Reform* (1780); World's Classics, Works of Burke, vol. II, p. 317

15 Yonge, op. cit., vol. I, pp. 3–4

CHAPTER 9 ALARM

1 Hon. G. Pellew, *Life and Correspondence of Henry Addington, First Viscount Sidmouth* (1847), vol. III, p. 85

2 ibid., vol. I, p. 270

3 ibid., vol. III, pp. 90 and 145

4 J. L. and B. Hammond, *The Skilled Labourer* (1919), p. 85

5 *Hansard, Parliamentary Debates*, XXXV, 568

6 ibid., XLI, 47 and 498

7 ibid., 47

8 See F. O. Darvall, *Public Order and Popular Disturbance in Regency England* (1934), ch. XII.

9 *The Times*, 1 and 4 July 1812

10 *Home Office Papers*, 'Disturbances 1812–20', 42, 153

11 Darvall, op. cit., p. 1

12 Additional Manuscripts, British Museum, 38280, fo. 205

13 Pellew, op. cit., vol. III, p. 152

14 ibid.

15 C. D. Yonge, *Life and Administration of Robert Banks Jenkinson, Second Earl of Liverpool* (1868), vol. II, p. 410

16 Pellew, op. cit., vol. III, p. 262

17 Add. MSS., British Museum, 38741, fo. 314

CHAPTER 10 THE MACHINE-BREAKERS

1 Hon. George Pellew, *Life and Correspondence of Henry Addington, First Viscount Sidmouth* (1847), vol. III, p. 93

2 *Annual Register*, vol. LV, p. 98

3 Pellew, op. cit., vol. III, pp. 84–5

4 ibid., pp. 93–6

5 ibid., p. 97

6 *Life and Correspondence of Robert Southey*, ed. C. Southey (1848–
   50), vol. III, pp. 326–7
7 J. L. and B. Hammond, *The Skilled Labourer* (1919), p. 281
8 Pellew, op. cit., vol. III, p. 86
9 J. L. and B. Hammond, op cit., ch. X
10 ibid.
11 ibid., pp. 325–9

CHAPTER 11   THE LONDON LEADERS

1 Edmund Burke, *Reflections on the French Revolution*, World's Classics, Works of Burke, vol. IV, p. 36
2 Sir Samuel Romilly, *Memoirs* (1840), vol. II, p. 537
3 F. D. Cartwright, *Life and Correspondence of Major John Cartwright* (1826), vol. II, p. 4
4 *Hansard, Parliamentary Debates*, XVII, 565
5 Cartwright, op. cit., vol. II, p. 43
6 ibid., p. 240
7 For some account of the Borough, and reform politics there, see
   Graham Wallas, *Life of Francis Place* (1908), ch. 2.
8 For Samuel Bamford at Westminster, see his *Passages in the Life of
   a Radical*, ed. H. Dunckley (1893), vol. II, chs. 3 and 4.
9 Wallas, op. cit., p. 117
10 ibid., p. 119
11 Alexander Bain, *James Mill* (1862), p. 433
12 For details of the career and character of Burdett, see M. W. Patter-
    son, *Sir Francis Burdett and his Times* (1931).
13 Cobbett's political opinion can best be studied in the anthological
    'life' put together by W. Reitzel in 1933, under the title *Progress
    of a Ploughboy to a Seat in Parliament.*
14 ibid., p. 225
15 William Cobbett, *Rural Rides*; Everyman edition, vol. I, p. 159
16 ibid.
17 Bamford, op. cit., vol. II, pp. 11–12
18 For details of Cartwright's life, see F. D. Cartwright, op. cit.
19 Cartwright, op. cit., vol. I, p. 45
20 ibid., pp. 86 and 221–2
21 ibid., pp. 84–5
22 ibid., vol. II, pp. 24–32, 72–3 and 86
23 ibid., vol. I, p. 115
24 Bamford, op. cit., vol. II, p. 12
25 Cartwright, op. cit., vol. II, pp. 31–2

26 *Political Register*, 15 February 1817 and 27 April 1816
27 Cartwright, op. cit., vol. II, p. 143
28 There is no adequate life of Henry Hunt. His own *Memoirs* (1820) are practically valueless.
29 See ch. 4, pp. 63–4
30 Bamford's portraits of the Spenceans are to be found in *Passages in the Life of a Radical* (1893), vol. II, ch. IV

CHAPTER 12 THE COUNTRY COUSINS

1 For some account, not necessarily very reliable, of these relations between Hunt and Burdett, see Hunt's pamphlet *The Green Bag Plot* (1819).
2 The best account of the Spa Fields Riot is contained in *State Trials*, ed. XXXII, Trial of Watson the elder on a charge of High Treason.
3 Samuel Bamford, *Passages in the Life of a Radical*, ed. H. Dunckley (1893), vol. II, chs. III and IV
4 *Political Register*, XXXI, 23 November 1816, p. 546
5 They are to be found in the *Annual Register*, 1817, pp. 6 seq., and Parliamentary Reports of Committees, 1817, vol. IV. The statutory provisions were framed in Geo. III, cap. 3, 6, 7, 19.

CHAPTER 13 SPIES AND INFORMERS

1 Samuel Bamford, *Passages in the Life of a Radical*, ed. H. Dunckley (1893), vol. II, pp. 32–5
2 Hon. G. Pellew, *Life and Correspondence of Henry Addington, First Viscount Sidmouth* (1847), vol. III, p. 178
3 Bamford, op. cit., vol. II, pp. 36–7
4 ibid., pp. 37–9
5 J. L. and B. Hammond, *The Skilled Labourer* (1919), pp. 350–53
6 *Hansard, Parliamentary Debates*, 12 and 20 June 1817
7 Bamford, op. cit., vol. II, chs. XIV–XVIII, XXI and XXII
8 ibid., pp. 135–7

CHAPTER 14 THE PENTRICH REVOLUTION

1 *Reports of Committees*, 1817, vol. IV
2 ibid.
3 See J. L. and B. Hammond, *The Skilled Labourer* (1919), ch. XII; and the important article by A. F. Fremantle, 'The truth about Oliver the Spy', in the *English Historical Review*, October 1932.

4 Hon. G. Pellew, *Life and Correspondence of Henry Addington, First Viscount Sidmouth* (1847), vol. III, p. 189

5 For details of the Pentrich rising, throughout, see *State Trials*, vol. XXXII, Trial of Jeremiah Brandreth and others for High Treason. There is also an account which was published at Ripley, Derbyshire, in 1895 : *The Pentrich Revolution*, by John Neal. The present account is based on these, and on information locally gathered by the writer.

6 In the possession of Dr Philip Turton, of Heanor, Derbyshire

CHAPTER 15 PETERLOO

1 Hon. G. Pellew, *Life and Correspondence of Henry Addington, First Viscount Sidmouth* (1847), vol. III, p. 199

2 ibid.

3 *Home Office Papers*, 'Disturbances 1812–20', 42, 178, 29 July

4 ibid., 179, 29 August

5 Quoted in J. L. and B. Hammond, *The Town Labourer* (1917), pp. 301–2. Bagguley's authorship is by no means certain.

6 Samuel Bamford, *Passages in the Life of a Radical*, ed. H. Dunckley (1893), vol. II, p. 141

7 See Grenville's *Memorandum*, 12 November 1819, C. D. Yonge, *Life and Administration of Robert Banks Jenkinson, Second Earl of Liverpool* (1868), vol. II, pp. 419–30.

8 See Bamford, op. cit., ch. XXV; also *Three Accounts of Peterloo*, ed. F. A. Bruton (1921).

9 *Three Accounts of Peterloo* (as above), p. 41

10 See Grenville's *Memorandum*, 12 November 1819, and Liverpool's reply. C. D. Yonge, op. cit., vol. II, pp. 419–34.

11 *Three Accounts of Peterloo* (as above), pp. 48–58

12 ibid., p. 14

13 ibid., pp. 52–3 and 49–50

14 ibid.

15 Arthur Aspinall, *Lord Brougham and the Whig Party* (1927), pp. 276–7

16 Pellew, op. cit., vol. III, p. 262

17 The story can be gleaned from the *Annual Register*, 1820, and from *State Trials*, vol. XXXIII; George Theodore Wilkinson, editor of the *Newgate Calendar Improved*, published an 'authentic history' at the time; and there is an essay on the subject in Sir Charles Oman's *The Unfortunate Colonel Despard* (1922).

18 Pellew, op. cit., vol. III, p. 321

INDEX

6124   62